The Self-Service Data Roadmap
Democratize Data and Reduce Time to Insight

Dr. Sandeep Uttamchandani

Beijing · Boston · Farnham · Sebastopol · Tokyo   

The Self-Service Data Roadmap

by Sandeep Uttamchandani

Published by O'Reilly Media, Inc., 1005 Gravenstein Highway North, Sebastopol, CA 95472.

O'Reilly books may be purchased for educational, business, or sales promotional use. Online editions are also available for most titles (*http://oreilly.com*). For more information, contact our corporate/institutional sales department: 800-998-9938 or *corporate@oreilly.com*.

Acquisitions Editor: Jessica Haberman
Developmental Editor: Corbin Collins
Production Editor: Beth Kelly
Copyeditor: Holly Bauer Forsyth
Proofreader: Piper Editorial, LLC

Indexer: nSight, Inc.
Interior Designer: David Futato
Cover Designer: Karen Montgomery
Illustrator: O'Reilly Media, Inc.

September 2020:   First Edition

Revision History for the First Edition
2020-09-10:   First Release

See *http://oreilly.com/catalog/errata.csp?isbn=9781492075257* for release details.

978-1-492-07525-7

[LSI]

For my parents; my teacher and mentor, Gul; my wife, Anshul; and my kids, Sohum and Mihika.

Table of Contents

Preface. xv

1. Introduction. 1
    Journey Map from Raw Data to Insights   3
        Discover   4
        Prep   6
        Build   7
        Operationalize   8
    Defining Your Time-to-Insight Scorecard   10
    Build Your Self-Service Data Roadmap   15

Part I.   Self-Service Data Discovery

2. Metadata Catalog Service. 21
    Journey Map   22
        Understanding Datasets   23
        Analyzing Datasets   23
        Knowledge Scaling   24
    Minimizing Time to Interpret   24
        Extracting Technical Metadata   24
        Extracting Operational Metadata   25
        Gathering Team Knowledge   26
    Defining Requirements   26
        Technical Metadata Extractor Requirements   27
        Operational Metadata Requirements   28
        Team Knowledge Aggregator Requirements   28
    Implementation Patterns   29

Source-Specific Connectors Pattern   29
Lineage Correlation Pattern   31
Team Knowledge Pattern   32
Summary   33

3. Search Service. 35
Journey Map   35
Determining Feasibility of the Business Problem   36
Selecting Relevant Datasets for Data Prep   36
Reusing Existing Artifacts for Prototyping   36
Minimizing Time to Find   37
Indexing Datasets and Artifacts   37
Ranking Results   37
Access Control   38
Defining Requirements   38
Indexer Requirements   39
Ranking Requirements   40
Access Control Requirements   40
Nonfunctional Requirements   40
Implementation Patterns   41
Push-Pull Indexer Pattern   42
Hybrid Search Ranking Pattern   44
Catalog Access Control Pattern   46
Summary   49

4. Feature Store Service. 51
Journey Map   52
Finding Available Features   53
Training Set Generation   53
Feature Pipeline for Online Inference   53
Minimize Time to Featurize   53
Feature Computation   54
Feature Serving   54
Defining Requirements   55
Feature Computation   55
Feature Serving   56
Nonfunctional Requirements   57
Implementation Patterns   57
Hybrid Feature Computation Pattern   58
Feature Registry Pattern   60
Summary   62

5. Data Movement Service. **63**

Journey Map   63
  Aggregating Data Across Sources   63
  Moving Raw Data to Specialized Query Engines   64
  Moving Processed Data to Serving Stores   64
  Exploratory Analysis Across Sources   64
Minimizing Time to Data Availability   64
  Data Ingestion Configuration and Change Management   65
  Compliance   65
  Data Quality Verification   65
Defining Requirements   66
  Ingestion Requirements   66
  Transformation Requirements   68
  Compliance Requirements   68
  Verification Requirements   69
  Nonfunctional Requirements   69
Implementation Patterns   70
  Batch Ingestion Pattern   70
  Change Data Capture Ingestion Pattern   72
  Event Aggregation Pattern   75
Summary   76

6. Clickstream Tracking Service. **77**

Journey Map   78
Minimizing Time to Click Metrics   79
  Managing Instrumentation   80
  Event Enrichment   81
  Building Insights   82
Defining Requirements   82
  Instrumentation Requirements Checklist   82
  Enrichment Requirements Checklist   83
Implementation Patterns   84
  Instrumentation Pattern   84
  Rule-Based Enrichment Patterns   85
  Consumption Patterns   87
Summary   89

Part II.   Self-Service Data Prep

7. Data Lake Management Service. **93**

Journey Map   94

Primitive Life Cycle Management   95
Managing Data Updates   96
Managing Batching and Streaming Data Flows   96
Minimizing Time to Data Lake Management   97
Requirements   97
Implementation Patterns   102
Data Life Cycle Primitives Pattern   103
Transactional Pattern   104
Advanced Data Management Pattern   105
Summary   106

8. Data Wrangling Service. **107**
Journey Map   108
Minimizing Time to Wrangle   109
Defining Requirements   110
Curating Data   110
Operational Monitoring   111
Defining Requirements   111
Implementation Patterns   111
Exploratory Data Analysis Patterns   112
Analytical Transformation Patterns   113
Summary   114

9. Data Rights Governance Service. **115**
Journey Map   117
Executing Data Rights Requests   117
Discovery of Datasets   118
Model Retraining   118
Minimizing Time to Comply   118
Tracking the Customer Data Life Cycle   118
Executing Customer Data Rights Requests   119
Limiting Data Access   119
Defining Requirements   119
Current Pain Point Questionnaire   120
Interop Checklist   120
Functional Requirements   121
Nonfunctional Requirements   122
Implementation Patterns   122
Sensitive Data Discovery and Classification Pattern   123
Data Lake Deletion Pattern   124
Use Case–Dependent Access Control   125
Summary   127

Part III.   Self-Service Build

10. Data Virtualization Service... **131**

Journey Map   132
   Exploring Data Sources   132
   Picking a Processing Cluster   132
Minimizing Time to Query   133
   Picking the Execution Environment   133
   Formulating Polyglot Queries   133
   Joining Data Across Silos   134
Defining Requirements   134
   Current Pain Point Analysis   134
   Operational Requirements   135
   Functional Requirements   135
   Nonfunctional Requirements   135
Implementation Patterns   136
   Automatic Query Routing Pattern   137
   Unified Query Pattern   138
   Federated Query Pattern   140
Summary   141

11. Data Transformation Service... **143**

Journey Map   144
   Production Dashboard and ML Pipelines   144
   Data-Driven Storytelling   144
Minimizing Time to Transform   144
   Transformation Implementation   144
   Transformation Execution   145
   Transformation Operations   145
Defining Requirements   145
   Current State Questionnaire   146
   Functional Requirements   146
   Nonfunctional Requirements   147
Implementation Patterns   147
   Implementation Pattern   148
   Execution Patterns   151
Summary   152

12. Model Training Service... **153**

Journey Map   154
   Model Prototyping   154
   Continuous Training   155

Model Debugging   156
Minimizing Time to Train   156
   Training Orchestration   156
   Tuning   157
   Continuous Training   157
Defining Requirements   158
   Training Orchestration   158
   Tuning   160
   Continuous Training   160
   Nonfunctional Requirements   160
Implementation Patterns   161
   Distributed Training Orchestrator Pattern   162
   Automated Tuning Pattern   163
   Data-Aware Continuous Training   164
Summary   166

13. Continuous Integration Service. **167**
Journey Map   168
   Collaborating on an ML Pipeline   168
   Integrating ETL Changes   168
   Validating Schema Changes   169
Minimizing Time to Integrate   169
   Experiment Tracking   169
   Reproducible Deployment   170
   Testing Validation   170
Defining Requirements   170
   Experiment Tracking Module   171
   Pipeline Packaging Module   171
   Testing Automation Module   172
Implementation Patterns   172
   Programmable Tracking Pattern   173
   Reproducible Project Pattern   174
Summary   175

14. A/B Testing Service. **177**
Journey Map   179
Minimizing Time to A/B Test   181
   Experiment Design   182
   Execution at Scale   182
   Experiment Optimization   183
Implementation Patterns   183
   Experiment Specification Pattern   184

Metrics Definition Pattern   185
Automated Experiment Optimization   185
Summary   186

Part IV.   Self-Service Operationalize

15. Query Optimization Service.   189
Journey Map   190
Avoiding Cluster Clogs   190
Resolving Runtime Query Issues   190
Speeding Up Applications   191
Minimizing Time to Optimize   191
Aggregating Statistics   191
Analyzing Statistics   192
Optimizing Jobs   193
Defining Requirements   194
Current Pain Points Questionnaire   194
Interop Requirements   195
Functionality Requirements   195
Nonfunctional Requirements   195
Implementation Patterns   196
Avoidance Pattern   196
Operational Insights Pattern   198
Automated Tuning Pattern   200
Summary   201

16. Pipeline Orchestration Service.   203
Journey Map   204
Invoke Exploratory Pipelines   205
Run SLA-Bound Pipelines   205
Minimizing Time to Orchestrate   205
Defining Job Dependencies   205
Distributed Execution   206
Production Monitoring   206
Defining Requirements   206
Current Pain Points Questionnaire   207
Operational Requirements   207
Functional Requirements   208
Nonfunctional Requirements   208
Implementation Patterns   209
Dependency Authoring Patterns   209

    Orchestration Observability Patterns   211
    Distributed Execution Pattern   212
  Summary   213

17. Model Deploy Service. **215**
  Journey Map   216
    Model Deployment in Production   216
    Model Maintenance and Upgrade   216
  Minimizing Time to Deploy   217
    Deployment Orchestration   217
    Performance Scaling   217
    Drift Monitoring   218
  Defining Requirements   218
    Orchestration   218
    Model Scaling and Performance   220
    Drift Verification   221
    Nonfunctional Requirements   221
  Implementation Patterns   221
    Universal Deployment Pattern   222
    Autoscaling Deployment Pattern   224
    Model Drift Tracking Pattern   225
  Summary   226

18. Quality Observability Service. **227**
  Journey Map   228
    Daily Data Quality Monitoring Reports   228
    Debugging Quality Issues   228
    Handling Low-Quality Data Records   229
  Minimizing Time to Insight Quality   229
    Verify the Accuracy of the Data   229
    Detect Quality Anomalies   230
    Prevent Data Quality Issues   231
  Defining Requirements   231
    Detection and Handling Data Quality Issues   232
    Functional Requirements   232
    Nonfunctional Requirements   233
  Implementation Patterns   233
    Accuracy Models Pattern   234
    Profiling-Based Anomaly Detection Pattern   235
    Avoidance Pattern   236
  Summary   238

19. Cost Management Service. **239**

  Journey Map   240

    Monitoring Cost Usage   240

    Continuous Cost Optimization   241

  Minimizing Time to Optimize Cost   241

    Expenditure Observability   241

    Matching Supply and Demand   242

    Continuous Cost Optimization   242

  Defining Requirements   243

    Pain Points Questionnaire   243

    Functional Requirements   243

    Nonfunctional Requirements   244

  Implementation Patterns   244

    Continuous Cost Monitoring Pattern   245

    Automated Scaling Pattern   246

    Cost Advisor Pattern   248

  Summary   249

Index. **251**

Preface

Conventions Used in This Book

The following typographical conventions are used in this book:

Italic
> Indicates new terms, URLs, email addresses, filenames, and file extensions.

`Constant width`
> Used for program listings, as well as within paragraphs to refer to program elements such as variable or function names, databases, data types, environment variables, statements, and keywords.

`Constant width bold`
> Shows commands or other text that should be typed literally by the user.

`Constant width italic`
> Shows text that should be replaced with user-supplied values or by values determined by context.

 This element signifies a tip or suggestion.

 This element signifies a general note.

This element indicates a warning or caution.

Using Code Examples

Supplemental material (code examples, exercises, etc.) is available for download at *https://oreil.ly/ssdr-book*.

If you have a technical question or a problem using the code examples, please send email to *bookquestions@oreilly.com*.

This book is here to help you get your job done. In general, if example code is offered with this book, you may use it in your programs and documentation. You do not need to contact us for permission unless you're reproducing a significant portion of the code. For example, writing a program that uses several chunks of code from this book does not require permission. Selling or distributing examples from O'Reilly books does require permission. Answering a question by citing this book and quoting example code does not require permission. Incorporating a significant amount of example code from this book into your product's documentation does require permission.

We appreciate, but generally do not require, attribution. An attribution usually includes the title, author, publisher, and ISBN. For example: "*The Self-Service Data Roadmap* by Sandeep Uttamchandani (O'Reilly). Copyright 2020 Sandeep Uttamchandani, 978-1-492-07525-7."

If you feel your use of code examples falls outside fair use or the permission given above, feel free to contact us at *permissions@oreilly.com*.

O'Reilly Online Learning

 For more than 40 years, *O'Reilly Media* has provided technology and business training, knowledge, and insight to help companies succeed.

Our unique network of experts and innovators share their knowledge and expertise through books, articles, and our online learning platform. O'Reilly's online learning platform gives you on-demand access to live training courses, in-depth learning paths, interactive coding environments, and a vast collection of text and video from O'Reilly and 200+ other publishers. For more information, visit *http://oreilly.com*.

How to Contact Us

Please address comments and questions concerning this book to the publisher:

O'Reilly Media, Inc.
1005 Gravenstein Highway North
Sebastopol, CA 95472
800-998-9938 (in the United States or Canada)
707-829-0515 (international or local)
707-829-0104 (fax)

We have a web page for this book, where we list errata, examples, and any additional information. You can access this page at *https://oreil.ly/ssdr*.

Email *bookquestions@oreilly.com* to comment or ask technical questions about this book.

For news and information about our books and courses, visit *http://oreilly.com*.

Find us on Facebook: *http://facebook.com/oreilly*.

Follow us on Twitter: *http://twitter.com/oreillymedia*.

Watch us on YouTube: *http://youtube.com/oreillymedia*.

CHAPTER 1
Introduction

Data is the new oil. There has been exponential growth in the amount of structured, semi-structured, and unstructured data collected within enterprises. Insights extracted from data are becoming a valuable differentiator for enterprises in every industry vertical, and machine learning (ML) models are used in product features as well as improved business processes.

Enterprises today are data-rich, but insights-poor. Gartner (*https://oreil.ly/kg3MU*) predicts that 80% of analytics insights will not deliver business outcomes through 2022. Another study (*https://oreil.ly/Z6wcN*) highlights that 87% of data projects never make it to production deployment. Sculley et al. (*https://oreil.ly/2xq7x*) from Google show that less than 5% of the effort of implementing ML in production is spent on the actual ML algorithms (as illustrated in Figure 1-1). The remaining 95% of the effort is spent on data engineering related to discovering, collecting, and preparing data, as well as building and deploying the models in production.

While an enormous amount of data is being collected within data lakes, it may not be consistent, interpretable, accurate, timely, standardized, or sufficient. Data scientists spend a significant amount of time on engineering activities related to aligning systems for data collection, defining metadata, wrangling data to feed ML algorithms, deploying pipelines and models at scale, and so on. These activities are outside of their core insight-extracting skills, and bottlenecked by dependency on data engineers and platform IT engineers who typically lack the necessary business context. The engineering complexity limits data accessibility to data analysts and scientists rather than democratizing it to a growing number of data citizens in product management, marketing, finance, engineering, and so on. While there is a plethora of books on advancement in ML programming, and deep-dive books on specific data technologies, there is little written about operational patterns for data engineering required to develop a self-service platform to support a wide spectrum of data users.

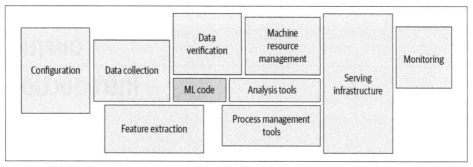

Figure 1-1. The study by Sculley et al. analyzed the time spent in getting ML models to production. ML code took 5% of time spent, while 95% of time spent was on the remaining boxes related to data engineering activities.

Several enterprises have identified the need to automate and make the journey from data to insight self-service. Google's TensorFlow Extended (TFX) (*https://oreil.ly/IzHKV*), Uber's Michelangelo (*https://oreil.ly/mZiAI*), and Facebook's FBLearner Flow (*https://oreil.ly/nOdbi*) are examples of self-service platforms for developing ML insights. There is no silver bullet strategy that can be adopted universally. Each enterprise is unique in terms of existing technology building blocks, dataset quality, types of use cases supported, processes, and people skills. For instance, creating a self-service platform for a handful of expert data scientists developing ML models using clean datasets is very different from a platform supporting heterogeneous data users using datasets of varying quality with homegrown tools for ingestion, scheduling, and other building blocks.

Despite significant investments in data technologies, there are three reasons, based on my experience, why self-service data platform initiatives either fail to take off or lose steam midway during execution:

Real pain points of data users getting lost in translation
    Data users and data platform engineers speak different languages. Data engineers do not have the context of the business problem and the pain points encountered in the journey map. Data users do not understand the limitations and realities of big data technologies. This leads to finger-pointing and throwing over problems between teams, without a durable solution.

Adopting "shiny" new technology for the sake of technology
    Given the plethora of solutions, teams often invest in the next "shiny" technology without clearly understanding the issues slowing down the journey map of extracting insights. Oftentimes, enterprises end up investing in technology for the sake of technology, without reducing the overall time to insight.

Tackling too much during the transformation process
> Multiple capabilities make a platform self-service. Teams often aim to work on all aspects concurrently, which is analogous to boiling the ocean. Instead, developing self-service data platforms should be like developing self-driving cars, which have different levels of self-driving capabilities that vary in level of automation and implementation complexity.

Journey Map from Raw Data to Insights

Traditionally, a data warehouse aggregated data from transactional databases and generated retrospective batch reports. Warehousing solutions were typically packaged and sold by a single vendor with integrated features for metadata cataloging, query scheduling, ingestion connectors, and so on. The query engine and data storage were coupled together with limited interoperability choices. In the big data era today, the data platform is a patchwork of different datastores, frameworks, and processing engines supporting a wide range of data properties and insight types. There are many technology choices across on-premise, cloud, or hybrid deployments, and the decoupling of storage and compute has enabled mixing and matching of datastores, processing engines, and management frameworks. The mantra in the big data era is using the "right tool for the right job" depending on data type, use case requirements, sophistication of the data users, and interoperability with deployed technologies. Table 1-1 highlights the key differences.

Table 1-1. The key differences in extracting insights from traditional data warehouses compared to the modern big data era

	Extracting insights in the data warehousing era	Extracting insights in the big data era
Data formats	Structured data	Structured, semi-structured, and unstructured data
Data characteristics	High-volume data	4 Vs (*https://oreil.ly/UgTk8*) of data: volume, velocity, variety, and veracity
Cataloging data	Defined at the time of aggregating data	Defined at the time of reading data
Freshness of insights	Insights are mainly retrospective (e.g., what happened in the business last week)	Insights are a combination of retrospective, interactive, real-time, and predictive
Query processing approach	Query processor and data storage coupled together as a single solution	Decoupled query processing and data storage
Data services	Integrated as a unified solution	Mix-and-match, allowing many permutations for selecting the right tool for the job

The journey map for developing any insight can be divided into four key phases: discover, prep, build, and operationalize (as shown in Figure 1-2). To illustrate the journey map, consider the example of building a real-time business insights dashboard that tracks revenue, marketing campaign performance, customer sign-ups and attrition, and so on. The dashboard also includes an ML forecasting model for revenue across different geographic locations.

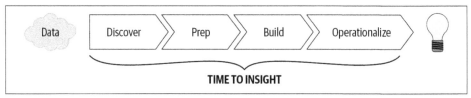

Figure 1-2. *The journey map for extracting insights from raw data.*

Discover

Any insights project starts with discovering available datasets and artifacts, as well as collecting any additional data required for developing the insight. The complexity of data discovery arises as a result of the difficulty of knowledge scaling within the enterprise. Data teams typically start small with team knowledge that is easily accessible and reliable. As data grows and teams scale, silos are created across business lines, leading to no single source of truth. Data users today need to effectively navigate a sea of data resources of varying quality, complexity, relevance, and trustworthiness. In the example of the real-time business dashboard and revenue forecasting model, the starting point for data users is to understand metadata for commonly used datasets, namely customer profile, login logs, billing datasets, pricing and promotions, and so on.

Discovering a dataset's metadata details

The first milestone is understanding the metadata properties, such as where the data originated, how the data attributes were generated, and so on. Metadata also plays a key role in determining the quality and reliability of the data. For instance, if the model is built using a table that is not populated correctly or has bugs in its data pipelines, the resulting model will be incorrect and unreliable. Data users start with team knowledge available from other users, which can be outdated and unreliable. Gathering and correlating metadata requires access to datastores, ingestion frameworks, schedulers, metadata catalogs, compliance frameworks, and so on. There is no standardized format to track the metadata of a dataset as it traverses being collected and transformed. The time taken to complete this milestone is tracked by the metric *time to interpret.*

Searching available datasets and artifacts

With the ability to understand a dataset's metadata details, the next milestone is to find all the relevant datasets and artifacts, namely views, files, streams, events, metrics, dashboards, ETLs, and ad hoc queries. In a typical enterprise, there are thousands or millions of datasets. As an extreme example, Google has 26 billion datasets (*https://oreil.ly/Feume*). Depending on the scale, data users can take days and weeks identifying relevant details. Today, the search relies heavily on team knowledge within data users and reaching out to application developers. The available datasets and artifacts are continuously evolving and need to be continuously refreshed. The time taken to complete this milestone is tracked by the metric *time to find.*

Reusing or creating features for ML models

Continuing the example, developing the revenue forecasting models requires training using historic values of revenue numbers by market, product line, and so on. Attributes like revenue that are an input to the ML model are referred to as features. An attribute can be used as a feature if historic values are available. In the process of building ML models, data scientists iterate on feature combinations to generate the most accurate model. Data scientists spend 60% of their time creating training datasets to generate features for ML models. Reusing existing features can radically reduce the time to develop ML models. The time taken to complete this milestone is tracked by the metric *time to featurize.*

Aggregating missing data

For creating the business dashboard, the identified datasets (such as customer activity and billing records) need to be joined to generate the insight of retention risk. Datasets sitting across different application silos often need to be moved into a centralized repository like a data lake. Moving data involves orchestrating the data movement across heterogeneous systems, verifying data correctness, and adapting to any schema or configuration changes that occur on the data source. Once the insights are deployed in production, the data movement is an ongoing task and needs to be managed as part of the pipeline. The time taken to complete this milestone is tracked by the metric *time to data availability.*

Managing clickstream events

In the business dashboard, assume we want to analyze the most time-consuming workflows within the application. This requires analyzing the customer's activity in terms of clicks, views, and related context, such as previous application pages, the visitor's device type, and so on. To track the activity, data users may leverage existing instrumentation within the product that records the activity or add additional instrumentation to record clicks on specific widgets, like buttons. Clickstream data needs to be aggregated, filtered, and enriched before it can be consumed for generating insights. For instance, bot-generated traffic needs to be filtered out of raw events. Handling a high volume of stream events is extremely challenging, especially in near real-time use cases such as targeted personalization. The time taken to complete this milestone of collecting, analyzing, and aggregating behavioral data is tracked by the metric *time to click metrics.*

Prep

The preparation phase focuses on getting the data ready for building the actual business logic to extract insights. Preparation is an iterative, time-intensive task that includes aggregating, cleaning, standardizing, transforming, and denormalizing data. It involves multiple tools and frameworks. The preparation phase also needs to ensure data governance in order to meet regulatory compliance requirements.

Managing aggregated data within a central repository

Continuing with the example, the data required for the business dashboard and forecasting model is now aggregated within a central repository (commonly referred to as a data lake). The business dashboard needs to combine historic batch data as well as streaming behavioral data events. The data needs to be efficiently persisted with respect to data models and on-disk format. Similar to traditional data management, data users need to ensure access control, backup, versioning, ACID properties for concurrent data updates, and so on. The time taken to complete this milestone is tracked by the metric *time to data lake management*.

Structuring, cleaning, enriching, and validating data

With the data now aggregated in the lake, we need to make sure that the data is in the right form. For instance, assume the records in the billing dataset have a null billing value for trial customers. As a part of the structuring, the nulls will be explicitly converted to zeroes. Similarly, there can be outliers in usage of select customers that need to be excluded to prevent skewing the overall engagement analysis. These activities are referred to as *data wrangling*. Applying wrangling transformations requires writing idiosyncratic scripts in programming languages such as Python, Perl, and R, or engaging in tedious manual editing. Given the growing volume, velocity, and variety of the data, the data users use low-level coding skills to apply the transformations at scale in an efficient, reliable, and recurring fashion. These transformations are not one-time but instead need to be reliably applied in an ongoing fashion. The time taken to complete this milestone is tracked by the metric *time to wrangle*.

Ensuring data rights compliance

Assume that the customer has not given consent to use their behavioral data for generating insights. Data users need to understand which customers' data can be used for which use cases. Compliance is a balancing act between better serving the customer experience with insights, and ensuring the data is being used in accordance with the customer's directives. There are no simple heuristics that can be universally applied to solving this problem. Data users want an easy way to locate all the available data for a given use case, without having to worry about compliance violations. There is no single identifier for tracking applicable customer data across the silos. The time taken to complete this milestone is tracked by the metric *time to compliance*.

Build

During the build phase, the focus is on writing the actual logic required for extracting the insight. The following are the key milestones for this phase.

Deciding the best approach for accessing and analyzing data

A starting point to the build phase is deciding on a strategy for writing and executing the insights logic. Data in the lake can be persisted as objects, or stored in specialized serving layers, namely key-value stores, graph databases, document stores, and so on. Data users need to decide whether to leverage native APIs and keywords of the data-stores, and decide on the query engine for the processing logic. For instance, short, interactive queries are run on Presto clusters, while long-running batch processes are on Hive or on Spark. Ideally, the transformation logic should be agnostic and should not change when data is moved to a different polyglot store, or if a different query engine is deployed. The time taken to complete this milestone is tracked by the metric *time to virtualize*.

Writing transformation logic

The actual logic for the dashboard or model insight is written either as an Extract-Transform-Load (ETL), Extract-Load-Transform (ELT), or a streaming analysis pattern. Business logic needs to be translated into actual code that needs to be performant and scalable as well as easy to manage for changes. The logic needs to be monitored for availability, quality, and change management. The time taken to complete this milestone is tracked by the metric *time to transform*.

Training the models

For the revenue forecasting example, an ML model needs to be trained. Historic revenue values are used to train the model. With growing dataset sizes and complicated deep learning models, training can take days and weeks. Training is run on a farm of servers consisting of a combination of CPUs and specialized hardware such as GPUs. Training is iterative, with hundreds of permutations of values for model parameters and hyperparameter values that are applied to find the best model. Model training is not one-time; models need to be retrained for changing data properties. The time taken to complete this milestone is tracked by the metric *time to train*.

Continuously integrating ML model changes

Assume in the business dashboard example that there is a change in the definition of how active subscribers are calculated. ML model pipelines are continuously evolving with source schema changes, feature logic, dependent datasets, data processing configurations, and model algorithms. Similar to traditional software engineering, ML models are constantly updated with multiple changes made daily across the teams. To integrate the changes, the data, code, and configuration associated with ML pipelines are tracked. Changes are verified by deploying in a test environment and using production data. The time taken to complete this milestone is tracked by the metric *time to integrate*.

A/B testing of insights

Consider a different example of an ML model that forecasts home prices for end customers. Assume there are two equally accurate models developed for this insight—which one is better? A growing practice within most enterprises is deploying multiple models and presenting them to different sets of customers. Based on behavioral data of customer usage, the goal is to select a better model. A/B testing—also known as bucket testing, split testing, or controlled experiment—is becoming a standard approach to making data-driven decisions. It is critical to integrate A/B testing as a part of the data platform to ensure consistent metrics definitions are applied across ML models, business reporting, and experimentation. Configuring A/B testing experiments correctly is nontrivial and must ensure there is no imbalance that would result in a statistically significant difference in a metric of interest across the variant populations. Also, customers must not be exposed to interactions between variants of different experiments. The time taken to complete this milestone is tracked by the metric *time to A/B test*.

Operationalize

In the operationalize phase of the journey map, the insight is deployed in production. This phase is ongoing until the insight is actively used in production.

Verifying and optimizing queries

Continuing the example of the business dashboard and revenue forecasting model, data users have written the data transformation logic either as SQL queries or big data programming models (such as Apache Spark or Beam) implemented in Python, Java, Scala, and so on. The difference between good and bad queries is quite significant; based on actual experiences, a query running for a few hours can be tuned to complete in minutes. Data users need to understand the multitude of knobs in query engines such as Hadoop, Spark, and Presto. Understanding which knobs to tune and their impact is nontrivial for most data users and requires a deep understanding of the inner workings of the query engines. There are no silver bullets—the optimal knob values for the query vary based on data models, query types, cluster sizes, concurrent query load, and so on. As such, query optimization is an ongoing activity. The time taken to complete this milestone is tracked by the metric *time to optimize*.

Orchestrating pipelines

The queries associated with the business dashboard and forecasting pipelines need to be scheduled. What is the optimal time to run the pipeline? How do we ensure the dependencies are correctly handled? Orchestration is a balancing act of ensuring pipeline service level agreements (SLAs) and efficient utilization of the underlying resources. Pipelines invoke services across ingestion, preparation, transformation, training, and deployment. Data users need to monitor and debug pipelines for correctness, robustness, and timeliness across these services, which is nontrivial. Orchestration of pipelines is multitenant, supporting multiple teams and business use cases. The time taken to complete this milestone is tracked by the metric *time to orchestrate*.

Deploying the ML models

The forecasting model is deployed in production such that it can be called by different programs to get the predicted value. Deploying the model is not a one-time task —the ML models are periodically updated based on retraining. Data users use non-standardized, homegrown scripts for deploying models that need to be customized to support a wide range of ML model types, ML libraries and tools, model formats, and deployment endpoints (such as IoT devices, mobile, browser, and web API). There are no standardized frameworks to monitor the performance of models and scale automatically based on load. The time taken to complete this milestone is tracked by the metric *time to deploy*.

Monitoring the quality of the insights

As the business dashboard is used daily, consider an example where it shows an incorrect value for a specific day. Several things can go wrong and lead to quality issues: uncoordinated source schema changes, changes in data element properties, ingestion issues, source and target systems with out-of-sync data, processing failures, incorrect business definitions for generating metrics, and many more. Data users need to analyze data attributes for anomalies and debug the root cause of detected quality issues. Data users rely on one-off checks that are not scalable with large volumes of data flowing across multiple systems. The goal is not just to detect data quality issues, but also to avoid mixing low-quality data records with the rest of the dataset partitions. The time taken to complete this milestone is tracked by the metric *time to insight quality*.

Continuous cost monitoring

We now have insights deployed in production with continuous monitoring to ensure quality. The last piece of the operationalized phase is cost management. Cost management is especially critical in the cloud where the pay-as-you-go model increases linearly with usage (in contrast to the traditional buy-up-front, fixed-cost model). With data democratization, where data users can self-serve the journey to extract insights, there is a possibility of significantly wasted resources and unbounded costs. A single bad query running on high-end GPUs can accumulate thousands of dollars in a matter of hours, typically to the surprise of the data users. Data users need to answer questions such as: a) what is the dollar spent per application? b) which team is projected to spend more than their allocated budgets? c) are there opportunities to reduce the spend without affecting performance and availability? and d) are the allocated resources appropriately utilized? The time taken to complete this milestone is tracked by the metric *time to optimize cost*.

Overall, in each phase of the journey today, data users spend a significant percentage of their time on data engineering tasks such as moving data, understanding data lineage, searching data artifacts, and so on. The ideal nirvana for data users is a self-service data platform that simplifies and automates these tasks encountered during the day-to-day journey.

Defining Your Time-to-Insight Scorecard

Time to insight is the overall metric that measures the time it takes to complete the entire journey from raw data into insights. In the example of developing the business dashboard and revenue forecasting model, time to insight represents the total number of days, weeks, or months to complete the journey map phases. Based on my experience managing data platforms, I have divided the journey map into 18 key milestones, as described in the previous section. Associated with each milestone is a metric such that the overall time to insight is a summation of the individual milestone metrics.

Each enterprise differs in their pain points related to the journey map. For instance, in the example of developing the business dashboard, an enterprise may spend a majority of time in *time to interpret* and *time to find* due to multiple silos and lack of documentation, while an enterprise in a regulated vertical may have *time to comply* as a key pain point in its journey map. In general, enterprises vary in their pain points due to differences in maturity of the existing process, technology, datasets, skills of the data team, industry vertical, and so on. To evaluate the current status of the data platform, we use a time-to-insight scorecard, as shown in Figure 1-3. The goal of the exercise is to determine the milestones that are the most time-consuming in the overall journey map.

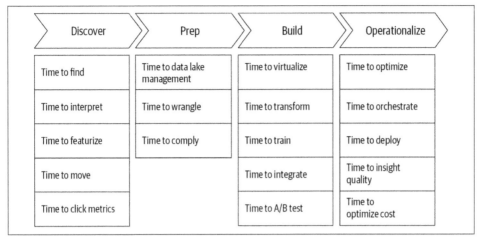

Figure 1-3. Scorecard for the time-to-insight metric as a sum of individual milestone metrics within the journey map.

Each chapter in the rest of the book corresponds to a metric in the scorecard and describes the design patterns to make them self-service. Following is a brief summary of the metrics:

Time to interpret

Associated with the milestone of understanding a dataset's metadata details before using it for developing insights. Incorrect assumptions about the dataset often leads to incorrect insights. The existing value of the metric depends on the process for defining, extracting, and aggregating technical metadata, operational metadata, and team knowledge. To minimize time to interpret and make it self-service, Chapter 2 covers implementation patterns for a metadata catalog service that extracts metadata by crawling sources, tracks lineage of derived datasets, and aggregates team knowledge in the form of tags, validation rules, and so on.

Time to find

Associated with the milestone of searching related datasets and artifacts. A high time to find leads to teams choosing to reinvent the wheel by developing clones of data pipelines, dashboards, and models within the enterprise, leading to multiple sources of truth. The existing value of the metric depends on the existing process to index, rank, and access control datasets and artifacts. In most enterprises, these processes are either ad hoc or have manual dependencies on the data platform team. To minimize time to find and make it self-service, Chapter 3 covers implementation patterns for a search service.

Time to featurize

Associated with the milestone of managing features for training ML models. Data scientists spend 60% of their time creating training datasets for ML models. The existing value of the metric depends on the process for feature computation and feature serving. To minimize time to featurize and make it self-service, Chapter 4 covers implementation patterns of a feature store service.

Time to data availability

Associated with the milestone of moving data across the silos. Data users spend 16% of their time moving data. The existing value of the metric depends on the process for connecting to heterogeneous data sources, data copying and verification, and adapting to any schema or configuration changes that occur on the data sources. To minimize time to data availability and make it self-service, Chapter 5 covers implementation patterns of a data movement service.

Time to click metrics

Associated with the milestone of collecting, managing, and analyzing clickstream data events. The existing value of the metric depends on the process of creating instrumentation beacons, aggregating events, enrichment by filtering, and ID stitching. To minimize time to click metrics and make it self-service, Chapter 6 covers implementation patterns of a clickstream service.

Time to data lake management

Associated with the milestone of managing data in a central repository. The existing value of the metric depends on the process of managing primitive data life cycle tasks, ensuring consistency of data updates, and managing batching and streaming data together. To minimize time to data lake management and make it self-service, Chapter 7 covers implementation patterns of a data lake management service.

Time to wrangle

Associated with the milestone of structuring, cleaning, enriching, and validating data. The existing value of the metric depends on the process of identifying data curation requirements for a dataset, building transformations to curate data at scale, and operational monitoring for correctness. To minimize time to wrangle and make it self-service, Chapter 8 covers implementation patterns of a data wrangling service.

Time to comply

Associated with the milestone of ensuring data rights compliance. The existing value of the metric depends on the process for tracking customer data across the application silos, executing customer data rights requests, and ensuring the use cases only use the data that has been consented to by the customers. To minimize time to comply and make it self-service, Chapter 9 covers implementation patterns of a data rights governance service.

Time to virtualize

Associated with the milestone of selecting the approach to build and analyze data. The existing value of the metric depends on the process to formulate queries for accessing data residing in polyglot datastores, queries to join data across the datastores, and processing queries at production scale. To minimize time to virtualize and make it self-service, Chapter 10 covers implementation patterns of a data virtualization service.

Time to transform

Associated with the milestone of implementing the transformation logic in data and ML pipelines. The transformation can be batch, near real-time, or real-time. The existing value of the metric depends on the process to define, execute, and operate transformation logic. To minimize time to transform and make it self-service, Chapter 11 covers implementation patterns of a data transformation service.

Time to train

Associated with the milestone of training ML models. The existing value of the metric depends on the process for orchestrating training, tuning of model parameters, and continuous retraining for new data samples. To minimize time to train and make it self-service, Chapter 12 covers implementation patterns of a model training service.

Time to integrate

Associated with the milestone of integrating code, data, and configuration changes in ML pipelines. The existing value of the metric depends on the process for tracking iterations of ML pipelines, creating reproducible packages, and validating the pipeline changes for correctness. To minimize time to integrate and make it self-service, Chapter 13 covers implementation patterns of a continuous integration service for ML pipelines.

Time to A/B test

Associated with the milestone of A/B testing. The existing value of the metric depends on the process for designing an online experiment, executing at scale (including metrics analysis), and continuously optimizing the experiment. To minimize time to A/B test and make it self-service, Chapter 14 covers implementation patterns of an A/B testing service as a part of the data platform.

Time to optimize

Associated with the milestone of optimizing queries and big data programs. The existing value of the metric depends on the process for aggregating monitoring statistics, analyzing the monitored data, and invoking corrective actions based on the analysis. To minimize time to A/B test and make it self-service, Chapter 15 covers implementation patterns of a query optimization service.

Time to orchestrate

Associated with the milestone of orchestrating pipelines in production. The existing value of the metric depends on the process for designing job dependencies, getting them efficiently executed on available hardware resources, and monitoring their quality and availability, especially for SLA-bound production pipelines. To minimize time to orchestrate and make it self-service, Chapter 16 covers implementation patterns of a pipeline orchestration service.

Time to deploy

Associated with the milestone of deploying insight in production. The existing value of the metric depends on the process to package and scale the insights available in the form of model endpoints, monitoring model drift. To minimize time to deploy and make it self-service, Chapter 17 covers implementation patterns of a model deploy service.

Time to insight quality

Associated with the milestone of ensuring correctness of the generated insights. The existing value of the metric depends on the process to verify accuracy of data, profile data properties for anomalies, and proactively prevent low-quality data records from polluting the data lake. To minimize time to insight quality and make it self-service, Chapter 18 covers implementation patterns of a quality observability service.

Time to optimize cost

Associated with the milestone of minimizing costs, especially while running in the cloud. The existing value of the metric depends on the process to select cost-effective cloud services, configuring and operating the services, and applying cost optimization on an ongoing basis. To minimize time to optimize cost and make it self-service, Chapter 19 covers implementation patterns of a cost management service.

The end result of this analysis is populating the scorecard corresponding to the current state of the data platform (similar to Figure 1-4). Each metric is color-coded based on whether the tasks associated with the metric can be completed, on the order of hours, days, or weeks. A metric that takes an order of weeks typically represents tasks that today are executed in an ad hoc fashion using manual, nonstandard scripts and programs and/or tasks requiring coordination between data users and data platform teams. Such metrics represent opportunities where the enterprise needs to invest in making the associated tasks self-service for data users.

The complexity associated with each of the scorecard metrics will differ between enterprises. For instance, in a startup with a handful of datasets and data team members, time to search and time to interpret can be accomplished in a matter of hours when relying solely on team knowledge, even though the process is ad hoc. Instead, the most time may be spent in data wrangling or tracking quality of the insights, given the poor quality of available data. Further, enterprises vary in the requirements associated with each service in the data platform. For instance, an enterprise deploying only offline trained ML models once a quarter (instead of online continuous training) may not prioritize improving the time to train metric even if it takes a number of weeks.

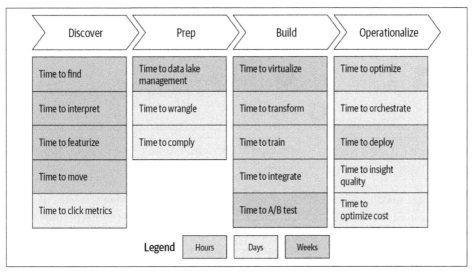

Figure 1-4. Example scorecard representing the current state of an enterprise's data platform.

Build Your Self-Service Data Roadmap

The first step in developing the self-service data roadmap is defining the scorecard for the current state of the data platform, as described in the previous section. The scorecard helps shortlist the metrics that are currently slowing down the journey from raw data to insights. Each metric in the scorecard can be at a different level of self-service, and prioritized for automation in the roadmap based on the degree to which it slows down the overall time to insight.

As mentioned earlier, each chapter covers design patterns to make the corresponding metric self-service. We treat self-service as having multiple levels, analogous to different levels of self-driving cars that vary in terms of the levels of human intervention required to operate them (as illustrated in Figure 1-5). For instance, a level-2 self-driving car accelerates, steers, and brakes by itself under driver supervision, while level 5 is fully automated and requires no human supervision.

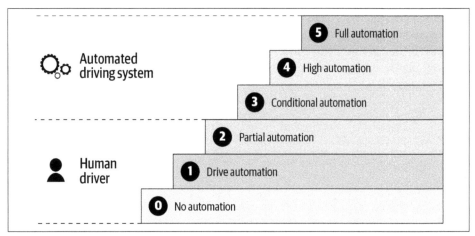

Figure 1-5. Different levels of automation in a self-driving car (from DZone (https://oreil.ly/j6e6P)).

Enterprises need to systematically plan the roadmap for improving the level of automation for each of the shortlisted metrics. The design patterns in each chapter are organized like Maslow's hierarchy of needs (*https://oreil.ly/74Rab*); the bottom level of the pyramid indicates the starting pattern to implement and is followed by two more levels, each building on the previous one. The entire pyramid within a given chapter represents the self-service, as shown in Figure 1-6.

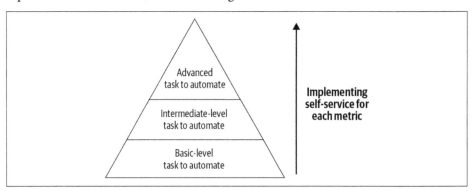

Figure 1-6. Maslow's hierarchy of task automation followed in each chapter.

In summary, this book is based on experience in implementing self-service data platforms across multiple enterprises. To derive maximum value from the book, I encourage readers to apply the following approach to executing their self-service roadmap:

1. Start by defining the current scorecard.

2. Identify two or three metrics that are most significantly slowing down the journey map based on surveys of the data users, and perform technical analysis of how the tasks are currently being implemented. Note that the importance of these metrics varies for each enterprise based on their current processes, data user skills, technology building blocks, data properties, and use case requirements.

3. For each of the metrics, start off with Maslow's hierarchy of patterns to implement. Each chapter is dedicated to a metric, and covers patterns with increasing levels of automation. Instead of recommending specific technologies that will soon become outdated in the fast-paced big data evolution, the book instead focuses on implementation patterns, and provides examples of existing technologies available on-premise as well as in the cloud.

4. Follow a phased crawl, walk, run strategy with a focus on doubling down on shortlisted metrics every quarter and making them self-service.

Finally, the book attempts to bring together perspectives of both the data users as well as data platform engineers. Creating a common understanding of requirements is critical in developing a pragmatic roadmap that intersects what is possible and what is feasible given the timeframe and resources available.

Ready! Set! Go!

PART I

Self-Service Data Discovery

CHAPTER 2

Metadata Catalog Service

Assume a data user is looking to develop a revenue dashboard. By talking to peer data analysts and scientists, the user comes across a dataset with details related to customer billing records. Within that dataset, they come across an attribute called "billing rate." What is the meaning of the attribute? Is it the source of truth, or derived from another dataset? Various other questions come up, such as, what is the schema of data? Who manages it? How was it transformed? How reliable is the data quality? When was it refreshed? and so on. There is no dearth of data within the enterprise, but consuming the data to solve business problems is a major challenge today. This is because building insights in the form of dashboards and ML models requires a clear understanding of the data properties (referred to as metadata). In the absence of comprehensive metadata, one can make inaccurate assumptions about the meaning of data and about its quality, leading to incorrect insights.

Getting reliable metadata is a pain point for data users. Prior to the big data era, data was curated before being added to the central warehouse—the metadata details, including schema, lineage, owners, business taxonomy, and so on, were cataloged first. This is known as *schema-on-write* (illustrated in Figure 2-1). Today, the approach with data lakes is to first aggregate the data and then infer the data details at the time of consumption. This is known as *schema-on-read* (illustrated in Figure 2-2). As such, there is no curated metadata catalog available to data users. An additional dimension of complexity is the siloed nature of metadata for a given dataset. For example, consider the sales dataset residing on a MySQL transactional database. To get this data in the lake, an ETL job is written in Spark and scheduled on Airflow. The transformed data is used by a TensorFlow ML model. Each of the frameworks has its own partial view of the end-to-end metadata. Given the wide variety of technologies for data persistence, scheduling, query processing, serving databases, ML frameworks, and so on, the lack of a single normalized representation of the end-to-end metadata makes consumption for data users even more difficult.

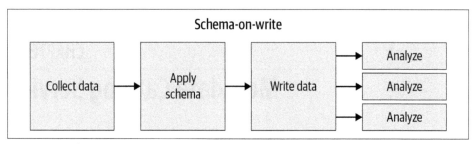

Figure 2-1. The traditional schema-on-write approach where data schema and other metadata are first cataloged before being written into the data warehouse.

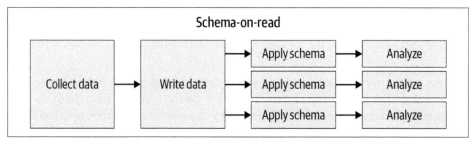

Figure 2-2. The modern big data approach of first aggregating the data in the lake and then making sense of the data schema and other metadata properties at the time of reading the data.

Ideally, data users should have a *metadata catalog service* that provides an end-to-end metadata layer across multiple systems and silos. The service creates an abstraction of a single data warehouse and is a single source of truth. Additionally, the catalog should allow users to enrich the metadata with team knowledge and business context. The metadata catalog also serves as a centralized service that various compute engines can use to access the different datasets. The success criteria of this service is to reduce the *time to interpret* data. This helps the overall time to insight by speeding up identification of the appropriate datasets as well as eliminating unnecessary iterations due to incorrect assumptions about availability and quality.

Journey Map

The need to interpret datasets is a starting point in the data scientist exploration. The following are the key day-to-day scenarios in the journey map for the metadata catalog service.

Understanding Datasets

As a first step in building a new model, instrumenting a new metric, or doing ad hoc analysis, data scientists need to understand the details of where the data originated, how it is used, how it is persisted, and so on. By understanding the data details, they can make informed decisions about shortlisting the correct datasets for further analysis in developing the insight. There are several aspects of understanding the data:

- What does the data represent logically? What is the meaning of the attributes? What is the source of truth of that data?
- Who and/or which team is the owner? Who are the common users?
- What query engines are used to access the data? Are the datasets versioned?
- Where is the data located? Where is it replicated to, and what is the format?
- How is the data physically represented, and can it be accessed?
- When was it last updated? Is the data tiered? Where are the previous versions? Can I trust this data?
- Are there similar datasets with common similar or identical content, both overall as well as for individual columns?

The metadata catalog becomes the single source of truth for these questions.

When a model or dashboard is deployed, the related dataset issues need to be actively monitored since they can impact the correctness and availability of the insight. The metadata catalog also stores the operational health of the datasets, and is used for impact analysis for any changes to the dataset schema or any bug discovered that other teams have consumed already. The information can help to quickly debug breakages in the data pipelines, alerting of SLA violations for delayed data availability, or data quality issues and other operational issues post-deployment.

Analyzing Datasets

There are many query engines available to analyze the datasets. Data scientists use the right tool for the job based on the dataset properties and query types. A single dataset can be consumed interchangeably by multiple query engines, such as Pig, Spark, Presto, Hive, and so on. For example, a Pig script reading data from Hive will need to read the table with Hive column types in Pig types. Similarly, processing may require data to be moved across datastores. During the process, the table in the destination datastore uses the destination table data types. To enable the use of multiple query processing frameworks, there is a need to map canonical data types to respective datastore and query engine types.

Knowledge Scaling

As data scientists work with different datasets for their projects, they discover additional details about business vocabulary, data quality, and so on. These learnings are referred to as *team knowledge*. The goal is to actively share team knowledge across data users by enriching the metadata catalog details for the datasets.

Minimizing Time to Interpret

Time to interpret represents the time taken by data scientists to understand the details of the dataset before building the insights. Given that this is the first step in the journey map, a higher time to interpret impacts the overall time to insight. In addition, an incorrect assumption about the datasets can lead to multiple needless iterations during the development of the insight, and it can limit the overall quality of the insight. The details of the dataset are divided into three buckets: technical, operational, and team metadata (as illustrated in Figure 2-3).

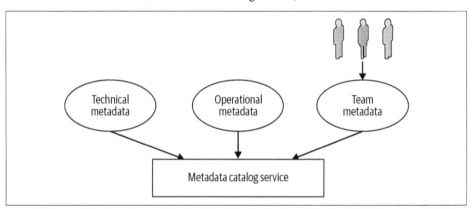

Figure 2-3. The different categories of information stored in the metadata catalog service.

Extracting Technical Metadata

Technical metadata consists of logical and physical metadata details of the dataset. *Physical metadata* covers details related to physical layout and persistence, such as creation and modification timestamps, physical location and format, storage tiers, and retention details. *Logical metadata* includes dataset schema, data source details, the process of generating the dataset, and owners and users of the dataset.

Technical metadata is extracted by crawling the individual data source without necessarily correlating across multiple sources. There are three key challenges in collecting this metadata:

Difference in formats

Each data platform stores metadata differently. For instance, Hadoop Distributed File System (HDFS) metadata is stored in terms of files and directories, while Kafka metadata is stored in terms of topics. Creating a single normalized metadata model that works for all platforms is nontrivial. The typical strategy is to apply the least common denominator, which will cause a leaky abstraction. Datasets reside in many different data formats and stores. Extracting metadata requires different drivers for connecting and extracting different systems.

Schema inference

Datasets that aren't self-describing are required to infer the schema. Schema for datasets is difficult to extract; inferring structure is hard for semi-structured datasets. There's no common way to enable access to data sources and generate DDLs.

Change tracking

Metadata is constantly changing. Keeping metadata updated is a challenge given the high churn and growing number of datasets.

Extracting Operational Metadata

Operational metadata consists of two key buckets:

Lineage

Tracking how the dataset was generated and its dependencies on other datasets. For a given dataset, lineage includes all the dependent input tables, derived tables, and output models and dashboards. It includes the jobs that implement the transformation logic to derive the final output. For example, if a job J reads dataset $D1$ and produces dataset $D2$, then the lineage metadata for $D1$ contains $D2$ as one of its downstream datasets, and vice versa.

Data profiling stats

Tracking availability and quality stats. It captures column-level and set-level characteristics of the dataset. It also includes execution stats that capture the completion times, data processed, and errors associated with the pipelines.

Operational metadata is not generated by connecting to the data source but rather by stitching together the metadata state across multiple systems. For instance, at Netflix, the data warehouse consists of a large number of datasets stored in Amazon S3 (via Hive), Druid, Elasticsearch, Redshift, Snowflake, and MySQL. Query engines, namely Spark, Presto, Pig, and Hive, are used for consuming, processing, and producing datasets.

Making sense of the overall data flow and lineage across the different processing frameworks, data platforms, and scheduling systems is a challenge given multiple different types of databases, schedulers, query engines, and business intelligence (BI) tools. The challenge is stitching together the details given the diversity of processing frameworks. Inferring lineage from code is not trivial, especially with UDFs, external parameters, and so on.

Another aspect of complexity is getting the complete lineage. The number of data-access events in the logs can be extremely high, and so can be the size of the transitive closure. Typically, there is a trade-off between completeness of the lineage associations and efficiency by processing only a sample of data-access events from the logs and by materializing only the downstream and upstream relations within a few hops, as opposed to computing the true transitive closure.

Gathering Team Knowledge

Team knowledge is an important aspect of metadata. As data science teams grow, it is important to persist these details for others to leverage. There are four categories:

- User-defined metadata in the form of annotations, documentation, and attribute description. This information is created via community participation and collaboration, enabling creation of a self-maintaining repository of documentation by encouraging conversations and pride in ownership.
- Business taxonomy or vocabulary to associate and organize data objects and metrics in a business-intuitive hierarchy. Also, business rules associated with datasets such as test accounts, strategic accounts, and so on.
- The state of the dataset in terms of compliance, personally identifiable information (PII) data fields, data encryption requirements, and so on.
- ML–augmented metadata in the form of the most popular tables, queries, etc., plus examining the source code and extracting any of the attached comments. These comments are often of high quality and their lexical analysis can provide short phrases that capture the semantics of the schema.

There are three key challenges related to team knowledge metadata:

- It is difficult to make it easy and intuitive for data users to share their team knowledge.
- The metadata is free-form, yet has to be validated to ensure correctness.
- The quality of the information is difficult to verify, especially if it is contradictory.

Defining Requirements

The metadata catalog service is a one-stop shop for metadata. The service is post hoc —i.e., it collects metadata after the datasets have been created or updated by various pipelines without interfering with dataset owners or users. It works in the background in a nonintrusive manner to gather the metadata about datasets and their usage. Post hoc is in contrast to traditional enterprise data management (EDM) that requires upfront management of datasets.

There are two interfaces to the service:

- A web portal that enables navigation, search, lineage visualization, annotation, discussion, and community participation.
- An API endpoint that provides a unified REST interface to access metadata of various datastores.

There are three key modules required for building the catalog service:

Technical metadata extractor
Focused on connecting to data sources and extracting basic metadata associated with the dataset.

Operational metadata extractor
Stitches the metadata across systems in the data transformation, creating an end-to-end (E2E) view.

Team knowledge aggregator
Enables users to annotate information related to datasets, allowing scaling of knowledge across the data teams.

Technical Metadata Extractor Requirements

The first aspect of the requirements is understanding the list of technologies needed to extract the technical metadata. The goal is to ensure that the appropriate support is available to extract the metadata, as well as represent the data model correctly. The list of systems involved can be divided into the following categories (as illustrated in Figure 2-4): schedulers (such as Airflow, Oozie, and Azkaban), query engines (such as Hive, Spark, and Flink), and relational and NoSQL datastores (such as Cassandra, Druid, and MySQL).

Another aspect is versioning support of the metadata—i.e., tracking versions of the metadata compared to the latest version. Examples include tracking the metadata changes for a specific column, or tracking table size trends over time. Being able to ask what the metadata looked like at a point in the past is important for auditing and debugging, and is also useful for reprocessing and rollback use cases. As a part of this requirement, it is important to understand the amount of history that is required to be persisted and to access the API to query the history of snapshots.

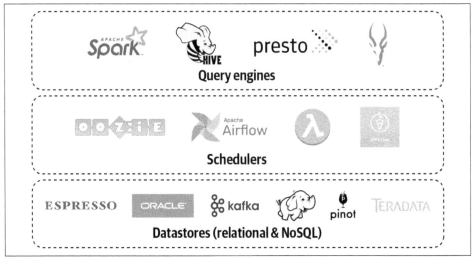

Figure 2-4. Different sources of technical metadata that needs to be collected.

Operational Metadata Requirements

To extract the lineage of processing jobs, the queries are parsed to extract the source and target tables. The requirement analysis involves getting an inventory of query types, including UDFs, across all the datastores and query engines (both streaming and batch processing). The goal is to find the appropriate query parser that supports these queries.

Another aspect of these requirements is related to data profiling stats—i.e., the need for monitoring, SLA alerting, and anomaly tracking. In particular, it is necessary to clarify whether support is required for a) availability alerts of datasets, b) anomaly tracking on the metadata as an indication of data quality, and c) SLA alerting of pipeline execution.

Team Knowledge Aggregator Requirements

For this module, we need to understand the following aspects of the requirements:

- Whether or not there is a need for a business vocabulary
- The need to limit the types of users who can add to the team knowledge—i.e., limiting access control and the approval process required to add to the team knowledge
- The need for validation rules or checks on the metadata
- The need to propagate team knowledge using lineage (e.g., if a table column is annotated with details, then subsequent derivations of the column are also annotated)

Implementation Patterns

There are three levels of automation for the metadata catalog service that correspond to the existing task map (as shown in Figure 2-5). Each level corresponds to automating a combination of tasks that are currently either manual or inefficient:

Source-specific connector pattern
Simplifies connecting to different data sources and extracting the metadata information associated with the data.

Lineage correlation pattern
Automates extracting the lineage of transformations correlating source and target tables.

Team knowledge pattern
Simplifies aggregating business context and sharing of knowledge among data users.

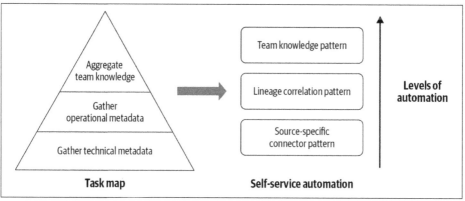

Figure 2-5. The different levels of automation for the metadata catalog service.

The metadata catalog service is being increasingly implemented as a part of data platforms. The popular open source implementations are FINRA's Herd (*https://oreil.ly/ YRXV0*), Uber's Databook (*https://oreil.ly/VFXXO*), LinkedIn's WhereHows (*https:// oreil.ly/MaSie*) and DataHub (*https://oreil.ly/oDsZg*), Netflix's Metacat (*https://oreil.ly/ js2JN*), and Apache's Atlas project (*https://oreil.ly/Ge-1D*), as well as cloud services such as AWS Glue (*https://oreil.ly/XbSXS*).

Source-Specific Connectors Pattern

The source-specific connectors pattern extracts metadata from sources to aggregate technical metadata. Datasets are identified using URN-based naming. There are two building blocks for this pattern:

Custom extractors

Source-specific connectors are used to connect and continuously fetch metadata. Custom extractors need appropriate access permissions to authorize credentials for connecting to datastores such as RDBMS, Hive, GitHub, and so on. For structured and semi-structured datasets, the extraction involves understanding the schema describing the logical structure and semantics of the data. Once the extractor connects to the source, it gathers details by implementing classifiers that determine the format, schema, and associated properties of the dataset.

Federated persistence

Metadata details are persisted in a normalized fashion. The respective systems are still the source of truth for schema metadata, so the metadata catalog does not materialize it in its storage. It only directly stores the business and user-defined metadata about the datasets. It also publishes all of the information about the datasets to the search service for user discovery.

An example of the source-specific connectors pattern is LinkedIn's WhereHows. Source-specific connectors are used to collect metadata from the source systems. For example, for Hadoop datasets, a scraper job scans through the folders and files on HDFS, reads and aggregates the metadata, then stores it back. For schedulers like Azkaban and Oozie, the connector uses the backend repository to get the metadata and aggregate and transform it to the normalized format before loading it into the WhereHows repository. Similar connectors are used for Kafka and Samza. Figure 2-6 shows another example of the pattern implemented in Netflix's Metacat catalog service.

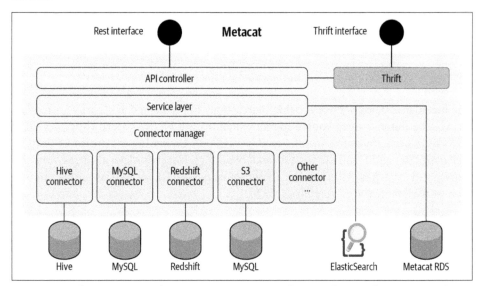

Figure 2-6. The source-specific connector pattern implemented in Netflix Metacat (from The Netflix Tech Blog (https://oreil.ly/Kov-O)).

Strengths of the source-specific connectors pattern:

- It exhaustively aggregates metadata across multiple systems, creating the abstraction of a single warehouse
- It normalizes the source-specific metadata into a common format

Weaknesses of the source-specific connectors pattern:

- It is difficult to manage in constantly keeping up with new adapters
- The post hoc approach of connecting to sources and extracting does not work at the extreme scale of millions of datasets

Lineage Correlation Pattern

The lineage correlation pattern stitches together operational metadata across data and jobs and combines with execution stats. By combining job execution records with lineage, the pattern can answer questions related to data freshness, SLAs, impacted downstream jobs for a given table, ranking of tables in a pipeline based on usage, and so on.

The pattern involves the following three building blocks:

Query parsing
Tracking data lineage is accomplished by analyzing the queries that are run either ad hoc or as scheduled ETLs. The queries are collected from job schedulers, datastore logs, streaming logs, GitHub repositories, and so on. The output of the query parsing is a list of input and output tables—i.e., tables that are read in and written out by the query. Query parsing is not a one-time activity but needs to continuously update based on query changes. Queries can be written in different languages, such as Spark, Pig, and Hive.

Pipeline correlation
A data or ML pipeline is composed of multiple data transformation jobs. Each job is composed of one or more scripts, and each script can have one or more queries or execution steps (as illustrated in Figure 2-7). The pipeline lineage view is constructed by joining the input and output tables associated with each query. This information is extracted from system-specific logs from ingestion frameworks, schedulers, datastores, and query engines.

Enriching lineage with execution stats
The execution stats, including completion time, cardinality of data processed, errors in execution, table access frequency, table counts, and so on, are added to the corresponding tables and jobs in the lineage view. This allows us to correlate table and job anomalies to the overall pipeline execution.

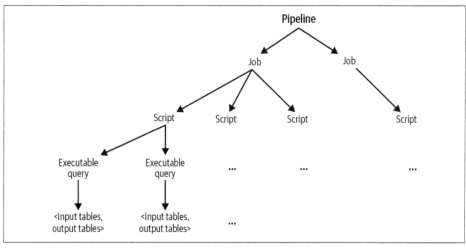

Figure 2-7. Generating lineage of data transformation jobs within a data or ML pipeline.

An example of the pattern is Apache Atlas, which extracts lineage across multiple Hadoop ecosystem components, namely Sqoop, Hive, Kafka, Storm, and so on. Given a Hadoop job ID, Atlas gathers the job conf query from the job history node. The query is parsed to generate the source and target tables. A similar approach is also applied to Sqoop jobs. In addition to table-level lineage, Atlas also supports column-level lineage by tracking the following types of dependencies:

Simple dependency
　　The output column has the same value as the input column.

Expression dependency
　　The output column is transformed by some expression at runtime (e.g., a Hive SQL expression) on the input columns.

Script dependency
　　The output column is transformed by a user-provided script.

The strength of this pattern is that it provides a nonintrusive way to reconstruct the dependencies. The weakness is that the lineage may not have 100% coverage with respect to query types and is approximate. The lineage correlation pattern is critical for deployments where hundreds of pipelines are run daily with guarantees for performance and quality SLA.

Team Knowledge Pattern

The team knowledge pattern focuses on metadata defined by data users to enrich the information associated with the datasets. The goal is for data users to share their experiences and help scale knowledge across teams. This is especially valuable when the datasets are not well documented, have multiple sources of truth, and vary in quality, and when a high percentage of datasets are no longer being maintained.

There are three key types of team knowledge:

Data documentation

This includes details of attribute meaning, enums, and data descriptions. Users can annotate the table columns with free-form metadata based on their usage experience. Also, dataset owners can annotate datasets with descriptions in order to help users figure out which datasets are appropriate for their use (e.g., which analysis techniques are used in certain datasets and which pitfalls to watch out for). Given the different levels of expertise, annotations from junior team members will be verified before being added to the catalog.

Business taxonomy and tags

This includes concepts used within the business as taxonomy to categorize data based on business domains and subject areas. Organizing datasets using business taxonomy helps data users browse based on topics of interest. Tags are used to identify tables for data life cycle management. Dataset auditors can tag datasets that contain sensitive information and alert dataset owners or prompt a review to ensure that the data is handled appropriately.

Pluggable validation

Table owners can provide audit information about a table as metadata. They can also provide column default values and validation rules to be used for writes into the table. Validations also include business rules used for developing the data.

Summary

In the big data era, there is a plethora of data available for generating insights. In order to succeed with the journey map of generating insights, it is critical to understand the metadata associated with the data: where, what, how, when, who, why, and so on. A metadata catalog service that centralizes this information as a single source of truth is indispensable in data platforms.

CHAPTER 3

Search Service

So far, given a dataset, we are able to gather the required metadata details to correctly interpret the properties and meaning of the attributes. The next challenge is, given thousands of datasets across enterprise silos, how we effectively locate the attributes required to develop the insight. For instance, when developing a revenue dashboard, how do we locate datasets of existing customers, products they use, pricing and promotions, activity, usage profiles, and so on? Further, how do we locate artifacts such as metrics, dashboards, models, ETLs, and ad hoc queries that can be reused in building the dashboard? This chapter focuses on finding the relevant datasets (tables, views, schema, files, streams, and events) and artifacts (metrics, dashboards, models, ETLs, and ad hoc queries) during the iterative process of developing insights.

A *search service* simplifies the discovery of datasets and artifacts. With a search service, data users express what they are looking for using keywords, wildcard searches, business terminology, and so on. Under the hood, the service does the heavy lifting of discovering sources, indexing datasets and artifacts, ranking results, ensuring access governance, and managing continuous change. Data users get a list of datasets and artifacts that are most relevant to the input search query. The success criteria for such a service is reducing the *time to find*. Speeding up time to find significantly improves time to insight, as data users are able to quickly search and iterate with different datasets and artifacts. A slowdown in the search process has a negative multiplicative effect on the overall time to insight.

Journey Map

The need to find datasets and artifacts is a starting point on the data scientist's journey map. This section discusses the key scenarios in the journey map for the search service.

Determining Feasibility of the Business Problem

Given a business problem, the first step in the discovery phase is to determine feasibility with respect to availability of relevant datasets. The datasets can be in one of the following availability states:

- Data does not exist and requires the application to be instrumented
- Data is available in the source systems but is not being aggregated in the data lake
- Data is available and is already being used by other artifacts

Feasibility analysis provides an early ballpark for the overall time to insight and is key for better project planning. The gaps discovered in data availability are used as requirements for the data collection phase.

Selecting Relevant Datasets for Data Prep

This is a key scenario for the search service, with the goal of shortlisting one or more datasets that can potentially be used for the next phases of the overall journey map. Selecting relevant datasets for data prep is an iterative process involving searching for datasets using keywords, sampling search results, and selecting deeper analysis of the meaning and lineage of data attributes. With well-curated data, this scenario is easier to accomplish. Often, the business definitions and descriptions are not updated, making identifying the right datasets difficult. A common scenario is the existence of multiple sources of truth where a given dataset can be present in one or more data silos with a different meaning. If existing artifacts are already using the dataset, that is a good indicator of the dataset quality.

Reusing Existing Artifacts for Prototyping

Instead of starting from scratch, the goal of this phase is to find any building blocks that can be reused. These might include data pipelines, dashboards, models, queries, and so on. A few common scenarios typically arise:

- A dashboard already exists for a single geographic location and can be reused by parameterizing geography and other inputs
- Standardized business metrics generated by hardened data pipelines can be leveraged
- Exploratory queries shared in notebooks can be reused

Minimizing Time to Find

Time to find is the total time required to iteratively shortlist relevant datasets and artifacts. Given the complexity of the discovery process, teams often reinvent the wheel, resulting in clones of data pipelines, dashboards, and models within the organization. In addition to causing wasted effort, this results in longer time to insight. Today, time to find is spent on the three activities discussed in this section. The goal of the search service is to minimize the time spent in each activity.

Indexing Datasets and Artifacts

Indexing involves two tasks:

- Locating sources of datasets and artifacts
- Probing these sources to aggregate details like schema and metadata properties

Both of these aspects are time-consuming. Locating datasets and artifacts across silos is currently an ad hoc process; team knowledge in the form of cheat sheets, wikis, anecdotal experiences, and so on is used to get information about datasets and artifacts. Team knowledge is hit-or-miss and not always correct or updated.

Probing sources for additional metadata, such as schema, lineage, and execution stats, requires APIs or CLIs specific to the source technology. There is no standardization to extract this information, irrespective of the underlying technology. Data users need to work with source owners and team knowledge to aggregate the meaning of column names, data types, and other details. Similarly, understanding artifacts like data pipeline code requires analysis of the query logic and how it can be reused. Given the diversity of technologies, representing the details in a common, searchable model is a significant challenge.

Indexing is an ongoing process as new applications and artifacts are continuously being developed. Existing datasets and artifacts are also continually evolving. Being able to update the results and keeping up with the changes is time-consuming.

Ranking Results

Today, a typical search ranking process starts by manually searching datastores, catalogs, Git repositories, dashboards, and so on. The search involves reaching out in Slack groups, looking through wikis, or attending brown bag sessions to gather team knowledge. Ranking results for the next phases of the analysis is time-consuming due to the following realities:

- Tables do not have clear names or a well-defined schema.
- Attributes within the table are not appropriately named.

- There are graveyard datasets and artifacts that are not actively being used or managed.

- The schema has not evolved in sync with how the business has evolved.

- Curation and best practices for schema design are not being followed. A common heuristic, or shortcut, is to only look at popular assets that are used across use cases and that have a high number of access requests. Also, new data users are wise to follow the activity of known data experts within the team.

Access Control

There are two dimensions of access control:

- Securely connecting to the dataset and artifact sources
- Limiting access to the search results

Connecting to the sources is time-consuming, requiring approvals from security and compliance teams that validate the usage. For encrypted source fields, appropriate decryption keys are also required. Read access permissions can limit the data objects that are allowed to be accessed, such as select tables, views, and schemas.

The other dimension is limiting access to search results to the right teams. Limiting the search results is a balancing act between being able to discover the presence of a dataset or artifact and gaining access to secure attributes.

Defining Requirements

The search service should be able to answer some data user questions. Are there datasets or artifacts related to topic X? The match to X can be related to names, descriptions, metadata, tags, categories, and so on. What are the most popular datasets and artifacts related to topic X and the related data user teams? What are the details of the metadata (such as lineage, stats, creation date, and so on) associated with a shortlisted dataset?

There are three key modules required to build the search service:

Indexer module
Discovers available datasets and artifacts, extracts schema and metadata properties, and adds to the catalog. It tracks changes and continuously updates the details.

Ranking module
Responsible for ranking the search results based on a combination of relevance and popularity.

Access module
    Ensures search results shown to a data user adhere to the access control policies.

Indexer Requirements

The indexer requirements vary from deployment to deployment, based on the types of datasets and artifacts to be indexed by the search service. Figure 3-1 illustrates the different categories of datasets and artifacts. Requirements gathering involves collecting an inventory of these categories and a list of deployed technologies. For instance, structured data in the form of tables and schema can be in multiple technologies, such as Oracle, SQL Server, MySQL, and so on.

Figure 3-1 shows the entities covered by the search service; it includes both data and artifacts. Datasets span structured, semi-structured, and unstructured data. Semi-structured NoSQL datasets can be key-value stores, document stores, graph databases, time-series stores, and so on. Artifacts include generated insights as well as recipes, such as ETLs, notebooks, ad hoc queries, data pipelines, and GitHub repos that can potentially be reused.

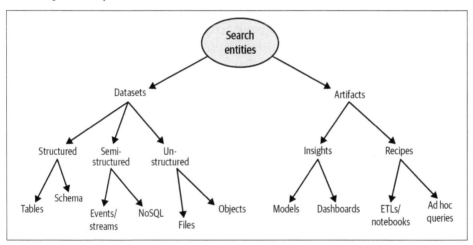

Figure 3-1. Categories of datasets and artifacts covered by the search service.

Another aspect of these requirements is updating the indexes as datasets and artifacts continuously evolve. It is important to define requirements according to how the updates are reflected within the search service:

- Determine how quickly indexes need to be updated to reflect the changes—i.e., determine the acceptable lag to refresh.

- Define indexes across versions and historic partitions—i.e., define whether the scope of search is limited only to the current partitions.

Ranking Requirements

Ranking is a combination of relevance and popularity. *Relevance* is based on the matching of name, description, and metadata attributes. As a part of the requirements, we can define the list of metadata attributes most relevant for the deployment. Table 3-1 represents a normalized model of metadata attributes. The metadata model can be customized based on the requirements of the data users.

Table 3-1. Categories of metadata associated with datasets and artifacts.

Metadata categories	Example properties
Basic	Size, format, last modified, aliases, access control lists
Content-based	Schema, number of records, data fingerprint, key fields
Lineage	Reading jobs, writing jobs, downstream datasets, upstream datasets
User-defined	Tags, categories
People	Owner, teams accessing, teams updating
Temporal	Change history

In addition to normalized metadata attributes, we can also capture technology-specific metadata. For instance, for Apache HBase, `hbase_namespace` and `hbase_col` `umn_families` are examples of technology-specific metadata. These attributes can be used to further search and filter the results.

Access Control Requirements

Access control policies for search results can be defined based on the specifics of the user, the specifics of the data attributes, or both. User-specific policies are referred to as role-based access control (RBAC), whereas attribute-specific policies are referred to as attribute-based access control (ABAC). For instance, limiting visibility for specific user groups is an RBAC policy, and a policy defined for a data tag or PII is an ABAC policy.

In addition to access policies, other special handling requirements might be required:

- Masking of row or column values.
- Time-varying policies such that datasets and artifacts are not visible until a specific timestamp (e.g., tables with quarterly results are not visible until the date the results are officially announced).

Nonfunctional Requirements

Similar to any software design, the following are some of the key nonfunctional requirements (NFRs) that should be considered in the design of a search service:

Response times for search
>It is important to have the search service respond to search queries on the order of seconds.

Scaling to support large indexes
>As enterprises grow, it is important that the search service scales to support thousands of datasets and artifacts.

Ease of onboarding for new sources
>Data source owners' experience when adding their sources to the search service should be simplified.

Automated monitoring and alerting
>The health of the service should be easy to monitor. Any issues during production should generate automated alerts.

Implementation Patterns

Corresponding to the existing task map, there are three levels of automation for the search service (as shown in Figure 3-2). Each level corresponds to automating a combination of tasks that are currently either manual or inefficient:

Push-pull indexer pattern
>Discovers and continuously updates available datasets and artifacts.

Hybrid search ranking pattern
>Ranks the results to help data users find the most relevant dataset and artifact to match the requirements of their data project.

Catalog access control pattern
>Limits access to datasets and artifacts visible in the search service based on the role of the data users and other attributes.

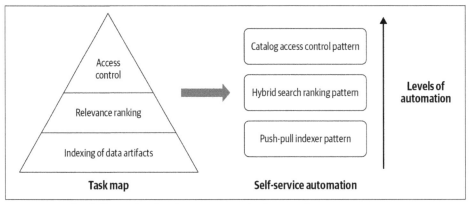

Figure 3-2. The different levels of automation for the search service.

Push-Pull Indexer Pattern

The push-pull indexer pattern discovers and updates available datasets and artifacts across the silos of an enterprise. The pull aspect of the indexer discovers sources, extracts datasets and artifacts, and adds them to the catalog. This is analogous to search engines crawling websites on the internet and pulling associated web pages to make them searchable. The push aspect is related to tracking changes in datasets and artifacts. In this pattern, sources generate update events that are pushed to the catalog for updating the existing details.

The push-pull indexer pattern has the following phases (as illustrated in Figure 3-3):

1. *Connect phase*

   The indexer connects to available sources, such as databases, catalogs, model and dashboard repositories, and so on. These sources are either added manually or discovered in an automated fashion. There are several ways for automated source discovery: scanning the network (similar to the approach used in vulnerability analysis), using cloud account APIs for discovering deployed services within the account, and so on.

2. *Extract phase*

   The next phase is extracting details such as name, description, and other metadata of the discovered dataset and artifacts. For datasets, the indexer provides source credentials to the catalog for extraction of the details (as covered in Chapter 2). There is no straightforward way to extract details of artifacts. For notebooks, data pipeline code, and other files persisted in Git repositories, the indexer looks for a metadata header, such as a small amount of structured metadata at the beginning of the file that includes author(s), tags, and a short description. This is especially useful for notebook artifacts where the entirety of the work, from the query to the transforms, visualizations, and write-up, is contained in one file.

3. *Update phase*

   Sources publish updates to datasets and artifacts on the event bus. These events are used to make updates to the catalog. For example, when a table is dropped, the catalog subscribes to this push notification and deletes the records.

An example of an artifacts repository is Airbnb's open source project called Knowledge Repo (*https://oreil.ly/hKl8e*). At the core, there is a GitHub repository to which notebooks, query files, and scripts are committed. Every file starts with a small amount of structured metadata, including author(s), tags, and a TL;DR. A Python script validates the content and transforms the post into plain text with Markdown syntax. A GitHub pull request is used to review the header contents and organize it by time, topic, or contents. To prevent low quality, similar to code reviews, peer review checks are done for methodological improvements, connections with preexisting work, and precision in details. Additionally, each post has a set of metadata tags, providing a many-to-one topic inheritance that goes beyond the folder location of the file. Users can subscribe to topics and get notified of a new contribution.

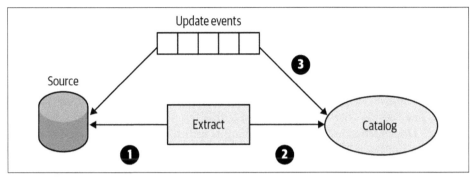

Figure 3-3. The connect, extract, and update phases of the push-pull indexer pattern.

An example of the push-pull indexer pattern implementation is Netflix's open source Metacat catalog (*https://oreil.ly/js2JN*), which is capable of indexing datasets. Metacat uses a pull model to extract dataset details, as well as a push notification model where data sources publish their updates to an event bus like Kafka. Data sources can also invoke an explicit REST API to publish a change event. In Metacat, changes are also published to Amazon SNS. Publishing events to SNS allows other systems in the data platform to "react" to these metadata or data changes accordingly. For example, when a table is dropped, the garbage collection service can subscribe to the event and clean up the data appropriately.

The strengths of the push-pull indexer pattern:

- Index updates are timely. New sources are crawled periodically, and change events are pushed on the event bus for processing.
- It's an extensible pattern for extracting and updating different categories of metadata attributes.
- It's scalable to support a large number of sources given the combination of push and pull approaches.

The weakness of the push-pull indexer pattern:

- Configuration and deployment for different source types can be challenging.
- To access details via pull, source permissions are required that might be a concern for regulated sources.

The push-pull indexer pattern is an advanced approach for implementing indexing (compared to a push-only pattern). To ensure sources are discovered, the onboarding process should include adding the source to the list of pull targets as well as creating a common set of access credentials.

Hybrid Search Ranking Pattern

Given a string input, the ranking pattern generates a list of datasets and artifacts. The string can be a table name, business vocabulary concept, classification tag, and so on. This is analogous to page ranking used by search engines for generating relevant results. The success criteria of the pattern is that the most relevant results are in the top five. The effectiveness of search ranking is critical for reducing time to insight. For instance, if the relevant result is in the top three on the first page instead of several pages down, the user won't waste time reviewing and analyzing several irrelevant results. The hybrid search ranking pattern implements a combination of relevance and popularity to find the most relevant datasets and artifacts.

There are three phases to the pattern (as illustrated in Figure 3-4):

1. Parsing phase

Search starts with an input string, typically in plain English. In addition to searching, there can be multiple criteria for filtering the results. The service is backed by a conventional inverted index for document retrieval, where each dataset and artifact becomes a document with indexing tokens derived based on the metadata. Each category of metadata can be associated with a specific section of the index. For example, metadata derived from the creator of the dataset is associated with the "creator" section of the index. Accordingly, the search `creator:x` will match keyword x on the dataset creator only, whereas the unqualified atom x will match the keyword in any part of a dataset's metadata. An alternative starting point to the parsing process is to browse a list of popular tables and artifacts and find the ones that are most relevant to the business problem.

2. Ranking phase

Ordering of the results is a combination of relevance and popularity. Relevance is based on fuzzy matching of the entered text to table name, column name, table description, metadata properties, and so on. Popularity-based matching is based on activity—i.e., highly queried datasets and artifacts show up higher in the list, while those queried less show up later in the search results. An ideal result is one that is both popular and relevant. There are several other heuristics to consider. For instance, newly created datasets have a higher weightage on relevance (since they are not yet popular). Another heuristic is to sort based on quality metrics, such as number of issues reported and whether the dataset is generated as part of a hardened data pipeline instead of an ad hoc process.

3. Feedback phase

Weightage between relevance and popularity needs to be adjusted based on feedback. The effectiveness of search ranking can be measured explicitly or implicitly: explicitly in the form of thumbs up/down ratings for the displayed results and implicitly in the form of the click-through rate (CTR) of top-five results. This will fine-tune the weightage and the fuzzy matching logic for relevance matching.

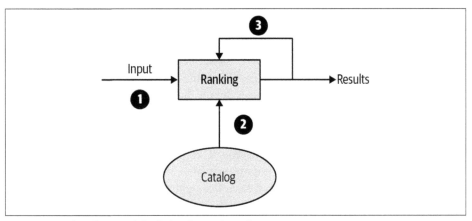

Figure 3-4. The phases of the hybrid search ranking pattern.

An example of the hybrid search ranking pattern is the Amundsen (*https://oreil.ly/BzyoZ*) open source project. Amundsen indexes datasets and artifacts. The input parsing implements type-ahead capability to improve the exact matching. The input string supports wildcards as well as keywords, categories, business vocabulary, and so on. The input can be further narrowed using different types of filters:

- Search by category, such as dataset, table, stream, tags, and so on
- Filter by `keyword: value`, such as `column: users` or `column_description: channels`

Amundsen enables fuzzy searches by implementing a thin Elasticsearch proxy layer to interact with the catalog. Metadata is persisted in Neo4j. It uses a data ingestion library for building the indexes. The search results show a subset of the inline metadata—a description of the table, as well the last date when the table was updated.

Scoring is generally a hard problem and involves tuning the scoring function based on users' experience. What follows are some of the heuristics used in the scoring function by Google's dataset search service (*https://oreil.ly/V2BEZ*):

The importance of a dataset depends on its type

The scoring function favors a structured table over a file dataset, all else being equal. The assumption is that a dataset owner has to register a dataset as a table explicitly, which in turn makes the dataset visible to more users. This action can be used as a signal that the dataset is important.

The importance of a keyword match depends on the index section
For instance, a keyword match on the path of the dataset is more important than a match on jobs that read or write the dataset, all else being equal.

Lineage fan-out is a good indicator of dataset importance, as it indicates popularity
Specifically, this heuristic favors datasets with many reading jobs and many downstream datasets. The assumption is that, if many production pipelines access the dataset, then the dataset is most likely important. One can view this heuristic as an approximation of PageRank in a graph where datasets and production jobs are vertices and the edges denote dataset accesses from jobs.

A dataset that carries an owner-sourced description is likely to be important
Our user interface enables dataset owners to provide descriptions for datasets that they want other teams to consume. The presence of such a description is treated as a signal of dataset importance. If a keyword match occurs in the description of a dataset, then this dataset is weighted higher as well.

Strengths of the hybrid search ranking pattern:

- It balances relevance and popularity, allowing data users to quickly shortlist the most relevant data.

- It is not bottlenecked by the need to add extensive metadata for relevance matching on day one. Metadata can be annotated incrementally while the pattern uses more of the popularity-based ranking.

Weaknesses of the hybrid search ranking pattern:

- It does not replace the need for curated datasets. The pattern relies on the correctness of the metadata details that are synchronized with the business details.

- Getting the right balance between popularity and relevance is difficult.

The hybrid search ranking pattern provides the best of both worlds. For datasets and artifacts where extensive amounts of metadata are available, it leverages the relevance matching. For assets that are not well curated, it relies on the popularity matching.

Catalog Access Control Pattern

The goal of the search service is to make it easy to discover datasets and artifacts. But it's equally important to ensure that access control policies aren't violated. The search results displayed to different users can exclude select datasets or vary in the level of metadata details. This pattern enforces access control at the metadata catalog and provides a centralized approach for fine-grained authorization and access control.

There are three phases to the catalog access control pattern:

Classify
> In this phase, users and datasets and artifacts are classified into categories. Users are classified into groups based on their role: data stewards, finance users, data quality admins, data scientists, data engineers, admins, and so on. The role defines the datasets and artifacts that are visible during the search process. Similarly, datasets and artifacts are annotated with user-defined tags, such as finance, PII, and so on.

Define
> Policies define the level of search details to be shown to a given user for a given dataset or artifact. For instance, tables related to financial results can be restricted to finance users. Similarly, data quality users can see advanced metadata and change log history. Policy definitions fall into two broad buckets: RBAC, where policies are defined based on users, and ABAC, where policies are defined based on attributes like user-defined tags, geographical tags based on IP address, time-based tags, and so on.

Enforce
> Typically, there are three ways to enforce access control policies in search results:
>
> - Basic metadata for everyone: In response to the search query, the results show basic metadata (such as name, description, owner, date updated, user-defined tags, and so on) to everyone, whether or not they have access. The reasoning for this approach is to ensure user productivity by showing the dataset and artifacts that exist. If the dataset matches the requirement, the user can request access.
>
> - Selective advanced metadata: Select users get advanced metadata like column stats and data previews based on the access control policies.
>
> - Masking of columns and rows: Based on access control, the same dataset will have a different number of columns as well as different rows in the data preview. Updates to the catalog are automatically propagated to the access control. For instance, if a column is labeled as sensitive, the search results will automatically start reflecting in the data preview.

An example of a popular open source solution for fine-grained authorization and access control is Apache Ranger (*https://oreil.ly/R2Op6*). It provides a centralized framework to implement security policies for the Atlas catalog and all Hadoop ecosystems. It supports RBAC and ABAC policies based on individual users, groups, access types, user-defined tags, dynamic tags like IP address, and more (as shown in Figure 3-5). Apache Ranger's policy model has been enhanced to support row-filtering and data-masking features so that users can only access a subset of rows in a table or masked/redacted values for sensitive data. Ranger's policy validity periods enable configuring a policy to be effective for a specified time range—for example, restricting access to sensitive financial information until the earnings release date.

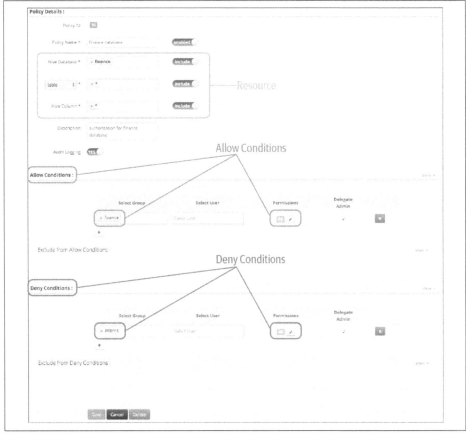

Figure 3-5. Screenshot of centralizd access control policy details available in Apache Ranger (from the Ranger wiki (https://oreil.ly/6e7Jl)).

Strengths of the catalog access control pattern:

- It's easy to manage given the centralized access control policies on the catalog level.
- It offers tunable access control based on different users and use cases.

Weaknesses of the catalog access control pattern:

- The catalog access control policies can get out of sync with the data source policies. For instance, the data user can access the metadata based on the catalog policies but not the actual dataset based on the backend source policy.

The catalog access pattern is a must-have for balancing discoverability and access control. It is a flexible pattern allowing simple heuristics as well as complex, fine-grained authorization and masking.

Summary

Real-world deployments have noncurated and siloed datasets and artifacts. They lack well-defined attribute names and descriptions and are typically out of sync with the business definitions. A search service can automate the process of shortlisting relevant datasets and artifacts, significantly simplifying the discovery phase in the journey map.

CHAPTER 4

Feature Store Service

So far, we have discovered the available datasets and artifacts that can be used to generate the required insight. In the case of ML models, there is an additional step of discovering features. For instance, a revenue forecasting model that needs to be trained would require the previous revenue numbers by market, product line, and so on as input. A *feature* is a data attribute that can be either extracted directly or derived by computing from one or more data sources—e.g., the age of a person, a coordinate emitted from a sensor, a word from a piece of text, or an aggregate value like the average number of purchases within the last hour. Historic values of the data attribute are required for using a feature in ML models.

Data scientists spend a significant amount of their time creating training datasets for ML models. Building data pipelines to generate the features for training, as well as for inference, is a significant pain point. First, data scientists have to write low-level code for accessing datastores, which requires data engineering skills. Second, the pipelines for generating these features have multiple implementations that are not always consistent—i.e., there are separate pipelines for training and inference. Third, the pipeline code is duplicated across ML projects and not reusable since it is embedded as part of the model implementation. Finally, there is no change management or governance of features. These aspects impact the overall time to insight. This is especially true as data users typically lack the engineering skills to develop robust pipelines and monitor them in production. Also, feature pipelines are repeatedly built from scratch instead of being shared across ML projects. The process of building ML models is iterative and requires exploration with different feature combinations.

Ideally, a *feature store service* should provide well-documented, governed, versioned, and curated features for training and inference of ML models (as shown in Figure 4-1). Data users should be able to search and use features to build models with minimal data engineering. The feature pipeline implementations for training as well as inference are consistent. In addition, features are cached and reused across ML projects, reducing training time and infrastructure costs. The success metric of this service is *time to featurize*. As the feature store service is built up with more features, it provides economies of scale by making it easier and faster to build new models.

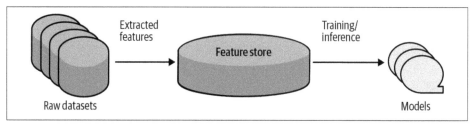

Figure 4-1. The feature store as the repository of features that are used for training and inference of models across multiple data projects.

Journey Map

Developing and managing features is a critical piece of developing ML models. Often, data projects share a common set of features, allowing reuse of the same features. An increase in the number of features reduces the cost of implementing new data projects (as shown in Figure 4-2). There is a good overlap of features across projects. This section discusses key scenarios in the journey map for the feature store service.

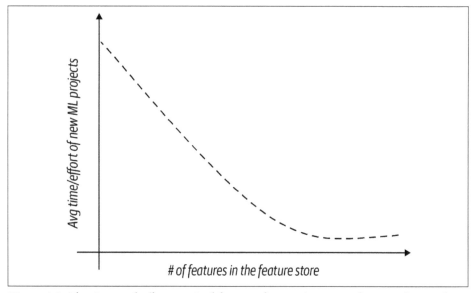

Figure 4-2. The time and effort required for new data projects goes down as the number of available features in the feature store grows.

Finding Available Features

As a part of the exploration phase, data scientists search for available features that can be leveraged to build the ML model. The goal of this phase is to reuse features and reduce the cost to build the model. The process involves analyzing whether the available features are of good quality and how they are being used currently. Due to a lack of a centralized feature repository, data scientists often skip the search phase and develop ad hoc training pipelines that have a tendency to become complex over time. As the number of models increases, it quickly becomes a pipeline jungle that is hard to manage.

Training Set Generation

During model training, datasets consisting of one or more features are required to train the model. The training set, which contains the historic values of these features, is generated along with a prediction label. The training set is prepared by writing queries that extract the data from the dataset sources and transform, cleanse, and generate historic data values of the features. A significant amount of time is spent in developing the training set. Also, the feature set needs to be updated continuously with new values (a process referred to as *backfilling*). With a feature store, the training datasets for features are available during the building of the models.

Feature Pipeline for Online Inference

For model inference, the feature values are provided as an input to the model, which then generates the predicted output. The pipeline logic for generating features during inference should match the logic used during training, otherwise the model predictions will be incorrect. Besides the pipeline logic, an additional requirement is having a low latency to generate the feature for inferencing in online models. Today, the feature pipelines embedded within the ML pipeline are not easily reusable. Further, changes in training pipeline logic may not be coordinated correctly with corresponding model inference pipelines.

Minimize Time to Featurize

Time to featurize is the time spent creating and managing features. Today, the time spent is broadly divided into two categories: feature computation and feature serving. Feature computation involves data pipelines for generating features both for training as well as inference. Feature serving focuses on serving bulk datasets during training, low-latency feature values for model inference, and making it easy for data users to search and collaborate across features.

Feature Computation

Feature computation is the process of converting raw data into features. This involves building data pipelines for generating historic training values of the feature as well as current feature values used for model inference. Training datasets need to be continuously backfilled with newer samples. There are two key challenges with feature computation.

First, there is the complexity of managing pipeline jungles. Pipelines extract the data from the source datastores and transform them into features. These pipelines have multiple transformations and need to handle corner cases that arise in production. Managing these at scale in production is a nightmare. Also, the number of feature data samples continues to grow, especially for deep learning models. Managing large datasets at scale requires distributed programming optimizations for scaling and performance. Overall, building and managing data pipelines is typically one of the most time-consuming parts of the overall time to insight of model creation.

Second, separate pipelines are written for training and inference for a given feature. This is because there are different freshness requirements, as model training is typically batch-oriented, while model inference is streaming with near real-time latency. Discrepancies in training and inference pipeline computation is a key reason for model correctness issues and a nightmare to debug at production scale.

Feature Serving

Feature serving involves serving feature values in bulk for training, as well as at low latency for inference. It requires features to be easy to discover and compare and analyze with other existing features. In a typical large-scale deployment, feature serving supports thousands of model inferences. Scaling performance is one of the key challenges, as is avoiding duplicate features given the fast-paced exploration of data users across hundreds of model permutations during prototyping.

Today, one of the common issues is that the model performs well on the training dataset but not in production. While there can be multiple reasons for this, the key problem is referred to as *label leakage*. This arises as a result of incorrect point-in-time values being served for the model features. Finding the right feature values is tricky. To illustrate, Zanoyan et al. (*https://oreil.ly/casp-*) cover an example illustrated in Figure 4-3. It shows the feature values selected in training for prediction at Time T1. There are three features shown: F1, F2, F3. For prediction P1, feature values 7, 3, 8 need to be selected for training features F1, F2, F3, respectively. Instead, if the feature values post-prediction are used (such as value 4 for F1), there will be feature leakage since the value represents the potential outcome of the prediction, and incorrectly represents a high correlation during training.

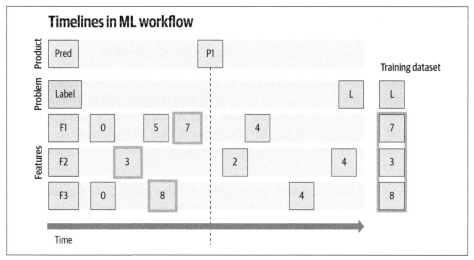

Figure 4-3. The selection of correct point-in-time values for features F1, F2, F3 during training for prediction P1. The actual outcome Label L is provided for training the supervised ML model.

Defining Requirements

Feature store service is a central repository of features, providing both the historical values of features over long durations like weeks or months as well as near real-time feature values over several minutes. The requirements of a feature store are divided into feature computation and feature serving.

Feature Computation

Feature computation requires deep integration with the data lake and other data sources. There are three dimensions to consider for feature computation pipelines.

First, consider the diverse types of features to be supported. Features can be associated with individual data attributes or are composite aggregates. Further, features can be relatively static instead of changing continuously relative to nominal time. Computing features typically requires multiple primitive functions to be supported by the feature store, similar to the functions that are currently used by data users, such as:

- Converting categorical data into numeric data
- Normalizing data when features originate from different distributions
- One-hot encoding or feature binarization
- Feature binning (e.g., converting continuous features into discrete features)

- Feature hashing (e.g., to reduce the memory footprint of one-hot-encoded features)
- Computing aggregate features (e.g., count, min, max, and stdev)

Second, consider the programming libraries that are required to be supported for feature engineering. Spark is a preferred choice for data wrangling among users working with large-scale datasets. Users working with small datasets prefer frameworks such as NumPy and pandas. Feature engineering jobs are built using notebooks, Python files, or .jar files and run on computation frameworks such as Samza, Spark, Flink, and Beam.

Third, consider the source system types where the feature data is persisted. The source systems can be a range of relational databases, NoSQL datastores, streaming platforms, and file and object stores.

Feature Serving

A feature store needs to support strong collaboration capabilities. Features should be defined and generated such that they are shareable across teams.

Feature groups

A feature store has two interfaces: writing features to the store and reading features for training and inference. Features are typically written to a file or a project-specific database. Features can be further grouped together based on the ones that are computed by the same processing job or from the same raw dataset. For instance, for a car-sharing service like Uber, all the trip-related features for a geographical region can be managed as a feature group since they can all be computed by one job that scans through the trip history. Features can be joined with labels (in the case of supervised learning) and materialized into a training dataset. Feature groups typically share a common column, such as a timestamp or customer ID, that allows feature groups to be joined together into a training dataset. The feature store creates and manages the training dataset, persisted as TFRecords, Parquet, CSV, TSV, HDF5, or .npy files.

Scaling

There are some aspects to consider with respect to scaling:

- The number of features to be supported in the feature store
- The number of models calling the feature store for online inferences
- The number of models for daily offline inference as well as training
- The amount of historic data to be included in training datasets
- The number of daily pipelines to backfill the feature datasets as new samples are generated

Additionally, there are specific performance scaling requirements associated with online model inference—e.g., TP99 latency value for computing the feature value. For online training, take into account time to backfill training sets and account for DB schema mutations. Typically, historical features need to be less than 12 hours old, and near real-time feature values need to be less than 5 minutes old.

Feature analysis

Features should be searchable and easily understandable, to ensure they are reused across ML projects. Data users need to be able to identify the transformations as well as analyze the features, finding outliers, distribution drift, and feature correlations.

Nonfunctional Requirements

Similar to any software design, the following are some of the key NFRs that should be considered in the design of a feature store service:

Automated monitoring and alerting
> The health of the service should be easy to monitor. Any issues during production should generate automated alerts.

Response times
> It is important to have the service respond to feature search queries on the order of milliseconds.

Intuitive interface
> For the feature store service to be effective, it needs to be adopted across all data users within the organization. As such, it is critical to have APIs, CLIs, and a web portal that are easy to use and understand.

Implementation Patterns

Corresponding to the existing task map, there are two levels of automation for the feature store service (as shown in Figure 4-4). Each level corresponds to automating a combination of tasks that are currently either manual or inefficient:

Hybrid feature computation pattern
> Defines the pattern to combine batch and stream processing for computing features.

Feature registry pattern
> Defines the pattern to serve the features for training and inference.

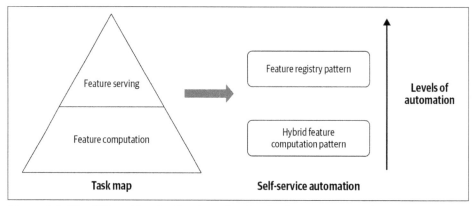

Figure 4-4. The different levels of automation for the feature store service.

Feature store services are becoming increasingly popular: Uber's Michelangelo (*https://oreil.ly/56ukj*), Airbnb's Zipline (*https://oreil.ly/cKwoi*), Gojek's Feast (*https://oreil.ly/foWgT*), Comcast's Applied AI (*https://oreil.ly/pw9it*), Logical Clock's Hopsworks (*https://oreil.ly/EMeHg*), Netflix's Fact Store (*https://oreil.ly/aiIZJ*), and Pinterest's Galaxy (*https://oreil.ly/sFSeL*) are some of the popular open source examples of a feature store service. A good list of emerging feature stores is available at featurestore.org. From an architecture standpoint, each of these implementations has two key building blocks: feature computation and serving.

Hybrid Feature Computation Pattern

The feature computation module has to support two sets of ML scenarios:

- Offline training and inference where bulk historic data is calculated at the frequency of hours
- Online training and inference where feature values are calculated every few minutes

In the hybrid feature computation pattern, there are three building blocks (as shown in Figure 4-5):

Batch compute pipeline
    Traditional batch processing runs as an ETL job every few hours, or daily, to calculate historic feature values. The pipeline is optimized to run on large time windows.

Streaming compute pipeline
    Streaming analytics performed on data events in a real-time message bus to compute feature values at low latency. The feature values are backfilled into the bulk historic data from the batch pipeline.

Feature spec

To ensure consistency, instead of data users creating pipelines for new features, they define a feature spec using a domain-specific language (DSL). The spec specifies the data sources and dependencies and the transformation required to generate the feature. The spec is automatically converted into batch and streaming pipelines. This ensures consistency in pipeline code for training as well as inference without user involvement.

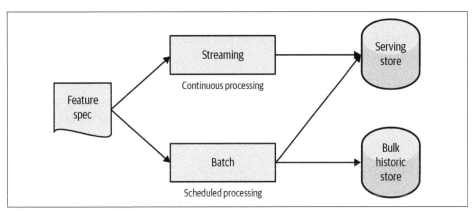

Figure 4-5. Parallel pipelines in the hybrid feature computation pattern.

An example of the hybrid feature computation pattern is Uber's Michelangelo (*https://oreil.ly/56ukj*). It implements a combination of Apache Spark and Samza. Spark is used for computing batch features and the results are persisted in Hive. Batch jobs compute feature groups and write to a single Hive table as a feature per column. For example, Uber Eats (Uber's food delivery service) uses the batch pipeline for features like a restaurant's average meal preparation time over the last seven days. For the streaming pipeline, Kafka topics are consumed with Samza streaming jobs to generate near real-time feature values that are persisted in key-value format in Cassandra. Bulk precomputing and loading of historical features happens from Hive into Cassandra on a regular basis. For example, Uber Eats uses the streaming pipeline for features like a restaurant's average meal preparation time over the last hour. Features are defined using a DSL that selects, transforms, and combines the features that are sent to the model at training and prediction times. The DSL is implemented as a subset of Scala, which is a pure functional language with a complete set of commonly used functions. Data users also have the ability to add their own user-defined functions.

Strengths of the hybrid feature computation pattern:

- It provides optimal performance of feature computation across batch and streaming time windows.
- The DSL to define features avoids inconsistencies associated with discrepancies in pipeline implementation for training and inference.

Weakness of the hybrid feature computation pattern:

- The pattern is nontrivial to implement and manage in production. It requires the data platform to be fairly mature.

The hybrid feature computation pattern is an advanced approach for implementing computation of features that is optimized for both batch and streaming. Programming models like Apache Beam are increasingly converging the batch and streaming divide.

Feature Registry Pattern

The feature registry pattern ensures it is easy to discover and manage features. It is also performant in serving the feature values for online/offline training and inference. The requirements for these use cases are quite varied, as observed by Li et al (*https:// oreil.ly/sFfDJ*). Efficient bulk access is required for batch training and inference. Low-latency, per-record access is required for real-time prediction. A single store is not optimal for both historical and near real-time features for the following reasons: a) datastores are efficient for either point queries or for bulk access, but not both, and b) frequent bulk access can adversely impact the latency of point queries, making them difficult to coexist. Irrespective of the use case, features are identified via canonical names.

For feature discovery and management, the feature registry pattern is the user interface for publishing and discovering features and training datasets. The feature registry pattern also serves as a tool for analyzing feature evolution over time by comparing feature versions. When starting a new data science project, data scientists typically begin by scanning the feature registry for available features, only adding new features that do not already exist in the feature store for their model.

The feature registry pattern has the following building blocks:

Feature values store
> Stores the feature values. Common solutions for bulk stores are Hive (used by Uber and Airbnb), S3 (used by Comcast), and Google BigQuery (used by Gojek). For online data, a NoSQL store like Cassandra is typically used.

Feature registry store

Stores code to compute features, feature version information, feature analysis data, and feature documentation. The feature registry provides automatic feature analysis, feature dependency tracking, feature job tracking, feature data preview, and keyword search on feature/feature group/training dataset metadata.

An example of the feature registry pattern is Hopsworks feature store (*https://oreil.ly/ 7c_fx*). Users query the feature store as SQL, or programmatically, and then the feature store returns the features as a dataframe (as shown in Figure 4-6). Feature groups and training datasets in the Hopsworks feature store are linked to Spark/NumPy/ pandas jobs, which enables the reproduction and recomputation of the features when necessary. In addition to a feature group or training dataset, the feature store does a data analysis step, looking at cluster analysis of feature values, feature correlation, feature histograms, and descriptive statistics. For instance, feature correlation information can be used to identify redundant features, feature histograms can be used to monitor feature distributions between different versions of a feature to discover covariate shift, and cluster analysis can be used to spot outliers. Having such statistics accessible in the feature registry helps users decide on which features to use.

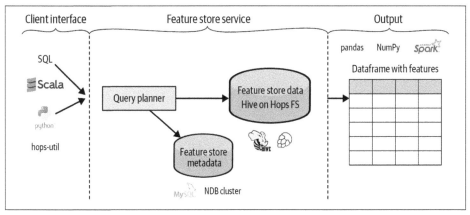

Figure 4-6. User queries to the feature store generate dataframes (represented in popular formats, namely pandas, NumPy, or Spark) (from the Hopsworks documentation (https://oreil.ly/2o1e0)).

Strengths of the feature registry pattern:

- It provides a performant serving of training datasets and feature values
- It reduces feature analysis time for data users

Weaknessess of the feature registry pattern:

- The potential performance bottleneck while serving hundreds of models
- Scaling for continuous feature analysis with a growing number of features

Summary

Today, there is no principled way to access features during model serving and training. Features cannot easily be reused between multiple ML pipelines, and ML projects work in isolation without collaboration and reuse. Given that features are deeply embedded in ML pipelines, when new data arrives, there is no way to pin down exactly which features need to be recomputed; rather, the entire ML pipeline needs to be run to update features. A feature store addresses these symptoms and enables economies of scale in developing ML models.

CHAPTER 5

Data Movement Service

In the journey of developing insights to solve business problems, we've discussed discovering existing datasets and their metadata, and reusable artifacts and features that can be used to develop the insights. Often, data attributes from different data warehouses or application databases must be aggregated for building insights. For example, the revenue dashboard will require attributes from billing, product codes, and special offers to be moved into a common datastore that is then queried and joined to update the dashboard every few hours or in real time. Data users spend 16% of their time moving data (*https://oreil.ly/qdbsF*). Today, data movement causes pain points for orchestrating the data movement across heterogeneous data sources, verifying data correctness between the source and target on an ongoing basis, and adapting to any schema or configuration changes that commonly occur on the data source.

Ensuring the data attributes from the different sources are available in a timely fashion is one of the major pain points. The time spent making data available impacts productivity and slows down the overall time to insight. Ideally, moving data should be *self-service* such that data users select a source, a target, and a schedule to move data. The success criteria for such a service is reducing the *time to data availability*.

Journey Map

This section talks about the different scenarios in the data scientist's journey map where data movement is required.

Aggregating Data Across Sources

Traditionally, data from transactional data sources was aggregated in a *data warehouse* for analytical purposes. Today, the variety of data sources has increased significantly to include structured, semi-structured, and unstructured data, including transactional databases, behavioral data, geospatial data, server logs, IoT sensors, and so on. Aggregating data from these sources is a challenge for data users.

To add to the complexity, data sources are getting increasingly siloed with the emergence of the microservices paradigm (*https://oreil.ly/2kHMq*) for application design. In this paradigm, developers can select different underlying datastores and data models best suited for their microservice. In the real world, a typical data user needs to grapple with different data silos, and typically coordinates across teams, managing product-based transactions, behavioral clickstream data, marketing campaigns, billing activity, customer support tickets, sales records, and so on. In this scenario, the role of the data movement service is to automate the aggregation of data within a central repository called a *data lake*.

Moving Raw Data to Specialized Query Engines

A growing number of query processing engines are optimized for different types of queries and data workloads. For instance, for slice-and-dice analysis of time-series datasets, data is copied into specialized analytical solutions like Druid (*https://oreil.ly/hmCP4*) and Pinot (*https://oreil.ly/_hu7N*). Simplifying data movement can help leverage the right analysis tool for the job. In cloud-based architectures, query engines increasingly run directly on the data lake, reducing the need to move data.

Moving Processed Data to Serving Stores

Consider the scenario where data is processed and stored as key-value pairs that need to be served by the software application to millions of end users. To ensure the right performance and scaling, the right NoSQL store needs to be selected as a serving store depending on the data model and consistency requirements.

Exploratory Analysis Across Sources

During the initial phases of model building, data users need to explore a multitude of data attributes. These attributes may not all be available in the data lake. The exploration phase doesn't require full tables but rather samples of the data for quick prototyping. Given the iterative nature of the prototyping effort, automating data movement as a point-and-click capability is critical. This scenario serves as a pre-step to deciding which datasets need to be aggregated within the data lake on a regular basis.

Minimizing Time to Data Availability

Today, time to data availability is spent on the four activities discussed in this section. The goal of the data movement service is to minimize this time spent.

Data Ingestion Configuration and Change Management

Data must be read from the source datastore and written to a target datastore. A technology-specific adapter is required to read and write the data from and to the datastore. Source teams managing the datastore need to enable the configuration to allow data to be read. Typically, concerns related to performance impact on the source datastore must be addressed. This process is tracked in Jira tickets and can take days.

After the initial configuration, changes to the schema and configuration can occur at the source and target datastores. Such changes can disrupt downstream ETLs and ML models relying on specific data attributes that may have been either deprecated or changed to represent a different meaning. These changes need to be proactively coordinated. Unless the data movement is one-time, ongoing change management is required to ensure source data is correctly made available at the target.

Compliance

Before the data can be moved across systems, it must be verified for regulatory compliance. For example, if the source datastore is under regulatory compliance laws like PCI (*https://oreil.ly/j8aBX*), the data movement must be documented with clear business justification. For data with personally identifiable information (PII) attributes, these must be encrypted during transit and on the target datastore. Emerging data rights laws such as the General Data Protection Regulation (*https://oreil.ly/K7Yqz*) (GDPR) and the California Consumer Privacy Act (CCPA) (*https://oreil.ly/eIBY6*) further limit the data that can be moved from source datastores for analytics. Compliance validations can take significant time depending on the applicable regulations.

Data Quality Verification

Data movement needs to ensure that source and target are in parity. In real-world deployments, quality errors can arise for a multitude of reasons, such as source errors, adapter failures, aggregation issues, and so on. Monitoring of data parity during movement is a must-have to ensure that data quality errors don't go unnoticed and impact the correctness of business metrics and ML models.

During data movement, data at the target may not exactly resemble the data at the source. The data at the target may be filtered, aggregated, or a transformed view of the source data. For instance, if the application data is sharded across multiple clusters, a single aggregated materialized view may be required on the target. Transformations need to be defined and verified before deploying in production.

Although there are multiple commercial and open source solutions available today, there is no one-size-fits-all solution for implementing a data movement service. The rest of the chapter covers requirements and design patterns for building the data movement service.

Defining Requirements

There are four key modules of a data movement service:

Ingestion module
> Responsible for copying data from the source to the target datastore, either one time or on an ongoing basis

Transformation module
> Responsible for transforming the data as it is copied from source to target

Compliance module
> Ensures data moved for analytical purposes meets compliance requirements

Verification module
> Ensures data parity between source and target

The requirements for each of these components varies from deployment to deployment depending on several factors, including industry regulations, maturity of the platform technology, types of insights use cases, existing data processes, skills of data users, and so on. This section covers the aspects data users need to consider for defining requirements related to the data movement service.

Ingestion Requirements

Three key aspects need to be defined as part of data ingestion requirements.

Source and target datastore technologies

A technology-specific adapter is required to read and write data from a datastore. Available solutions vary in the adapters they support. As such, it is important to list the datastores currently deployed. Table 5-1 lists the popular categories of datastores.

Table 5-1. Categories of datastores to be collected as part of the requirements gathering.

Datastore category	Popular examples
Transactional databases	Oracle, SQL Server, MySQL
NoSQL datastores	Cassandra, Neo4j, MongoDB
Filesystems	Hadoop FileSystem, NFS appliance, Samba
Data warehouses	Vertica, Oracle Exalogic, AWS Redshift
Object store	AWS S3
Messaging frameworks	Kafka, JMS
Event logs	Syslog, NGNIX logs

Data scale

The key aspects of scale that data engineers need to understand are:

- How big are the tables in terms of number of rows; that is, do they have thousands or billions of rows?
- What is the ballpark size of the tables in TB?
- What is the ballpark of the number of tables to be copied on an ongoing basis?

Another aspect of scale is the rate of change: an estimation of whether the table is fast changing with regard to the number of inserts, updates, and deletes. Using the size of the data and rate of updates, data engineers can estimate the scaling requirements.

Acceptable refresh lag

For exploratory use cases, the data movement is typically a one-time move. For the ongoing copy of data, there are a few different options, as shown in Figure 5-1. In the figure, scheduled data copy can be implemented as a batch (periodic) instead of a continuous operation. Batch operations can be either full-copy of the table or incremental copy of only the changes from the last change. For continuous copy, changes on the source are transmitted to the target in near real-time (on the order of seconds or minutes).

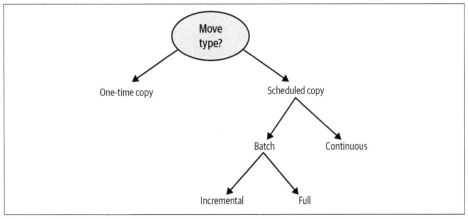

Figure 5-1. Decision tree showing the different types of data movement requests.

Transformation Requirements

During data movement, the target may not be the exact replica of the source. As part of the data movement service, it is important to define the different types of transformations that need to be supported by the service. There are four categories of transformation:

Format transformation
> The most common form is for the target data to be a replica of the source table. Alternatively, the target can be an append log of updates or a list of change events representing updates, inserts, or deletes on the table.

Automated schema evolution
> For scheduled data movement, the schema of the source table can get updated. The data movement service should be able to automatically adapt to changes.

Filtering
> The original source table or event may have fields that need to be filtered from the target. For instance, only a subset of columns from the source table may be required on the target. Additionally, filtering can be used for deduping duplicate records. Depending on the type of analytics, filtering of deleted records may need special handling. For example, financial analytics require deleted records to be available marked with a delete flag (called a *soft delete*) instead of the actual delete (a *hard delete*).

Aggregation
> In scenarios where the source data is sharded across multiple silos, the transformation logic aggregates and creates a single materialized view. Aggregation can also involve enriching data by joining across sources.

Compliance Requirements

During data movement, you should consider multiple aspects of compliance. Figure 5-2 shows Maslow's hierarchy of requirements that should be considered. At the bottom of the triangle are the three As of compliance: authentication, access control, and audit tracking. Above that are considerations for handling PII with regard to encryption as well as masking. Next up are any requirements specific to regulatory compliance, such as SOX, PCI, and so on. At the top is data rights compliance, with laws such as CCPA, GDPR, and so on.

Figure 5-2. Hierarchy of compliance requirements to be considered during data movement.

Verification Requirements

Ensuring the source and target are at parity is critical for the data movement process. Different parity check requirements can be defined depending on the type of analytics and the nature of data involved. For instance, row count parity ensures all the source data is reflected on the target. There is also sampling parity, where a subset of rows is compared to verify that records on source and target match exactly and that there was no data corruption (such as data columns appearing as null) during the data movement. There are multiple other quality checks, such as column value distributions and cross-table referential integrity, which are covered in Chapter 9. If errors are detected, the data movement service should be configured to either raise the alert or make the target data unavailable.

Nonfunctional Requirements

Similar to any software design, the following are some of the key NFRs that should be considered in the design of a data movement service:

Ease of onboarding for new source datastores
Simplify the experience for data source owners onboarding to the service and support a wide range of source and target datastores.

Automated monitoring and failure recovery
The service should be able to checkpoint and recover from any data movement failures. This is especially important when large tables are being moved. The solution also should have a comprehensive monitoring and alerting framework.

Minimizing performance impact on data source performance
Data movement should not slow down performance of data sources, as this can directly impact application user experience.

Scaling of the solution
Given the constant growth of data, the service should support thousands of daily scheduled data moves.

Open source technology used extensively by the community
In selecting open source solutions, be aware that there are several graveyard projects. Ensure the open source project is mature and extensively used by the community.

Implementation Patterns

The data movement service needs to accomplish four key tasks: ingestion, transformation, compliance, and verification modules. This chapter focuses on the patterns that implement the ingestion and transformation modules. The patterns for the compliance and verification modules are generic building blocks and are covered in Chapter 9 and Chapter 18, respectively. Corresponding to the existing task map for ingestion and transformation, there are three levels of automation for the data movement service (as shown in Figure 5-3).

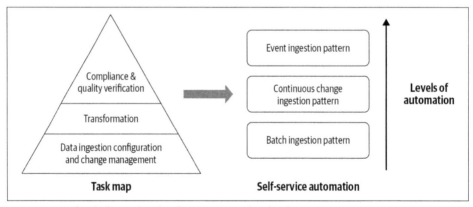

Figure 5-3. The different levels of automation for the data movement service.

Batch Ingestion Pattern

Batch ingestion is a traditional pattern that was popular in the early days of the big data evolution. It is applicable for both one-time as well as scheduled data movement. The term *batch* implies that updates on the sources are grouped together and then periodically moved to the target. Batch ingestion is typically used for data movement of large sources without a requirement for real-time updates. The batch process is typically scheduled every 6–24 hours.

There are three phases to the batch ingestion pattern (as shown in Figure 5-4):

1. *Partition phase*

   The source table to be copied is logically partitioned into smaller chunks to parallelize the data move.

2. *Map phase*

   Each chunk is allocated to a mapper (in the MapReduce terminology). A mapper fires queries to read data from the source table and copies to the target. Using more mappers will lead to a higher number of concurrent data transfer tasks, which can result in faster job completion. However, it will also increase the load on the database, potentially saturating the source. For incremental table copies, the mappers process the inserts, updates, and deletes to the source table since the last update.

3. *Reduce phase*

   The output of the mappers is stored as staging files and combined by the reducer into a single materialized view on the target data store. Reducers can also implement transformation functions.

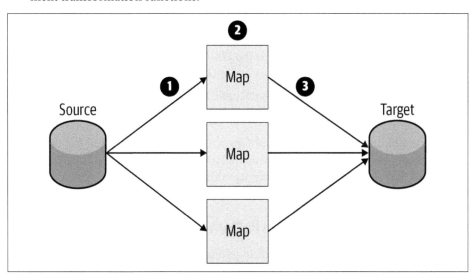

Figure 5-4. The batch ingestion pattern involves using the map phase (of MapReduce) to partition the source data object and parallel copy into the target data object.

A popular implementation of the batch ingestion pattern is Apache Sqoop (*https://oreil.ly/iqArX*). Sqoop is used for bulk data movement, typically between relational databases and filesystems to Hadoop Distributed File System (HDFS) and Apache

Hive. It is implemented as a client-server model: the clients are installed on source and target datastores and the data movement is orchestrated as MapReduce jobs by the Sqoop server that coordinates with the clients. The technology-specific adapters for connecting to the datastores are installed on the client (in the newer Sqoop2 version, the drivers are installed on the server). Data movement is a MapReduce job where the mappers on the source clients would be transporting the data from the source, while the reducers on the target clients would be copying and transforming the data. Sqoop supports both full table refresh and incremental table copy based on a high watermark.

Strengths of the batch ingestion pattern:

- It is a traditional data movement pattern applicable to a wide range of source and target datastores. Minimal effort is required for data source owners to onboard, manage, and maintain their source datastores.
- It supports scaling to thousands of daily scheduled data moves. It implements failure recovery by leveraging MapReduce.
- It has built-in support for data validation after copy.

Weaknesses of the batch ingestion pattern:

- It does not support data refresh in near real time.
- It can potentially impact the performance of source datastores. There is also a potential compliance concern with the JDBC connection used to connect source datastores that are under regulatory compliance.
- It has limited support for incremental table refresh with hard deletes and for data transformation capabilities.

Batch ingestion is a good starting point for organizations early in their big data journey. Depending on the maturity of the analytics teams, batch-oriented might be sufficient. Data engineering teams typically use this pattern to get fast coverage on the available data sources.

Change Data Capture Ingestion Pattern

As organizations mature beyond batch ingestion, they move to the change data capture (CDC) pattern. It is applicable for ongoing data movement where the source updates need to be available on the target with low latency (on the order of seconds or minutes). CDC implies capturing every change event (updates, deletes, inserts) on the source and applying the update on the target. This pattern is typically used in conjunction with batch ingestion that is used for the initial full copy of the source table while the continuous updates are done using the CDC pattern.

There are three phases to the CDC ingestion pattern (as shown in Figure 5-5):

1. *Generating CDC events*
   A CDC adapter is installed and configured on the source database. The adapter is a piece of software that is specific to the source datastore for tracking inserts, updates, and deletes to the user-specified table.

2. *CDC published on event bus*
   CDC is published on the event bus and can be consumed by one or more analytics use cases. The events on the bus are durable and can be replayed in case there are failures.

3. *Merge of events*
   Each event (insert, delete, update) is applied to the table on the target. The end result is a materialized view of the table that lags the source table with a low latency. The metadata corresponding to the target table is updated in the data catalog to reflect the refresh timestamp and other attributes.

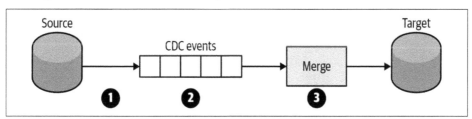

Figure 5-5. The phases of a CDC ingestion pattern.

There is a variant of the CDC ingestion pattern where the events can be consumed directly instead of through a merge step (that is, excluding step 3 in Figure 5-5). This is typically applicable for scenarios where raw CDC events are transformed into business-specific events. Another variant is to store the CDC events as a time-based journal, which is typically useful for risk and fraud detection analytics.

A popular open source implementation of the CDC ingestion pattern is Debezium (*https://debezium.io*) combined with Apache Kafka (*https://oreil.ly/mH9yU*). Debezium is a low-latency CDC adapter. It captures committed database changes in a standardized event model, irrespective of the database technologies. The event describes what changed, when, and where. Events are published on Apache Kafka in one or more Kafka topics (typically one topic per database table). Kafka ensures that all the events are replicated and totally ordered, and allows many consumers to independently consume these same data change events with little impact on the upstream system. In the event of failures during the merge process, it can be resumed exactly where it left off. The events can be delivered exactly-once or at-least-once—all data change events for each database/table are delivered in the same order they occurred in the upstream database.

For merging the CDC records into a materialized target table, the popular approaches are either batch-oriented using MapReduce, or streaming-oriented using technologies like Spark. Two popular open source solutions are Apache Gobblin (*https://oreil.ly/8rvyX*), which uses MapReduce (shown in Figure 5-6) and Uber's Marmaray (*https://oreil.ly/Va_Vc*), which uses Spark. The merge implementation in Gobblin includes deserialization/extract, convert format, validate quality, and write to the target. Both Gobblin and Marmaray are designed for any source to any target data movement.

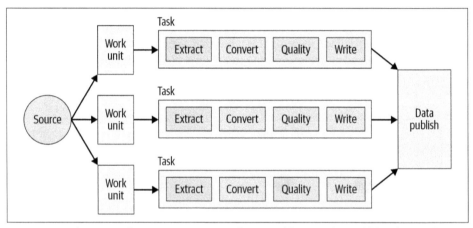

Figure 5-6. The internal processing steps implemented by Apache Gobblin during data movement from source to target (from SlideShare (https://oreil.ly/yDSUB)).

Strengths of the CDC pattern:

- The CDC pattern is a low-latency solution to update the target with minimal performance impact on the source datastore.
- CDC adapters are available for a wide range of datastores.
- It supports filtering and data transformation during the data movement process.
- It supports large tables using incremental ingestion.

Weaknesses of the CDC pattern:

- Ease of onboarding is limited given the expertise required for selecting optimal configuration options of CDC adapters.
- Merge implementations using Spark (instead of Hadoop MapReduce) may encounter issues for very large tables (on the order of a billion rows).

- It requires a table with a CDC column to track incremental changes.

- It supports limited filtering or data transformation.

This approach is great for large, fast-moving data. It is employed widely and is one of the most popular approaches. It requires operational maturity across source teams and data engineering teams to ensure error-free tracking of updates and merging of the updates at scale.

Event Aggregation Pattern

The event aggregation pattern is a common pattern for aggregating log files as well as application events where the events are required to be aggregated on an ongoing basis in real time for fraud detection, alerting, IoT, and so on. The pattern is increasingly applicable with the growing number of logs, namely web access logs, ad logs, audit logs, and syslogs, as well as sensor data.

The pattern involves aggregating from multiple sources, unifying into a single stream, and making it available for batch or streaming analytics. There are two phases to the pattern (as shown in Figure 5-7):

1. *Event forwarding*

   Events and logs from edge nodes, log servers, IoT sensors, and so on, are forwarded to the aggregation phase. Lightweight clients are installed to push logs in real time.

2. *Event aggregation*

   Events from multiple sources are normalized, transformed, and made available to one or more targets. Aggregation is based on streaming data flows; streams of events are buffered and periodically uploaded to the datastore targets.

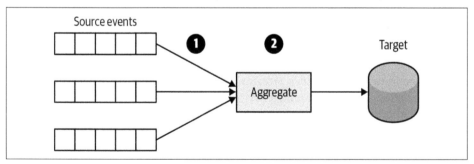

Figure 5-7. The phases of an event aggregation pattern.

A popular implementation of the pattern is Apache Flume (*https://oreil.ly/Dvyf_*). As a part of the data movement, a configuration file defines the sources of events and the target where the data is aggregated. Flume's source component picks up the log files and events from the sources and sends them to the aggregator agent where the data is processed. Log aggregation processing is stored in the memory and streamed to the destination.

Flume was originally designed to quickly and reliably stream large volumes of log files generated by web servers into Hadoop. Today, it has evolved to handle event data, including data from sources like Kafka brokers, Facebook, and Twitter. Other popular implementations are Fluent Bit (*https://fluentbit.io*) and Fluentd (*https://oreil.ly/FjUAB*), which are popular as open source log collectors and log aggregators.

Strengths of the event aggregation pattern:

- The event aggregation pattern is a real-time solution optimized for logs and events. It is highly reliable, available, and scalable (horizontally).
- It has minimal impact on source performance.
- It is highly extensible and customizable, and it incurs minimal operational overhead.
- It supports filtering and data transformation during the data movement process.
- It scales to deal with large volumes of log and event data.

Weakness of the event aggregation pattern:

- It does not provide ordering guarantee for the source events.
- Its at-least-once instead of exactly-once delivery of messages requires the target to deal with duplicate events.

In summary, this pattern is optimized for logs and events data. While it is easy to get started, it is designed for analytics use cases that can handle out-of-ordering of data as well as duplicate records.

Summary

Data can be in the form of tables, streams, files, events, and so on. Depending on the type of analytics, the data movement may have different requirements with respect to refresh lag and consistency. Depending on the requirements and the current state of the data platform, the movement service should be designed to move data between any source to any target using one or more patterns in this chapter.

CHAPTER 6

Clickstream Tracking Service

In the journey of creating insights, one of the increasingly important ingredients is collecting, analyzing, and aggregating behavioral data, known as *clickstream data*. Clickstream is a sequence of events that represent visitor actions within the application or website. It includes clicks, views, and related context, such as page load time, browser or device used by the visitor, and so on. Clickstream data is critical for business process insights like customer traffic analysis, marketing campaign management, market segmentation, sales funnel analysis, and so on. It also plays a key role in analyzing the product experience, understanding user intent, and personalizing the product experience for different customer segments. A/B testing uses clickstream data streams to compute business lifts or capture user feedback to new changes in the product or website.

As clickstream data is used by a growing spectrum of data users, namely marketers, data analysts, data scientists, and product managers, there are three key pain points related to the collection, enrichment, and consumption of clickstream data. First, data users need to continuously add new tracking beacons in the product and web pages based on their analytics needs. Adding these beacons is not self-service and requires expertise to determine where to add the instrumentation beacons, what instrumentation library to use, and what event taxonomy to use. Even existing tracking code has to be repeatedly updated to send events to new tools for marketing, email campaigns, and so on. Second, clickstream data needs to be aggregated, filtered, and enriched before it can be consumed for generating insights. For instance, raw events need to be filtered for bot-generated traffic. Handling such data at scale is extremely challenging. Third, clickstream analytics requires access to both transactional history as well as real-time clickstream data. For several clickstream use cases, such as targeted personalization for better user experience, the analysis must be near real-time. These pain points impact *time to click* metrics, which in turn impacts the overall time to insight for a growing number of use cases, namely personalization, experimentation, and marketing campaign performance.

Ideally, a self-service *clickstream service* simplifies the authoring of instrumentation beacons within the SaaS application as well as marketing web pages. The service automates the aggregation, filtering, ID stitching, and context enrichment of the event data. Data users can consume the data events as both batch and streaming depending on the use case needs. Using the service automation, the time to click metrics are improved across collection, enrichment, and consumption, optimizing the overall time to insight. In this chapter, we cover enrichment patterns specifically for clickstream data, while Chapter 8 covers the generic data preparation patterns.

Journey Map

In marketing campaigns, there can be different optimization objectives: for example, increasing sales monetization, improving customer retention, or extending brand reach. Insights need to be extracted from raw data consisting of web tracking events (clicks, views, conversions), ad tracking events (ad impressions, costs), inventory databases (products, inventory, margins), and customer order tracking (customers, orders, credits). The insight provides a correlation between running the online advertisement and its impact on the objective function—clicks, views, view time, advertisement cost/conversion ratio, and so on. The insights allow marketers to understand the journey that leads customers to their brand and provide a structured way to understand where new subscribers are coming from (brand new, winback, or cross-sell customers). Similarly, web traffic analysis provides insights about sources bringing traffic, popular keywords, conversion rates from different traffic source visitors, cohort analysis linked to campaigns, and so on. Understanding product flows helps uncover scenarios like a trial customer struggling with the invoicing feature, who may need customer care help.

Clickstream data is used by a variety of personas:

- Marketers aiming to improve brand, monetization, and retention via different kinds of marketing campaigns. Using clickstream and offline data, marketers create a 360-degree profile of the customer experience. Figure 6-1 shows how the aggregated clickstream events are used to construct the journey map experience of different customers.

- Data analysts aiming to use clickstream insights to uncover customer segmentation, product flows requiring improvements, and so on.

- Application developers using clickstream analysis for building personalization into the product to better cater to different customer segments.

- Experimenters running A/B scenarios using clickstream metrics to evaluate impact.

- Data scientists using standardized clickstream events for predictive modeling for adoption of production features.
- Product managers interested in real-time data about how product features are performing.

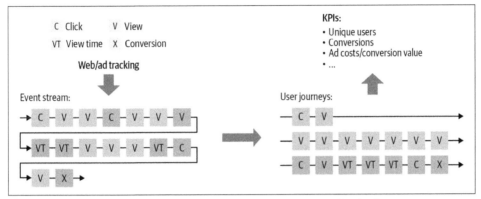

Figure 6-1. Aggregated clickstream events used to construct individual customer experience map (from the Spark Summit (https://oreil.ly/aacWw)).

Each of the clickstream use cases involves three key building blocks:

- Adding tracking code in product and web pages to capture clicks and views from customers
- Collecting data from the beacons, which is then aggregated, correlated, cleaned, and enriched
- Generating insights by combining real-time clickstream events and historic data in the lake

Minimizing Time to Click Metrics

Time to click metrics include time for managing instrumentation, enriching collected events, and analytics for consumption of the data (as illustrated in Figure 6-2).

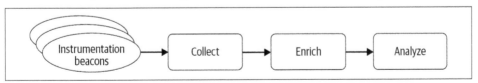

Figure 6-2. The key building blocks for the clickstream service.

Managing Instrumentation

Generating clickstream events requires instrumentation beacons within the product or web pages. Typically, beacons implement a JavaScript tracker, which is loaded with the page on every request, and sends a JSON POST request to a collector service with details of the views, clicks, and other behavioral activity. The beacon events can be collected from both the client side (for example, a mobile app where the customer presses the pay button) and the server side (for example, completion of customer's billing payment transaction).

Today, there are several challenges in managing instrumentation at scale within enterprises. First, there are multiple clones of libraries and collection frameworks. The frameworks may not be reliable. Second, the beacons have to be updated constantly to accommodate third-party integrations, namely email marketing tools, experimentation tools, campaign tools, and so on. Integrating a tool requires tracking these events directly in the beacon code, catching the data, and sending it to the corresponding service. Specific tracking code needs to be added for each new service. Third, the tracking schema has inconsistent standards of event properties and attributes, resulting in dirty data. Overall, there is no consistency in architecture and no visibility or control over data collection and distribution, as shown in Figure 6-3.

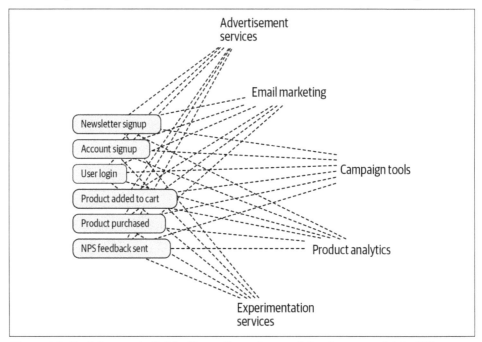

Figure 6-3. Each beacon individually configured to send the data to multiple different tools and frameworks.

Event Enrichment

The events collected by the instrumentation beacons need to be cleaned and enriched. There are four key aspects required for a majority of use cases:

Bot filtering

Bots across the internet are crawling web pages. Typically, one-third or more of website traffic is caused by bots. Events triggered by the bots need to be filtered out since they skew critical metrics related to customer interactions and conversions per visitor. This impacts the validity of insights related to marketing campaigns, experimentation, attribution, optimizations, and so on. The challenge is accurately identifying bot-related traffic. The approach today is based on rules to analyze access pattern details.

Sessionization

To better understand customer behavior, raw clickstream events are divided into sessions. A session (*https://oreil.ly/-BrSZ*) is a short-lived and interactive exchange between two or more devices and/or users—for instance, a user browsing and then exiting the website, or an IoT device periodically waking up to perform a job and then going back to sleep. The interactions result in a series of events that occur in sequence, with a start and an end. In web analytics, a session represents a user's actions during one particular visit to the website. Using sessions enables the answering of questions about things like most frequent paths to purchase, how users get to a specific page, when and why users leave, whether some acquisition funnels more efficient than others, and so on. A start and an end of a session is difficult to determine and is often defined by a time period without a relevant event associated with it. A session starts when a new event arrives after a specified "lag" time period (determined via iterative analysis) has passed without an event arriving. A session ends in a similar manner, when a new event does not arrive within the specified lag period.

Rich context

To effectively extract insights, the clickstream events are enriched with additional context, such as user agent details like device type, browser type, and OS version. IP2Geo adds geolocations based on IP address by leveraging lookup services such as MaxMind (*https://oreil.ly/Ak6TQ*). This is accomplished using a JavaScript tag on the client side to gather user interaction data, similar to many other web tracking solutions.

Overall, enriching data at scale is extremely challenging, especially event ordering, aggregation, filtering, and enrichment. It involves millions of events processed in real time for insights analysis.

Building Insights

Real-time dashboards are used for visibility into the E2E customer journey, customer 360 profiles, personalization, and so on. Tracking user behavior in real time allows for updating recommendations, performing advanced A/B testing, and pushing notifications to customers. Building insights requires complex correlations between event streams as well as batch data. The processing involves millions of events per second, with subsecond event processing and delivery. For global enterprises, the processing needs to be globally distributed.

For the processing, the customer IDs need to be correlated (known as *identity stitching*). Identity stitching matches the customers to as many available identifiers as possible in order to have an accurately matching profile. This helps with making a more accurate analysis of the raw events as well as tailoring the customer experience to all the touch points. Customers today interact using multiple devices. They may start the website exploration on a desktop machine, continue on a mobile device, and make the buy decision using a different device. It is critical to know if this is the same customer or a different one. By tracking all the events in a single pipeline, the customer events can be correlated by matching IP addresses. Another example of a correlation is using cookie IDs when a customer opens an email, then having the cookie track the email address hashcode.

Today, a challenge is lag in creating E2E dashboards; this usually takes up to 24 hours for product analytics dashboards. The customers' online journey map is incredibly complex, with dozens of different touchpoints and channels influencing the ultimate decision to purchase. Using the enterprise's own website to track customer behavior is akin to using a last-touch attribution model and does not provide a complete picture.

Defining Requirements

The clickstream platform supports a wide range of use cases, and the pain points vary. The following are checklists for prioritizing the pain points.

Instrumentation Requirements Checklist

Most enterprises today do not have a well-defined event taxonomy or standardized tools to instrument web pages and product pages. This checklist focuses on the event types and sources that need to be aggregated:

Attributes captured in the event
    Define the attributes of the event, namely who, what, where, and domain details, as well as the type of events, namely page views, clicks, and so on.

Collecting client-side events
    Take an inventory of mobile clients, desktop applications, and web applications.

Collecting third-party sources
Determine whether there is a need to aggregate log data and statistics from third-party sources such as Google, Facebook Pixel, advertisement agencies, and so on. For each of the agencies, identify the corresponding webhooks.

Collecting server-side events
Determine whether there is a need to capture events from backend application servers.

Speeds and feeds
Get a ballpark estimate of the number of beacons, the rate of events generated, and the retention time frame of the events.

Enrichment Requirements Checklist

Raw clickstream data is typically enriched depending on the requirements of the use case. The enrichment is a combination of cleaning unwanted events, joining additional information sources, summarization over different time granularities, and ensuring data privacy. The following is a checklist of potential enrichment tasks:

Bot filtering
Filtering bot traffic from real user activity, especially for use cases predicting the engagement of users in response to product changes.

User agent parsing
Additional details, such as browser type and mobile versus desktop, are associated with the clickstream events. This is required for use cases aimed at correlating user activity differences with such attributes.

IP2Geo
Tracking geographical locations to better understand product usage differences across geographies.

Sessionization
For use cases analyzing a user's activity during a given session and across sessions.

Summarization of events data over different timeframes
For use cases that vary in their requirements for individual event details versus general user activity trends over longer time periods.

Privacy filtering
For use cases like removing IP addresses for user privacy regulatory compliance.

Certain use cases may require access to raw data as well as defining custom topic structures and partitioning schemes for the clickstream events. It is important to understand the different options being used to identify users, namely account sign-ins (a small subset of users), cookie identification (this does not work cross-device and is subject to deletion, expiration, and blocking), device fingerprinting (a probabilistic way of identifying users), and IP matching (which is problematic with dynamic and shared IPs).

Implementation Patterns

Corresponding to the existing task map, there are three levels of automation for the clickstream service (as shown in Figure 6-4). Each level corresponds to automating a combination of tasks that are currently either manual or inefficient:

Instrumentation pattern
    Simplifies managing tracking beacons within the product and marketing web pages.

Enrichment patterns
    Automate cleaning and enrichment of clickstream events.

Consumption patterns
    Automate processing of the events to generate real-time insights for multiple use cases.

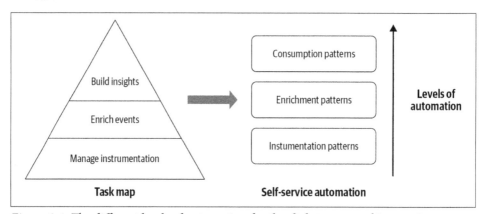

Figure 6-4. The different levels of automation for the clickstream tracking service.

Instrumentation Pattern

The instrumentation pattern simplifies the management of instrumentation beacons across the product and web pages. It makes updating, adding, and listing the available beacons self-service for data users. Traditionally, beacons are implemented as JavaScript trackers that are loaded with the page. The beacon sends a JSON POST request to providers for email campaign management, experimentation platforms, web analytics services, and so on. As teams add new providers, the beacon code needs to be updated to send the events to the providers. Instead of updating each of the existing beacons with forwarding logic, the instrumentation pattern implements a proxy model that works as follows:

Collect events

Events are generated by web pages, mobile apps, desktop apps, and backend servers. Also, events from third-party servers are collected using webhooks. Client-side events are in the form of JavaScript trackers and pixels. Each event has a taxonomy in the form of event name, event properties, and event value definition. The events are sent to a proxy endpoint.

Verify events

Events are verified at the endpoint for schema properties and data. Nonconforming events are used to trigger violations or even block access. Verifying the quality of events helps to create proactive detection and feedback loops.

Proxy events to targets

Events are forwarded to multiple providers without loading multiple tags on the site. The advantage of this approach is that you load fewer beacons without complicating the tracking code.

The open source implementations of this pattern are Segment (*https://oreil.ly/DPDue*) and RudderStack (*https://oreil.ly/7BUGK*).

To illustrate the pattern, we cover Segment. It implements a proxy for clickstream events using a publisher-subscriber approach. The events are added to a message bus (such as Kafka). The providers for email tools, web analytics, and other deployed solutions are added as subscribers. As new solutions are added, the beacons do not have to change, but simply require subscribers to be added to the event message bus. Given the simplicity of the beacons, it is easier for data users to add and manage beacons themselves.

Rule-Based Enrichment Patterns

These patterns focus on enriching clickstream data to extract insights. The enrichment patterns analyze, filter, and enhance the raw events. The patterns are rule-based and need to be extensible by data users to evolve the heuristics. The key enrichment patterns are related to bot filtering, sessionization, and user context enrichment.

Bot-filtering pattern

This pattern defines rules to distinguish between a human user and a bot. The rules are based on detailed analysis of several patterns and implemented using Spark or R (*https://oreil.ly/kdomJ*) packages. A few common checks to distinguish bot access are:

- Turning off images
- Empty referrers

- Page hit rate is too fast
- Depth-first or breadth-first search of site
- Originating from cloud providers
- Not accepting cookies (making each hit its own unique visitor)
- Frequently coming from a Linux or unknown operating system
- Using a spoofed user agent string with an outdated or unknown browser version

A combination of these rules is often a good predictor of bot traffic.

Bot-filtering analysis is typically rolled up by IP address, user agent, and operating system rather than by visitor ID; since there are no cookies, every bot hit generates a new visitor. Bots also have a predictable access timestamp for each page. Linear regression, when applied to extremely predictable access timestamps, have an R-squared value very close to 1 and are a good indicator of bot traffic.

Sessionization pattern

This pattern is based on rules. A common approach is a lag time period (typically 30 minutes) that passes without an event arriving. For the sessionization, SQL queries execute continuously over the clickstream events and generate session markers. These queries are called window SQL functions and specify bounded queries using a window defined in terms of time or rows. AWS Kinesis (*https://oreil.ly/gm-tC*) provides three types of windowed query functions: sliding windows, tumbling windows, and stagger windows. For sessionization, stagger windows are a good alternative, as they open when the first event that matches a partition key condition arrives. Also, they do not rely on the order the events arrive in the stream, but rather on when they are generated.

User context enrichment pattern

To effectively extract insights, clickstream events are enriched with additional context, such as geolocation and user agent details like browser version. An implementation of the pattern is the open source Divolte Collector (*https://divolte.io*), which collects the beacons and enriches the events (as shown in Figure 6-5). During enrichment, domain-specific identifiers from the URL structure (e.g., product IDs, page types, etc.) are parsed. User agent and IP2Geo information is extracted on the fly. The resulting click events are published on Kafka queues and are directly usable for insights generation without any ETL or log file parsing.

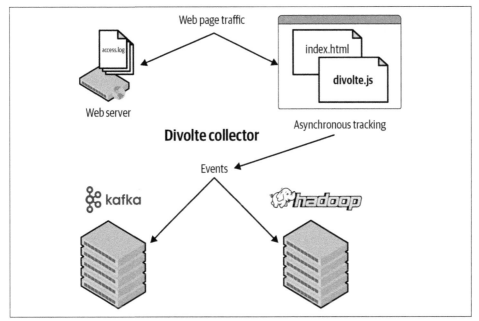

Figure 6-5. The flow of beacon data via the open source Divolte Collector (from https:// divolte.io).

Consumption Patterns

Consumption patterns focus on consumption of the clickstream data to power ML models and real-time dashboards related to how marketing campaigns are performing; how experiments are impacting retention, growth, and upselling; and so on. The processing pattern combines streaming data correlated with batch metrics and referred to as *complex event processing* (CEP). The CEP pattern involves a generic search and correlation of patterns across events in time within or across batches using windowing functions. There are two approaches to implementing CEP within the context of clickstream consumption:

- Using message processing frameworks, such as Apache NiFi and Pulsar (*https:// oreil.ly/MZQE2*), that allow processing of the individual events identified by timestamps.

- Using a serving layer in the form of a time-series datastore, such as Apache Druid (*https://oreil.ly/nbgYO*), Pinot, and Uber's M3 (*https://oreil.ly/RTb6P*), which handles both record-level updates and batch bulk loads.

To illustrate the messaging frameworks pattern, we cover Apache Pulsar. Pulsar is a powerful pub-sub model built on a layered architecture that comes out of the box with geo-replication, multitenancy, unified queuing, and streaming. Data is served by stateless "broker" nodes, whereas data storage is handled by "bookie" nodes. This architecture has the benefit of scaling brokers and bookies independently. This is more resilient and scalable compared to existing messaging systems (such as Apache Kafka) that colocate data processing and data storage on the same cluster nodes. Pulsar is operated with a SQL-like event processing language. For processing, Pulsar CEP processing logic is deployed on many nodes (called CEP cells). Each CEP cell is configured with an inbound channel, outbound channel, and processing logic. Events are typically partitioned based on a key such as user ID. All events with the same partitioned key are routed to the same CEP cell. In each stage, events can be partitioned based on a different key, enabling aggregation across multiple dimensions.

To illustrate the time-series serving layer, we cover Apache Druid. Druid implements column-oriented storage, with each column stored individually. This allows reading only the columns needed for a particular query, which supports fast scans, rankings, and groupbys. Druid creates inverted indexes for string values for fast search and filter and gracefully handles evolving schemas and nested data (*https://oreil.ly/ayC-b*). It partitions data intelligently, based on time, by sharding the data across multiple data workers (as shown in Figure 6-6). As a result, time-based queries are significantly faster than traditional databases. In addition to its native JSON-based language (*https://oreil.ly/JK7MR*), Druid supports SQL (*https://oreil.ly/4Ver2*) over either HTTP or JDBC. It can scale to ingest millions of events per second, retain years of data, and provide subsecond queries. Scale up or down by just adding or removing servers, and Druid automatically rebalances.

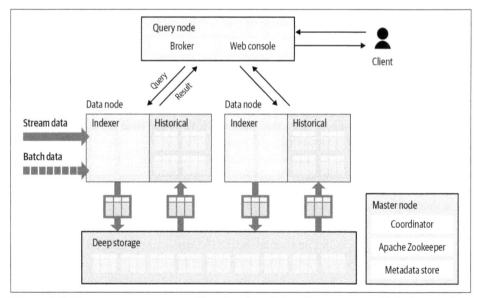

Figure 6-6. The user query processed by time-based sharding across multiple data nodes in Apache Druid (from http://druid.apache.org).

Summary

Clickstream data represents a critical dataset for several insights, such as online experimentation, marketing, and so on, that are related to customer behavior. With millions of customers and fine-grained instrumentation beacons, automating ingestion and analysis of clickstream data is a key capability for most SaaS enterprises.

PART II

Self-Service Data Prep

CHAPTER 7

Data Lake Management Service

Now that we have discovered and collected the required data to develop the insights, we enter the next phase of preparing the data. Data is aggregated in the data lake. Data lakes have become the central data repositories for aggregating petabytes of structured, semi-structured, and unstructured data. Consider the example of developing a model to forecast revenue. Data scientists will often explore hundreds of different models over a period of weeks and months. When they revisit their experiments, they need a way to reproduce the models. Typically, the source data has been modified by upstream pipelines, making it nontrivial to reproduce their experiments. In this example, the data lake needs to support versioning and rollback of data. Similarly, there are other data life cycle management tasks, such as ensuring consistency across replicas, schema evolution of the underlying data, supporting partial updates, ACID consistency for updates to existing data, and so on.

While data lakes have become popular as central data warehouses, they lack the support for traditional data life cycle management tasks. Today, multiple workarounds need to be built and lead to several pain points. First, primitive data life cycle tasks have no automated APIs and require engineering expertise for reproducibility and rollback, provisioning data-serving layers, and so on. Second, application workarounds are required to accommodate lack of consistency in the lake for concurrent read-write operations. Also, incremental updates, such as deleting a customer's records for compliance, are highly nonoptimized. Third, unified data management combining stream and batch is not possible.

The alternatives require separate processing code paths for batch and stream (referred to as *lambda architecture*) or converting all data as events (referred to as *kappa architecture*), which are nontrivial to manage at scale. Figure 7-1 shows the lambda and kappa architectures. These impact the *time to data lake management*, slowing down the overall process of building insights. Given the lack of self-service, data users are bottlenecked by data engineering teams to perform data lake management operations.

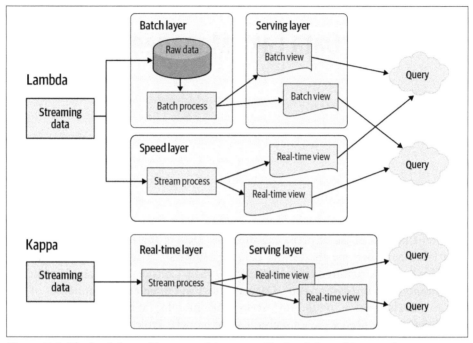

Figure 7-1. The lambda and kappa architectures. The lambda architecture has separate batch and speed processing layers, whereas kappa as a unified real-time event processing layer (from Talend (https://oreil.ly/qZPqV)).

Ideally, a self-service *data lake management service* automates the execution of primitive data life cycle management capabilities and provides APIs and policies for data users to invoke. The service provides transactional ACID capabilities for the lake and optimizes the incremental updates required for the data. It unifies streaming and batch views by allowing events to be added to batch tables; data users can leverage existing query frameworks to build insights combining historic and real-time records. Overall, given that data lake management tasks are fundamental to every data pipeline, automating these tasks improves the overall time to insight.

Journey Map

In the overall journey map, executing on data management tasks today is analogous to a tango between data engineers and data users. Data users create Jira tickets for the execution of these tasks. Data engineers execute on them with typical back-and-forth and delays due to competitive priorities across multiple project teams. This is usually not scalable and slows down the overall journey map. With the data lake management service, data users are empowered to execute these tasks without getting bottlenecked. The interaction touchpoints during the overall journey map are covered in the rest of the section.

Primitive Life Cycle Management

When the data is ingested within the lake, a bucket is created in the object store to persist the files associated with the data. The bucket is added to the metadata catalog and becomes accessible to different processing engines. Table 7-1 summarizes the pain points of basic data life cycle management tasks on the lake.

Table 7-1. The pain points related to primitive data life cycle management in the lake.

Primitive life cycle task	Pain point	Workarounds applied
Versioning of data required for exploration, model training, and resolving corruption due to failed jobs that have left data in an inconsistent state, resulting in a painful recovery process.	There are no clear processes for creating and restoring snapshots. There is no easy way to get values of specific table attributes at a specific point in time. There is no way to roll back failed jobs/transactions based on version or timestamp.	Snapshots are created based on policies. Multiple copies of the data are created for reproducibility of models, leading to increased storage costs. For accessing historical data, the entire snapshot is restored in a sandbox namespace and made accessible for analysis. The process requires the help of data engineers.
Schema evolution to manage the changes in the source datasets.	Schema evolution can lead to broken downstream analytics. There is no support to validate the schema of the dataset at the time of lake ingestion.	Creating isolation data layers between source datasets and downstream analytics. This is not foolproof and does not work for all schema changes.
Data-serving layers to efficiently expose the lake data to web applications and analytics.	Read-write on processed lake data may not be efficient for all data models, such as key-value, graph, document, and time-series. Data users settle for suboptimal one-size-fits-all relational models.	Modifying the data model of the application to fit the relational model.
Centralized **tracking of data access and usage.** Auditing data changes is critical both in terms of data compliance as well as simple debugging to understand how data has changed over time.	Difficult-to-track updates and access to the datasets across multiple users and services. Lack of centralized auditing leads to blindspots with respect to access control.	Ad hoc scripts and audit monitoring.

One of the common tasks is data rollback. Data pipelines write bad data for downstream consumers because of issues ranging from infrastructure instabilities to messy data to bugs in the pipeline. For pipelines with simple appends, rollbacks are addressed by date-based partitioning. When updates and deletes to previous records are involved, rollback becomes very complicated, requiring data engineers to deal with such complex scenarios.

In addition, incremental updating of data is a primitive operation. Big data formats were originally designed for immutability. With the emergence of data rights compliance, where customers can request that their data be deleted, updating lake data has become a necessity. Because of the immutability of big data formats, deleting a record translates to reading all the remaining records and writing them in a new partition. Given the scale of big data, this can create significant overhead. A typical workaround today is to create fine-grained partitions to speed up rewriting of data.

Managing Data Updates

A table in the data lake can translate into multiple file updates (as shown in Figure 7-2). Data lakes do not provide the same integrity guarantees that ACID databases do. Isolation guarantees that are missing impact readers that get partial data while the write operation is updating the data. Similarly, concurrent write operations can corrupt the data. Another aspect of update consistency is that the write may not have propagated to all the replicas given the eventual consistency model. Read-after-write operations may sometimes return errors. To accommodate the missing ACID guarantees, workarounds are implemented in the application code: retries when the updates are missing; blackout time such that consuming applications are restricted from consuming data during execution to avoid reading corrupt data; and updates are manually tracked for completion as well as for rolling back in the event of an error.

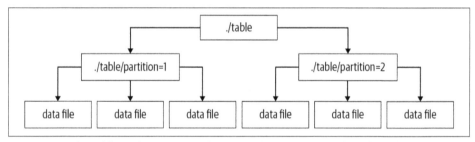

Figure 7-2. The table update can translate to updating multiple data files (from Slide-Share (https://oreil.ly/phZmD)).

Managing Batching and Streaming Data Flows

Traditionally, insights were retrospective and operated as batch processing. As insights are becoming real-time and predictive, they need to analyze both the ongoing stream of updates as well as historic data tables. Ideally, streaming events can be added to the batch tables, allowing data users to simply leverage the existing queries on the table. Existing data lake capabilities have several limitations (*https://oreil.ly/GmR0*): reading consistent data while data is being written, handling late-arriving data without having to delay downstream processing, reading incrementally from a large table with good throughput, and so on. The workarounds applied today are the lambda and kappa architectures discussed previously.

Minimizing Time to Data Lake Management

Time to data lake management includes the time spent in primitive life cycle management, correctness of data updates, and managing batching and streaming data together. Each of these are time-consuming, and the technical challenges were covered previously in "Journey Map" on page 94.

Requirements

Besides the functional requirements, there are three categories of requirements to understand for the existing deployment: namespace management requirements, supported data formats in the lake, and types of data-serving layers.

Namespace zones

Within a data lake, zones allow the logical and/or physical separation of data. The namespace can be organized into many different zones based on the current workflows, data pipeline process, and dataset properties. What follows is the typical (*https://oreil.ly/qrd5j*) namespace configuration (as shown in Figure 7-3) that is used by most enterprises in some shape and form to keep the lake secure, organized, and agile.

Bronze zone

> This is for raw data ingested from transactional datastores. It is a dumping ground for raw data and long-term retention. The sensitive data is encrypted and tokenized. Minimal processing is done in this zone to avoid corrupting the raw data.

Silver zone

> This is the staging zone containing intermediate data with filtered, cleaned, augmented data. After data quality validation and other processing is performed on data in the bronze zone, it becomes the "source of truth" in this zone for downstream analysis.

Gold zone

> Contains clean data that is ready for consumption along with business-level aggregates and metrics. This represents the traditional data warehouse. The processed output and standardized data layers are stored in this zone.

Besides the pre-created namespaces, data users may want the ability to create sandbox namespaces for exploration. Sandbox zones have minimal governance and are typically deleted after 30 days. Also, with growing regulatory compliance, a new zone, called sensitive zone or red zone, is being created. This zone has restricted access to select data stewards with heavy governance. It is used for select use cases like fraud detection, financial reporting, and so on.

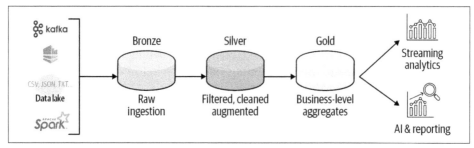

Figure 7-3. A typical namespace configuration within the data lake (from Databricks (https://oreil.ly/eROqr)).

Supported file formats

Data in the lake can be in different formats. Data formats play an important role in the context of performance and scaling for insights. As a part of the requirements gathering, understanding the current deployed formats as well as investing in transformation of the file formats ensures a better match for the use case requirements.

Data formats need to balance concerns about robustness of the format (i.e., how well tested is the format for data corruption scenarios) and interoperability with popular SQL engines and analytics platforms. The following are the different requirements to consider:

Expressive
> Can the format express complex data structures, such as maps, records, lists, nested data structures, etc.?

Robust
> Is the format well defined and well understood? Is it well tested with respect to corruption scenarios and other corner cases? Another important aspect of robustness is simplicity of the format. The more complex the format, the higher the probability of bugs in the serialization and deserialization drivers.

Space efficient
> A compact representation of the data is always an optimization criteria. Space efficiency is based on two factors: a) ability to represent data as binary, and b) ability to compress the data.

Access optimized
> This criteria minimizes the amount of data (in bytes) that is accessed in response to application queries. There is no silver bullet, and it depends heavily on the

type of queries (e.g., select * queries versus a query that filters based on a limited number of column values). Another aspect of access optimization is the ability to split the file for parallel execution.

There are several good articles on the available formats (*https://oreil.ly/kT-5b*). The key ones are:

Text files
This is one of the oldest formats. While it is human-readable and interoperable, it is fairly inefficient in terms of space and access optimization.

CSV/TSV
These formats have limitations with respect to inefficient binary representation and access. Also, it is difficult to express complex data structures in these formats.

JSON
This is one of the most expressive and general-purpose formats for application developers. It is unoptimized both in terms of space and access compared to some of the other formats in this list.

SequenceFile
This is one of the oldest file formats in Hadoop. Data was represented as key-value pairs. It was popular when Java was the only way to access Hadoop using a writable interface. The biggest issue was interoperability, and it did not have a generic definition.

Avro
This is similar to SequenceFile except that the schema is stored with the file header. The format is expressive and interoperable. The binary representation has overheads and is not the most optimized. Overall, it is great for general-purpose workloads.

ORCFile
This is a column-oriented format that is used in high-end commercial databases. Within the Hadoop ecosystem, this format is considered the successor of the RCFile format, which was inefficient in storing data as strings. ORCFile has strong Hortonworks support and interesting recent advancements (*https://oreil.ly/Pfmyt*), namely Push Predicate Down (PPD) and improved compression.

Parquet
This is similar to ORCFile and has support from Cloudera. Parquet implements the optimizations from the Google Dremel paper (*https://oreil.ly/M7xBw*).

Combined with encoding, there are various popular compression techniques, such as zlib, gzip, LZO, and Snappy. While compression techniques are largely encoding independent, it is important to distinguish between columnar compression techniques that depend primarily on individual values (such as tokenization, prefix compression, etc.) and those that depend on sequences of values (such as run-length encoding [RLE] or delta compression). Table 7-2 summarizes the discussion of on-disk layout formats.

Table 7-2. A comparison of data persistence file formats.

	Expressive	Robust	Binary & Compressed	Access Optimized	Ecosystem
Text File	◗	●	○	○	●
CSV/TSV	◗	◕	◗	○	●
JSON	◕	●	◗	○	●
SequenceFile	◕	◕	◗	○	○
Avro	●	●	◕	◗	◕
ORCFile	●	●	●	●	●
Parquet	●	◕	●	●	●

Serving layers

Data persisted in the lake can be structured, semi-structured, and unstructured. For semi-structured data, there are different data models such as key-value, graph, document, and so on. Depending on the data model, an appropriate datastore should be leveraged for optimal performance and scaling. There is a plethora of NoSQL solutions supporting different data models. NoSQL is often emphasized as "nonSQL" given the trade-off of transactional SQL capabilities in lieu of scaling, availability, and performance (CAP theorem being the poster child). It's important to realize that NoSQL is less about the SQL fidelity and more about the variety of data models supported—it should be remembered as "nonrelational SQL" that reduces the impedance mismatch between the application and datastore by selecting the right data model. I like the Wikipedia definition of NoSQL (*https://oreil.ly/pURvC*): "A NoSQL (originally referring to "nonSQL" or "nonrelational") database provides a mechanism for storage and retrieval of data that is modeled in means other than the tabular relations used in relational databases." There are several books on the topic of NoSQL solutions. What follows is a brief summary of the most commonly used data models.

Key-value data model.　This is the easiest of the data models. An application stores arbitrary data as a set of values or blobs (there might be limits on the maximum size). The stored values are opaque—any schema interpretation must be done by the application. The key-value store simply retrieves or stores the value by key. Popular examples are Riak, Redis, Memcache, Hazelcast, Aerospike, and AWS DynamoDB.

Wide-column data model.　A wide-column database organizes data into rows and columns, similar to a relational database. Logically related columns are divided into groups known as column families. Within a column family, new columns can be added dynamically, and rows can be sparse (that is, a row doesn't need to have a value for every column). Implementations like Cassandra allow creating indexes over specific columns in a column family, retrieving data by column value rather than row key. Read and write operations for a row are usually atomic with a single column family, although some implementations provide atomicity across the entire row, spanning multiple column families. Popular examples include Cassandra, HBase, Hypertable, Accumulo, and Google Bigtable.

Document data model.　Unlike key-value stores, the fields in documents can be used to query and filter data by using the values in these fields. A single document may contain information that would be spread across several relational tables in an RDBMS. MongoDB and other implementations support in-place updates, enabling an application to modify the values of specific fields in a document without rewriting the entire document. Read and write operations over multiple fields in a single document are atomic. When the data fields to be stored may vary between the different elements, a relational or column-oriented storage may not be best, as there would be a lot of empty columns. A document store does not require that all documents have the same structure. Popular examples include MongoDB, AWS DynamoDB (limited capabilities), Couchbase, CouchDB, and Azure Cosmos DB.

Graph data model.　A graph database stores two types of information: nodes and edges. Nodes are entities, and edges specify the relationships between nodes. Both nodes and edges can have properties that provide information about that node or edge, similar to columns in a table. Edges can also have a direction indicating the nature of the relationship. Popular examples include Neo4j, OrientDB, Azure Cosmos DB, Giraph, and Amazon Neptune.

Beyond the data models listed previously, there are others, such as message stores, time-series databases, multimodel stores, and so on. Figure 7-4 illustrates the datastores available within the cloud using AWS as an example.

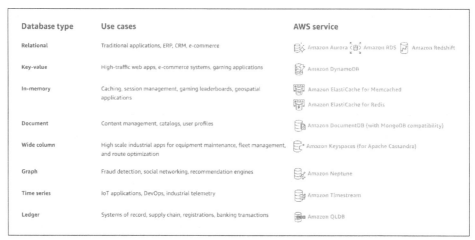

Figure 7-4. The growing list of data models supported in AWS Cloud (from AWS (https://oreil.ly/Na6aQ)).

Implementation Patterns

Corresponding to the existing task map, there are three levels of automation for the data life cycle management service (as shown in Figure 7-5). Each level corresponds to automating a combination of tasks that are currently either manual or inefficient:

Data life cycle primitives pattern
Simplifies primitive operations as well as incremental data updates.

Transactional pattern
Supports ACID transactions in data lake updates.

Advanced data management pattern
Unifies streaming and batch data flows.

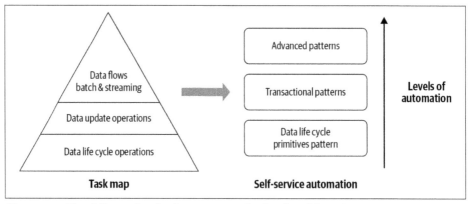

Figure 7-5. The different levels of automation for the data life cycle management service.

Data Life Cycle Primitives Pattern

The goal of this pattern is to empower data users to execute the primitive operations via policies and APIs. This includes policies for namespace creation, storing data in data-serving layers, creating partitions, creating audit rules, handling schema evolution, and versioning of data. Additionally, updating data is a primitive operation, and the goal is to optimize it. We cover details of patterns related to schema evolution, data versioning, and incremental data updates.

Schema evolution

The goal is to automatically manage schema changes such that the downstream analytics are not impacted by the change. In other words, we want to reuse existing queries against evolving schemas and avoid schema mismatch errors during querying. There are different kinds of schema changes, such as rename columns; add columns at the beginning, middle, or end of the table; remove columns; reorder columns; and change column data types. The approach (*https://oreil.ly/QElz_*) is to use the data format that can handle both backward and forward evolution. With backward compatibility, a new schema can be applied to read data created using previous schemas, and with forward compatibility, an older schema can be applied to read data created using newer schemas. Applications may not be updated immediately and should always read data in a new schema without benefiting from new features.

To generalize, schema evolution is a function of the data format, type of schema change, and the underlying query engine. Depending on the type of schema change and the schema, the change may be disruptive to downstream analytics. For instance, Amazon Athena (*https://oreil.ly/TF3Q0*) is a schema-on-read query engine. When a table is created in Athena, it applies schemas when reading the data. It does not change or rewrite the underlying data. Parquet and ORC are columnar data storage formats that can be read by index or by name. Storing data in either of these formats ensures no schema mismatch errors while running Athena queries.

Data versioning

The goal of this pattern is to implement a time travel capability such that users can query the data at a specific point in time. This is required for training reproducibility, rollbacks, and auditing. Databricks Delta (*https://oreil.ly/8BX-4*) is an example implementation of this pattern. In writing into a Delta table or directory, every operation is automatically versioned. There are two different ways to access the different versions: using a timestamp or using a version number. Under the covers, every table is the result of the sum total of all of the commits recorded in the Delta Lake transaction log. The transaction log records the details to get from the table's original state to its current state. After 10 commits to the transaction log, Delta Lake saves a checkpoint file in Parquet format. Those files enable Spark to skip ahead to the most recent checkpoint file, which reflects the state of the table at that point.

Incremental updates

This pattern aims to optimize making incremental updates in the data lake. An example of the pattern is Hudi (*https://oreil.ly/GKXKG*) (Hadoop Upsert Delete and Incremental), which enables applying mutations to data in HDFS on the order of a few minutes. Hudi loads the Bloom filter index (*https://oreil.ly/5ffCm*) from all Parquet files in the involved partitions and tags the record as either an update or insert by mapping the incoming keys to existing files for updates. Hudi groups inserts per partition, assigns a new field, and appends to the corresponding log file until the log file reaches the HDFS block size. A scheduler kicks off a time-limited compaction process every few minutes, which generates a prioritized list of compactions. Compaction runs asynchronously. On every compaction iteration, the files with the most logs are compacted first, whereas small log files are compacted last since the cost of rewriting the Parquet file is not amortized over the number of updates to the file.

Transactional Pattern

This pattern focuses on implementing atomicity, consistency, isolation, durability (ACID) transactions on the data lake. There are several implementations of the pattern, namely Delta Lake, Iceberg (*https://oreil.ly/Tqs_B*), and Apache ORC (*https://oreil.ly/ocz2F*) (in Hive 3.x).

To illustrate the pattern, we cover the high-level details of the Delta Lake ACID implementation. For comprehensive details of the implementation, refer to Databricks (*https://oreil.ly/O8jyD*).

Whenever a user performs an operation to modify a table (such as insert, update, or delete), Delta Lake breaks that operation down into a series of discrete steps. Those actions are then recorded in the transaction log as ordered, atomic units known as commits. The Delta Lake transaction log is an ordered record of every transaction that has ever been performed on a Delta Lake table since its inception. When a user reads a Delta Lake table for the first time or runs a new query on an open table that has been modified since the last time it was read, Spark checks the transaction log to see what new transactions have posted to the table, then updates the end user's table with those new changes. This ensures that a user's version of a table is always synchronized with the master record as of the most recent query.

Atomicity guarantees that operations (like insert or update) performed on the lake either complete fully or don't complete at all. The transaction log is the mechanism through which Delta Lake is able to offer the guarantee of atomicity. Delta Lake supports serializable isolation by only recording transactions that execute fully and completely and using that record as the single source of truth. For concurrent write-write updates, it uses optimistic concurrency control. Currently, Delta Lake does not support multi-table transactions and foreign keys.

Advanced Data Management Pattern

The advanced data management pattern combines streaming event data within a single existing table (as illustrated in Figure 7-6). Data users can access the combined streaming and batch data using existing queries using time-window functions. This allows for processing data continuously and incrementally as new data arrives without having to choose between batch or streaming.

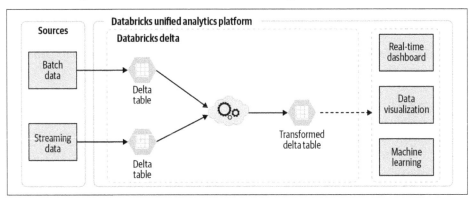

Figure 7-6. The merging of batch and stream data into a single Databricks Delta Table (from Caserta (https://oreil.ly/Mi4uo)).

Batch and streaming analytics have traditionally been handled separately since the basic functionality building blocks have been missing in the lake. For instance, there is no mechanism to track records that have changed in the partition since the last time it was consumed. Although upserts can solve the problem of publishing new data to a partition quickly, downstream consumers do not know what data has changed since a point in the past. In the absence of the primitive to identify the new records, scanning and recomputing everything is required for the entire partition or table, which can take a lot of time and is not feasible at scale. There are other patterns required to implement the unified streaming and batch view. Figure 7-7 illustrates these missing primitives as well as how they are implemented in Delta Lake. Streaming data ingest, batch historic backfill, and interactive queries work out of the box without additional effort.

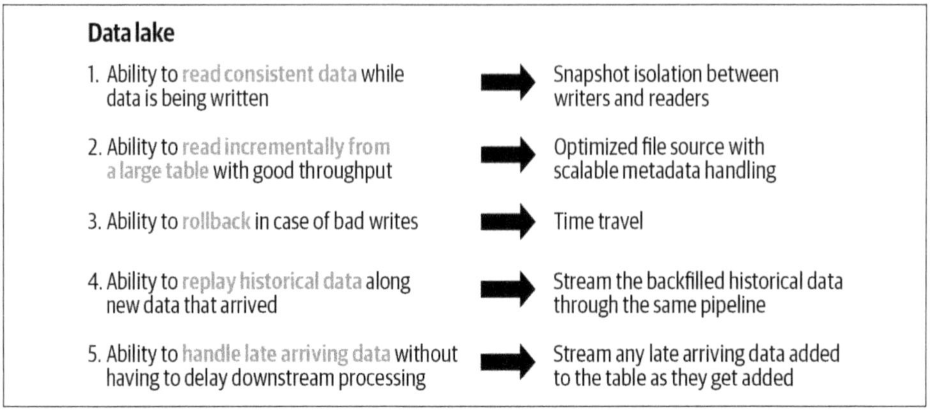

Data lake

1. Ability to read consistent data while data is being written → Snapshot isolation between writers and readers

2. Ability to read incrementally from a large table with good throughput → Optimized file source with scalable metadata handling

3. Ability to rollback in case of bad writes → Time travel

4. Ability to replay historical data along new data that arrived → Stream the backfilled historical data through the same pipeline

5. Ability to handle late arriving data without having to delay downstream processing → Stream any late arriving data added to the table as they get added

Figure 7-7. The required data lake primitives and how they are implemented in Delta Lake (from Databricks (https://oreil.ly/b-n0v)).

Summary

Traditionally, data was aggregated in data warehouses and analyzed with batch processing. The needs of data life cycle management were supported by the warehouse. Fast-forwarding to data lakes, the same data life cycle management requirements need to be supported within a complex combination of datastores, processing engines, and streaming and batch processes. The goal of the data lake management service is to automate these tasks similar to traditional data warehouses.

CHAPTER 8
Data Wrangling Service

With the data now aggregated within the lake, we are now ready to focus on wrangling the data, which typically includes structuring, cleaning, enriching, and validating the data. Wrangling is an iterative process to curate errors, outliers, missing values, imputing values, data imbalance, and data encoding. Each step during the process exposes new potential ways that the data might be "re-wrangled," with the goal of generating the most robust data values for generating the insights. Also, wrangling provides insights into the nature of data, allowing us to ask better questions for generating insights.

Data scientists spend a significant amount of time and manual effort on wrangling (as shown in Figure 8-1). In addition to being time-consuming, wrangling is incomplete, unreliable, and error prone, and comes with several pain points. First, data users touch on a large number of datasets during exploratory analysis, so it is critical to discover the properties of the data and detect wrangling transformations required for preparation quickly. Currently, evaluating dataset properties and determining the wrangling to be applied is ad hoc and manual. Second, applying wrangling transformations requires writing idiosyncratic scripts in programming languages like Python, Perl, and R, or engaging in tedious manual editing using tools like Microsoft Excel. Given the growing volume, velocity, and variety of the data, the data users require low-level coding skills to apply the transformations at scale in an efficient, reliable, and recurring fashion. The third pain point is operating these transformations reliably on a day-to-day basis and proactively preventing transient issues from impacting data quality. These pain points impact the *time to wrangle*, which represents the time required to make the data credible for generating productive and reliable insights. Wrangling is a key step in generating insights and impacts the overall time to insight.

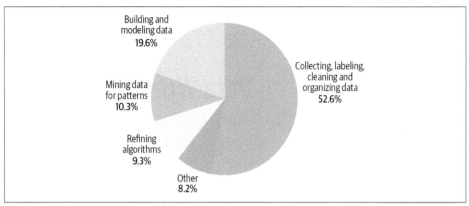

Figure 8-1. Time spent by data scientists on various activities based on the 2017 Data Scientist Report. (https://oreil.ly/5nW30)

Ideally, the *self-service data wrangling service* expedites the process to visualize, transform, deploy, and operationalize at production scale. Given the diverse domain ontologies, data extraction and transformation rules, and schema mappings, there is no one-size-fits-all for data wrangling. The service provides data users with an interactive and detailed visual representation, allowing for deeper data exploration and understanding of the data at a granular level. It intelligently assesses the data at hand to recommend a ranked list of suggested wrangling transformations for users. Data users can define transformations easily without low-level programming—the transformation functions automatically compile down into the appropriate processing framework, with best-fit execution for the scale of data and transformation types. Data users can define quality verification rules for datasets and proactively prevent low-quality data from polluting the cleansed datasets. Overall, the service provides a broad spectrum of data users with intelligent, agile data wrangling, which ultimately produces more accurate insights.

Journey Map

Irrespective of the project, the data wrangling journey typically consists of the following tasks:

Discovering
> This is typically the first step. It leverages the metadata catalog to understand the properties of data and schema and the wrangling transformations required for analytic explorations. It is difficult for nonexpert users to determine the required transformations. The process also involves record matching—i.e., finding the relationship between multiple datasets, even when those datasets do not share an identifier or when the identifier is not very reliable.

Validating

There are multiple dimensions of validation, including verifying whether the values of a data field adhere to syntactic constraints like Boolean true/false as opposed to 1/0. Distributional constraints verify value ranges for data attributes. Cross-attribute checks verify cross-database referential integrity—for example, a credit card updated in the customer database being correctly updated in the subscription billing database.

Structuring

Data comes in all shapes and sizes. There are different data formats that may not match the requirements for downstream analysis. For example, a customer shopping transaction log may have records with one or more items while individual records of the purchased items might be required for inventory analysis. Another example is standardizing particular attributes like zip codes, state names, and so on. Similarly, ML algorithms often do not consume data in raw form and typically require encoding, such as categories encoded using one-hot encoding.

Cleaning

dThere are different aspects of cleaning. The most common form is removing outliers, missing values, null values, and imbalanced data that can distort the generated insights. Cleaning requires knowledge about data quality and consistency—i.e., knowing how various data values might impact your final analysis. Another aspect is deduplication of records within the dataset.

Enriching

This involves joining with other datasets, such as enriching customer profile data. For instance, agricultural firms may enrich production predictions with weather information forecasts. Another aspect is deriving new forms of data from the dataset.

Data quality issues such as missing, erroneous, extreme, and duplicate values undermine analysis and are time-consuming to find and resolve. With enterprises becoming data-driven, data wrangling is being used by a wide range of data users, namely data analysts, scientists, product managers, marketers, data engineers, application developers, and so on. The wrangling journey map also needs to deal with the four Vs of big data: volume, velocity, variety, and veracity.

Minimizing Time to Wrangle

Time to wrangle includes exploratory data analysis, defining the data transformations, and implementing them at production scale.

Defining Requirements

When determining data wrangling requirements, define them by interactive and iterative exploration of the data properties. Given the spectrum of data users, data wrangling requires tools to support both programmers and nonprogrammer data users. Data scientists typically use programming frameworks like Python pandas and R libraries, whereas nonprogrammers rely on visualization solutions.

Visualization tools come with a few challenges. First, visualization is difficult given multiple dimensions and growing scale. For large datasets, enabling rapid-linked selections like dynamic aggregate views is challenging. Second, different types of visualizations are best suited to different forms of structured, semi-structured, and unstructured data. Too much time is spent manipulating data just to get analysis and visualization tools to read it. Third, it is not easy for visualization tools to help reason with dirty, uncertain, or missing data. Automated methods can help identify anomalies, but determining the error is context-dependent and requires human judgment. While visualization tools can facilitate this process, analysts must often manually construct the necessary views to contextualize anomalies, requiring significant expertise.

Curating Data

Based on the requirements for wrangling, this step focuses on building the functions for transformation of data at scale. Data users need to automate the data transformations in order to have them applied in an ongoing fashion and at scale. While there are generic patterns for implementing data transformations at scale (covered in the next chapter), a popular approach is using visual analytics tools that translate iterative visual edits of data into wrangling rules that are applied to the dataset (see the paper by Kandel et al. (*https://oreil.ly/RbAcE*)).

Visual analytics frameworks for data curation present a few key challenges:

- Scalability for large datasets
- Intelligence to automatically apply to similar datasets (reducing manual intervention)
- Support for specification of correctness, data quality issues, data reformatting, and conversions between data values of different types
- Learning from human input and leveraging interactive transform histories for the data transformation process

Overall, visual analytics is an active area of research. Experts are working to determine how appropriate visual encodings can facilitate detection of data issues and how interactive visualizations facilitate the creation of data transformation specifications.

Operational Monitoring

Once the curation is deployed in production, it needs to be monitored continuously for correctness and performance SLAs. This includes creating models for data accuracy, running the verification as scheduled jobs, extending the wrangling functions, and debugging for operational issues.

The key challenges are handling processing failures, implementing job retries and optimization, and debugging patterns of data issues. We cover the topic of operational monitoring for data quality in detail in Chapter 18.

Defining Requirements

Enterprises differ in terms of the current state of their data organization, the sensitivity of generated insights to data quality, and the expertise of their data users. The approach in building the wrangling service is to first focus on tasks in the journey map that are slowing down the time to curate. We refer readers to the book (*https://oreil.ly/iZ50D*) *Principles of Data Wrangling* (*https://oreil.ly/QSN_6*), which includes questionnaires for evaluating the pain points during the understanding, validating, structuring, cleaning, and enriching phases of the wrangling journey.

Implementation Patterns

Corresponding to the existing task map, there are three levels of automation for the wrangling service (as shown in Figure 8-2). Each level corresponds to automating a combination of tasks that are currently either manual or inefficient:

Exploratory data analysis patterns
Expedite the understanding of the datasets to define the wrangling transformations.

Analytical transformation patterns
Implement the transformations at production scale.

Automated quality enforcement patterns
Operationalize monitoring for tracking and debugging of data quality. We cover the details related to this pattern in Chapter 18.

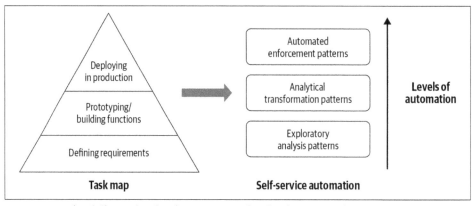

Figure 8-2. The different levels of automation for the data wrangling service.

Exploratory Data Analysis Patterns

Exploratory data analysis (EDA) patterns focus on understanding and summarizing the dataset to determine the data wrangling transformations required for the data. It is a crucial step to take before diving into ML or dashboard modeling. There are three distinct components of data understanding:

- Structure discovery helps determine whether your data is consistent and formatted correctly.

- Content discovery focuses on data quality. Data needs to be formatted, standardized, and properly integrated with existing data in a timely and efficient manner.

- Relationship discovery identifies connections between different datasets.

Understanding the data makeup helps to effectively select predictive algorithms.

Given the spectrum of data users, there are three different EDA patterns, listed in ascending order of programming skills required:

- Visual analysis provides an easy-to-read, visual perspective of data integrity, statistical distribution, completeness, and so on. A few example implementations that provide data visualizations and relevant data summaries are Profiler (*https://oreil.ly/NtROm*), Data Wrangler (*https://oreil.ly/SKUba*), and Trifacta. RapidMiner (*https://oreil.ly/ZqwIB*) provides an intuitive graphical user interface for the design of analysis processes and requires no programming.

- Traditional programming libraries like Python's pandas (*https://oreil.ly/gDhMe*) library allow data users to analyze and transform with a single Python statement. Similarly, the dplyr library in R provides a fast, consistent tool for working with DataFrame-like objects, both in memory and out of memory.

- Big data programming APIs like Apache Spark provide developers with easy-to-use APIs for operating on large datasets across languages: Scala, Java, Python, and R. Traditional programming libraries are typically great for working with samples of data but are not scalable. Spark provides different API abstractions to analyze the properties of data, namely RDD, DataFrame, and Datasets. Depending on the use case, the appropriate APIs need to be selected depending on structured versus semi-structured or unstructured data. A good analysis with pros and cons for RDD, DataFrame, Datasets is covered in the Databricks blog (*https://oreil.ly/v518s*).

ML techniques are increasingly being applied to searching and learning the data wrangling transformations to be used for any particular problem. The manual understanding of data properties is complemented with machine learning, making understanding achievable for a much larger group of users and in a shorter amount of time.

Analytical Transformation Patterns

These patterns focus on applying wrangling transformations to the data at production scale. Besides programming, the two common patterns are visual analytics and drag-and-drop ETL definition frameworks. In this section, we focus on visual analytics, which is used mainly in the context of data wrangling. The other transformation patterns are generic; they're covered in Chapter 11.

Visual analytics allows wrangling data through interactive systems that integrate data visualization, transformation, and verification. The pattern significantly reduces specification time and promotes the use of robust, auditable transforms instead of manual editing. The pattern works as follows:

1. Data users interact with the data visualization to understand the properties of the data. Transformation functions can be defined during the data exploration process.

2. The visual analytics pattern automatically maps the transformation functions to broader datasets. Based on user input, the tool learns patterns that can be applied across datasets.

3. The transformations are automatically converted into reusable ETL processes that continuously run on a schedule, enlisting regular data loads. The transformation can also be applied in the context of streaming analytics.

By pulling interactive data visualization and transformation into one environment, the pattern radically simplifies the process of building transformations.

To illustrate the pattern, Stanford's Wrangler (*https://oreil.ly/k5w_q*) is an interactive system for creating data transformations. Wrangler combines direct manipulation of visualized data with automatic inference of relevant transforms, enabling analysts to iteratively explore the space of applicable operations and preview their effects. Wrangler leverages semantic data types to aid validation and type conversion. Interactive histories support review, refinement, and annotation of transformation scripts. With just a few clicks, users are able to set null fields to a specific value, take out unnecessary or outlier data, and perform data transformation on fields to normalize them.

Summary

Data wrangling is the process of making data useful. Raw data is not always credible and may not be suitably representative of reality. By investing in self-service frameworks for data wrangling, enterprises can significantly reduce the overall time to insight. A wrangling service automates the process by integrating data visualization, transformation, and verification.

CHAPTER 9

Data Rights Governance Service

With the data now wrangled, we are ready to build insights. There is one additional step, as a wide majority of data used for extracting insights is gathered directly or indirectly from customer interactions. If the datasets include customer details, especially PII such as name, address, social security number, and so on, enterprises need to ensure that the use of the data is in compliance with the user's data preferences. There is a growing number of data rights regulations like GDPR (*https://oreil.ly/ KsoJf*), CCPA (*https://oreil.ly/LaVGj*), Brazilian General Data Protection Act (*https:// oreil.ly/K6dCp*), India Personal Data Protection Bill (*https://oreil.ly/VZXG9*), and several others, as shown in Figure 9-1. These laws require the customer data to be collected, used, and deleted based on their preferences. There are different aspects to data rights, namely:

Collection of data rights
    The right to be informed about the collection of personal data and the categories of information collected

Use of data rights
    The right to restrict processing (i.e., how the data is used); the right to opt out of the sale of personal information; the identities of third parties to which information is sold

Deletion of data rights
    The right to erasure of personal data shared with the application as well as data shared with any third party

Access to data rights
    The right to access the customer's personal data; the right to rectification if data is inaccurate or incomplete; the right to data portability, which allows individuals to obtain and reuse personal data

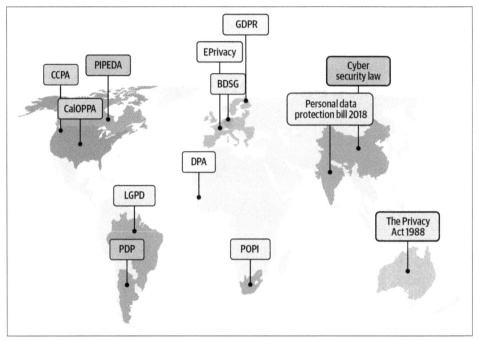

Figure 9-1. The emerging data rights laws across the world (from Piwik PRO (https://oreil.ly/zxVMi)).

Ensuring compliance requires data users and data engineers to work together. Data scientists and other data users want an easy way to locate all the available data for a given use case without having to worry about compliance violations. Data engineers have to ensure they have located all the customer data copies correctly and execute the rights of users in a comprehensive, timely, and auditable fashion.

As mentioned in Chapter 1, *Introduction*, compliance is a balancing act between the ability to better serve the customer experience using insights while ensuring the data is being used in accordance with the customer's directives—and there are no simple heuristics that can be applied universally to solve the problem. Today, there are a few pain points associated with data governance.

First, ensuring a customer's data is used only for the right use cases is difficult as those use cases become increasingly fine-grained. Data users must understand which customer's data can be used for which use cases. Second, tracking applicable customer data is nontrivial given silos of data and a lack of a single identifier to map as customer key (especially the ones acquired over time). Without strict coordination with data users, finding derivations is difficult. A comprehensive catalog of the original data, historic copies, derived data, and third-party datasets is required. Third, executing customer data rights requests must be timely and audited. Appropriate measures are required to ensure the requests aren't fraudulent. It's nontrivial to package all of the customer's personal data in an interoperable format while ensuring the internal schema is not exposed for reverse engineering.

These pain points impact the time to comply, which will slow down the overall time to insight. New use cases take longer since they first need to identify the available permissible data. There's an ongoing cost, as existing use cases need to be reevaluated constantly for scope of data given evolving global laws. Also, data engineering teams spend significant time scaling to support millions of customers and their requests.

Ideally, a self-service *data rights governance service* tracks the life cycle of the data: where it is generated, how it is transformed, and how it is used in different use cases. The service automates the execution of data rights requests and automatically ensures data is accessed only for the right use cases. Minimizing the *time to comply* improves the overall time to insight.

Journey Map

Data is the lifeblood of experiences and is required during all phases of the journey map: discovery, building, training, and post-deployment refinement. Data rights allow users full control over the personal data shared with any enterprise. The role of the governance service is ongoing, as customers may change their consent for using their data for different use cases. Enterprises running their applications are responsible for collecting, managing, and providing access to the customer data and are defined as *data controllers*. If the enterprise uses third-party tools for email marketing, SEO, and so on, those vendors are the *data processors*. The controller is responsible for enforcing data rights across the processors as well.

Executing Data Rights Requests

Customers can request to enforce their data rights. Customers have various expectations with respect to enforcement of their data rights:

- Personal data should only be stored where necessary
- Personal data should be deleted when requested, or when the account is closed
- Personal data should be processed only with user consent

In most enterprises today, the request handling is semi-automated and involves dedicated teams of data engineers. Automating these requests requires identifying what data was collected from the customer, how it is identified, where it is located across all the data sources and the data lake, how the customer preferences are persisted, how the data is used for insights generation, how the data is shared with partners, and what use cases process the data and lineage of the generated insights. Data engineers then need to codify workflows to execute the customer request.

Discovery of Datasets

The quality of the insights generated from the raw data is a function of the available data. Data scientists, analysts, and broader users need to understand what data is available for a given use case. In particular, data users want to analyze as much data as possible so the models are accurate. They want to discover and access the data that is available for analysis based on customer preferences as quickly as possible. The challenge today is persisting these fine-grained preferences, which can be considered a matrix of customer's data elements and the different use cases. For each use case, there is a need to create a filtered view of the customer data, and logic needs to be built in the data collection and dataset preparation to filter data for the use cases.

Customers may want to be excluded from specific use cases. For example, in the case of professional networking portals like LinkedIn (*https://oreil.ly/JwxUG*), a user may want their profile data to be used to recommend new connections but not job recommendations. There's another aspect of customer preferences that may not be honored fully. Consider a scenario of online payment fraud, where the legal investigation may require access to deleted data records to establish a transaction trail.

Model Retraining

Customer data rights preferences change continuously. These changes need to be taken into account during refreshing models and other insights. Currently, model training adds new samples incrementally for training and discards old samples based on a retention time window. Typically, the problem is simplified with a coarse-grained software agreement. An alternative approach has been to mask the PII data in the training process, eliminating the need to discard. Masking may not always be an option due to reidentification risk.

Minimizing Time to Comply

Time to comply includes time spent in tracking the life cycle of data and customer preferences, executing customer data rights requests, and ensuring the right data is used in accordance with customer preferences.

Tracking the Customer Data Life Cycle

This includes tracking how data is collected from the customer, how the data is stored and identified, how the customer preferences are persisted, how data is shared with third-party processors, and how data is transformed by different pipelines.

Tracking customer data presents a couple of key challenges today. First, customers are identified by multiple different IDs. This is especially true for enterprise products integrated via acquisitions. For data shared among services, it is critical to identify dependencies where deletion of records can impact product functionality. Second, PII data needs to be handed with appropriate levels of encryption and access control. PII data needs to be classified based on understanding the semantics of data (not just the schema).

Executing Customer Data Rights Requests

This includes executing customer data rights related to collection, use, deletion, and access to data. Beyond the data management challenges, minimizing the time to execute customer requests needs to address a few challenges. First, the requests need to be validated to prevent fraudulent requests. This involves identifying the user and ensuring they have the right role to issue the request. Second, you need the ability to delete specific data associated with customers from all data systems. Given immutable storage formats, erasing data is difficult and requires understanding of formats and namespace organization. The deletion operation has to cycle through the datasets asynchronously within the compliance SLA without affecting the performance of running jobs. Records that can't be deleted need to be quarantined and the exception records need to be manually triaged. This processing needs to scale to tens of PBs of data as well as for third-party data. Third, you need to make sure not to give away intellectual property secrets as part of the portability requests in order to prevent reverse engineering of the internal formats.

Limiting Data Access

Limiting data access includes ensuring customer data is used for the right use cases based on their preferences. It requires understanding what data elements the use case requires, the type of insight the use case will generate, and whether the data is shared with partners.

The matchmaking of customer preference to use cases requires a complex maze of access policies. Metadata to persist usage preferences should be able to accommodate fine-grained use cases. The metadata needs to be performant and able to accommodate changing customer preferences, and it needs to be evaluated each time. For example, if a user has opted out of email marketing, the next time emails are sent, the customer should be excluded.

Defining Requirements

There is no silver bullet for implementing a data rights governance service. Enterprises differ along the following key dimensions in the context of data governance needs:

- Maturity of the data management in the lake and transactional systems
- Compliance requirements for different industry verticals

- Categories of use cases related to data analytics and ML
- Granularity of user preferences and data elements

Current Pain Point Questionnaire

The goal is to understand the key gaps in the existing data platform deployment. Evaluate the following aspects:

Identification of customer data
> Is the customer data identified uniformly with a primary key across the data silos? The key identifies the customer data across transactional datastores as well as the data lake.

Ability to track lineage
> For datasets derived from raw data, is there clear lineage on how data is derived?

Inventory of use cases
> Is there a clear inventory of all the use cases that operate on the data? You need to have an understanding of the data being used for each use case. More importantly, understand whether the use case benefits the customer experience (for instance, more relevant messages in their feed) as opposed to building a better overall prediction model based on aggregates of customer data.

Managing PII data
> Are there clear standards to identify data attributes that are PII? Are there clear policies associated with masking, encryption, and access to PII data?

Speeds and feeds
> This is related to the scale of data governance operations. The key KPIs are number of regulated datasets, number of customer requests, and number of systems involved in delete and access operations.

Interop Checklist

The governance service needs to work with existing systems. The following is a checklist of the key building blocks to consider in terms of interoperability (as shown Figure 9-2):

Storage systems
> S3, HDFS, Kafka, relational databases, NoSQL stores, etc.

Data formats
> Avro, JSON, Parquet, ORC, etc.

Table management
> Hive, Delta Lake, Iceberg, etc.

Processing engines
Spark, Hive, Presto, TensorFlow, etc.

Metadata catalog
Atlas, Hive Metastore, etc.

Third-party vendors as data processors
Email campaign management tools, customer relationship management, etc.

Figure 9-2. Key systems to consider for interoperability of the data governance service (from Databricks (https://oreil.ly/x7uV0)).

Functional Requirements

The data governance solution needs to have the following features:

- Delete personal data from backups and third parties when it's no longer neces-sary or when consent has been withdrawn. You need the ability to delete a spe-cific subset of data or all data associated with a specific customer from all systems.

- Manage the customer's preferences for data to be collected, behavioral data track-ing, use cases for the data, and communication. *Do not sell data preferences.*

- Discover violations, such as datasets containing PII or highly confidential data that are incorrectly accessible to specific data users or specific use cases. Also, dis-cover datasets that have not been purged within the SLA.

- Verify data rights requests based on user roles and permissions.

- Support different levels of access restrictions. These can range from basic restric-tion (where access to a dataset is based on business need), to privacy by default (where data users shouldn't get raw PII access by default), to consent-based access (where access to data attributes is only available if the user has consented for the particular use case).

Nonfunctional Requirements

Similar to any software design, the following are some of the key NFRs that should be considered in the design of the data rights governance service:

Intuitive data portability
When customers request their data, it needs to be provided in a readable format that is easily portable and broadly applicable.

Scales to handle bursts of requests
SaaS applications can have millions of customers. The service should have the ability to handle bursts of customer requests and complete them in a timely fashion.

Intuitive for customers to enforce data rights
Customers should be able to easily discover how to enforce their data rights.

Extensible for systems
As new building blocks are added to the platform, the data rights governance service should be able to interoperate easily.

Implementation Patterns

Corresponding to the existing task map, there are three levels of automation for the data rights governance service. Each level corresponds to automating a combination of tasks that are currently either manual or inefficient (as shown in Figure 9-3).

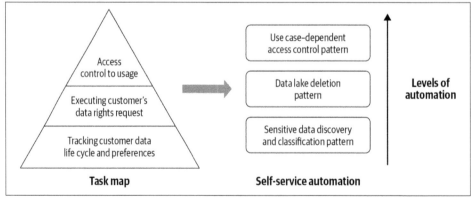

Figure 9-3. Different levels of automation for the data rights governance service.

Sensitive Data Discovery and Classification Pattern

The scope of the sensitive data discovery and classification pattern is discovery and classification of sensitive customer data. The goal is to enable organizations to locate and label their most sensitive data (data containing PII or business secrets) in order to correctly execute customer data rights. Data discovery is the process of locating where user data resides and detecting sensitive PII data for data rights compliance. Classification is the process of labeling the data logically to give context and understanding of the type of information. For example, a table containing social security details could effectively be labeled as PII and given a risk score to denote sensitive data. As a part of the discovery and classification, the pattern helps detect data use cases that are in violation of user preferences. Examples of the pattern include the Amazon Macie (*https://oreil.ly/b7esZ*) and Apache Atlas (*https://oreil.ly/vr3AY*) lineage-based classification.

The pattern works as follows:

- Data discovery daemons collect hundreds of data point values about each data field. It extracts a fingerprint of the data, which is an approximation of the values contained in each field and can easily be used to find similar fields.

- ML algorithms, such as clustering algorithms, allow grouping of similar fields— often hundreds of them, including derived fields of data.

- As data fields are classified in the metadata catalog, the labels are propagated across all the other fields in the lineage. As data users passively train the data catalog with labels or by adding missing or incorrect tags, ML learns from these actions and continuously improves its ability to recognize and accurately tag data.

To illustrate, consider the example of Amazon Macie, which uses machine learning to automatically discover, classify, and protect sensitive data in AWS. Macie understands the data and tracks data access (as shown in Figure 9-4). Macie recognizes sensitive data such as PII, source code, SSL certificates, iOS and Android app signing, OAuth API keys, and so on. It classifies the data based on content, regex, file extension, and PII classifier. Additionally, Macie provides a library of content types (*https://oreil.ly/jTd2z*), each with a designated sensitivity level score. Macie supports multiple compression and archive file formats like bzip, Snappy, LZO, and so on. It continuously monitors data access activity for anomalies and generates alerts. It applies patterns related to which users have access to what data objects and their content visibility (personal data, credentials, sensitivity), as well as access behavior in terms of identification of overly permissive data and unauthorized access to content.

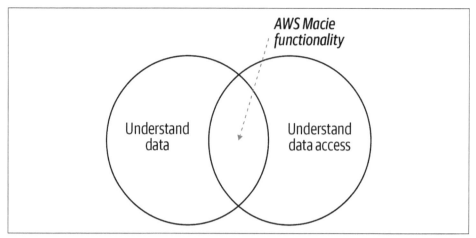

Figure 9-4. The Amazon Macie functionality that combines both the understanding of data as well as tracking of data access.

To illustrate the pattern of label propagation, consider the example of Apache Atlas (*https://oreil.ly/ITcfs*). Classification propagation enables classifications associated with a data entity (e.g., a table) to be automatically associated with other related entities based on data lineage. For instance, for a table classified as `PII tag`, all the tables or views that derive data from this table will also be automatically classified as PII. The classification propagation is policy controlled by the users.

Data Lake Deletion Pattern

This pattern focuses on deleting data in the data lake associated with the customer. Data from the transactional datastores is ingested in the lake for downstream analytics and insights. To meet compliance requirements, a customer delete request needs to ensure data is deleted from the original and derived datasets as well as from all the copies of data in the lake. At a high level, the process works as follows:

- When a customer deletion request is received, it is soft-deleted in the transactional sources.

- During the ingestion process, the records related to the customer are deleted. Given the immutability of the data formats, the delete leads to a massive write operation (i.e., read all the records and rewrite). Delete records are also sent to the third-party processors.

- For historic partitions, the deletion is handled as a batched asynchronous process. The deleted records of multiple customers are tracked in a separate table and bulk-deleted in a batch operation while still ensuring the compliance SLA.

To illustrate the process, we cover Apache Gobblin as an example. Gobblin tracks the Hive partitions associated with the data. During ingestion from the transactional source tables, if the customer data needs to be purged, then those corresponding records will be dropped during the merge process of the ingestion pipeline. This is also applicable to stream processing. The cleaning of historic data records in the lake can be triggered via API. For instance, in the open source Delta Lake project, the vac uum (*https://oreil.ly/niVKY*) command deletes the records from the history.

To illustrate managing the third-party processors, the OpenDSR (*https://oreil.ly/5rX1v*) specification defines a common approach for data controllers and processors to build interoperable systems for tracking and fulfilling data requests. The specification provides a well-defined JSON specification supporting request types of erasure, access, and portability. It also provides a strong cryptographic verification of request receipts to provide chain of processing assurance and demonstrate accountability to regulatory authorities.

Use Case–Dependent Access Control

The goal of this pattern is to ensure data is used for the appropriate use case based on the customer's preferences. Data users extracting insights should not have to worry about violations related to the usage of data. The customer may want different elements of their data used for specific use cases. The customer's preference can be considered as a bitmap (as illustrated in Table 9-1) with different data elements, such as profile, location, clickstream activity, and so on, permissible for different use cases, such as personalization, recommendations, and so on. These preferences are not static and need to be enforced as quickly as possible. For instance, data marketing campaign models should only process the email addresses that have consented to receive communications.

Table 9-1. Bitmap of data elements within the application that are permitted to be used for different use cases based on customer preferences

Data elements	Use case 1	Use case 2	Use case 3
Email address	Yes	No	Yes
Customer support chats	Yes	No	No
User-entered data	Yes	Yes	No
...	...	...	...

There are two broad approaches to implementing this pattern:

Out-of-band control
> Accomplished using fine-grained access control of files, objects, tables, and columns. Based on the attributes associated with the data objects, access is limited to teams corresponding to the specific use cases.

In-bound control

Accomplished using logical tables and views generated dynamically from the underlying physical data at the time of access.

Implementing in-bound access control requires a significant engineering investment to introduce a layer of indirection between the existing clients and the datastores. The in-bound control is much more fine-grained, fool proof, and reactive to changing customer preferences.

To illustrate out-of-bound control, we cover Apache Atlas and Ranger. Atlas is the catalog that allows metadata and tags to be defined for data entities. Ranger provides a centralized security framework that enforces access based on attributes defined for the data entities. It also allows defining column-level or row-level attribute-based access control for data-masking or row-filtering. Figure 9-5 illustrates an example where datasets have different visibility to support teams based on classification in Atlas and enforced by Ranger during access. Another example of the out-of-band control pattern is AWS Data Lake Formation (*https://oreil.ly/G6g5d*), which enforces access policies across AWS services like AWS Redshift, EMR, Glue, and Athena, ensuring users only see tables and columns to which they have access, including logging and auditing all the access.

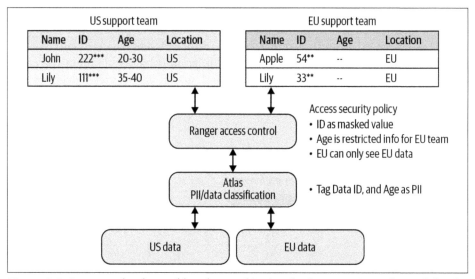

Figure 9-5. An example of out-of-band control in Apache Ranger using policies defined in Apache Atlas (from Hands-On Security in DevOps (https://oreil.ly/fn-V2)).

To illustrate the in-bound control pattern, we cover LinkedIn's Dali (*https://oreil.ly/W-67Q*) project. Dali's design principle is to treat data like code. It provides a logical data-access layer for Hadoop and Spark, as well as streaming platforms. The physical schema can be consumed using multiple external schemas, including creating logical flattened views across multiple datasets applying union, filter, and other transformations (as illustrated Figure 9-6). Given a dataset, its metadata, and use case, it generates a dataset and column-level transformations (mask, obfuscate, and so on). The dataset is automatically joined with member privacy preferences, filtering out non-consented data elements. Dali also combines with Gobblin to purge the datasets on the fly by joining with pending customer delete requests. Under the hood, Dali consists of a catalog to define and evolve physical and virtual datasets and a record-oriented dataset layer for applications. The queries issued by the data users are transformed seamlessly to leverage the Dali views. Toward that end, the SQL is translated into a platform-independent intermediate representation using Apache Calcite. The UDFs for the views use the open source Transport UDFs APIs for running seamlessly on Spark, Samza, and other technologies. There is ongoing (*https://oreil.ly/-eVbn*) work to intelligently materialize the views and query rewrite to use the materialized views.

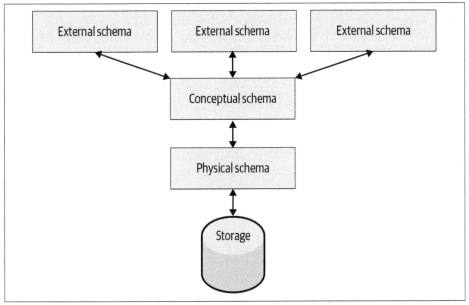

Figure 9-6. Dali's code-based transformation of the physical schema into multiple external use case–specific external schema (from Databricks (https://oreil.ly/uy-KJ)).

Summary

Data governance is a balancing act between the ability to better serve the customer experience with insights while ensuring data is being used in accordance with the customer's directives. The governance service is a must-have for enterprises with a large number of SaaS customers with fine-grained preferences associated with the usage of their personal data.

PART III

Self-Service Build

CHAPTER 10

Data Virtualization Service

With the data ready, we can now start writing the processing logic for generating the insights. There are three trends in big data deployments that need to be taken into account to effectively design the processing logic. First is the polyglot data models associated with the datasets. For instance, graph data is best persisted and queried in a graph database. Similarly, there are other models, namely key-value, wide-column, document, and so on. Polyglot persistence is applicable both for lake data as well as application transactional data. Second, the decoupling of query engines from data storage persistence allows different query engines to run queries on data persisted in the lake. For instance, short, interactive queries are run on Presto clusters, whereas long-running batch processes are on Hive or Spark. Typically, multiple processing clusters are configured for different combinations of query workloads. Selecting the right cluster types is key. Third, for a growing number of use cases like real-time BI, the data in the lake is joined with the application sources in real time. As insights generation becomes increasingly real-time, there is a need to combine historic data in the lake with real-time data in application datastores.

Given these trends, data users need to keep up with the changing technology landscape and gain expertise in evolving data models and query engines and efficiently joining data across silos. This leads to a few pain points. First, as data resides across polyglot datastores within the lake as well as in application data sources, writing queries requires a learning curve for the datastore-specific dialects. Second, there is a need to combine data across datastores within a single query. The approach of first aggregating data, converting it into a normalized form, and then querying it does not meet the needs of a growing number of real-time analytics. The third challenge is deciding on the right query processing cluster. Data users need to pick the right query engine and the appropriate processing cluster, which varies in configuration optimized for SLA workloads, ad hoc, testing, and so on. With decoupled architectures, different query engines can be selected for executing the query on the data based on the data cardinality, query type, and so on.

Ideally, the *data virtualization service* should hide the details associated with the underlying datastores and clusters. The data user submits a SQL-like query. The service automatically federates the query across datastores, optimizing to the specific primitives of the datastores. The properties of the query are used to take into account the appropriate query processing engine cluster. By automating the details of datastore-specific queries, the service reduces the time to query tasks for the data users. Given the iterative nature of defining queries, this has a multiplicative effect on overall time to insight.

Journey Map

The query virtualization service is applicable during all phases of the journey map (the discover, prep, build, and operationalize phases).

Exploring Data Sources

During the discovery phase, data residing in application polyglot stores, warehouses, and lakes is accessed to understand and iterate on the required data properties. Data can be in different forms: structured, semi-structured, and unstructured. While structured relational data is fairly well-established, semi-structured data models are nontrivial and come with a learning curve. This slows down the iterations, impacting the overall time to insight. In some scenarios, running the exploratory queries can slow down or impact serving the application data traffic.

The ability to query and join data across multiple silos is also applicable to the operationalize phase. As applications are being developed as microservices, there is a growing number of polyglot data store silos (e.g., sales data, product data, and customer support data). Building models or dashboards joined across data silos in real time is nontrivial. Today, the approach is to first aggregate the data within the data lake, which may not be feasible for real-time requirements. Instead, data users should be able to access the data as a single namespace assuming a single logical database encompassing all silos.

Picking a Processing Cluster

With decoupling of query engines and data persistence, the same data can be analyzed using different query engines run on different query clusters. Data users need to track the different clusters and pick the right one. The clusters vary in configuration (optimized for long-running, memory-intensive queries versus short-running compute queries), intended use cases (testing versus SLA-centric), allocations to business organizations, and so on. Choosing the appropriate cluster is challenging given the growing number of query processing engines; selecting the right engine based on the properties of the query requires a certain level of expertise. The processing cluster selection also needs to take into account dynamic properties like load balancing and maintenance schedules like blue-green.

Minimizing Time to Query

Time to query is a summation of the time taken to develop the query that accesses data across polyglot datastores and picking the processing environment to execute the query. The time spent is divided into the following categories.

Picking the Execution Environment

As mentioned previously, multiple processing clusters are configured to support different properties of queries. Picking the execution environment involves routing the query to the right processing cluster based on the query type. This requires tracking the inventory of existing environments and their properties, analyzing the properties of the query, and tracking load on the clusters. The challenges are the overhead in tracking the inventory of clusters, continuously updating the current state of the clusters for loads and availability, and routing the requests transparently without requiring client-side changes.

Formulating Polyglot Queries

Data is typically spread across a combination of relational databases, nonrelational datastores, and data lakes. Some data may be highly structured and stored in SQL databases or data warehouses. Other data may be stored in NoSQL engines, including key-value stores, graph databases, ledger databases, or time-series databases. Data may also reside in the data lake, stored in formats that may lack schema or that may involve nesting or multiple values (e.g., Parquet (*https://oreil.ly/sDN7H*) and JSON). Every different type and flavor of datastore may suit a particular use case, but each also comes with its own query language. Polyglot query engines, NewSQL, and NoSQL datastores provide semi-structured data models (typically JSON-based) and respective query languages. The lack of formal syntax and semantics, idiomatic language constructs, and large variations in syntax, semantics, and actual capabilities pose problems even for experts—it is hard to understand, compare, and use these languages.

Also, there is a tight coupling between the query language and the format in which data is stored. If the data needs to be changed to another format or if the query engine needs to change, then the application and queries must also change. This is a large obstacle to the agility and flexibility needed to effectively use data.

Joining Data Across Silos

Data resides across multiple sources in polyglot datastores. Running queries on siloed data requires first aggregating the data in the lake, which may not be feasible given real-time requirements. The challenge today is to balance the load on the application datastores with traffic from the analytical systems. Traditional query optimizers take into account cardinality and data layout, which is difficult to accomplish across the data silos. Typically, the data of the application datastores is also cached as materialized views to support repeating queries.

Defining Requirements

The data virtualization service has multiple levels of self-service automation. This section covers the current level of automation and the requirements for deployment of the service.

Current Pain Point Analysis

The following considerations will help you get a pulse of the current status:

Need for data virtualization
> Ask the following questions to understand the urgency of automating data virtualization: Are multiple query engines being used? Is polyglot persistence within the data lake or application datastores being used? Is there a need to join across transactional stores? If the answers to these questions aren't "yes," then implementing the data virtualization service should be treated as a lower priority.

Impact of data virtualization
> Review the following considerations to quantify the improvements implementing the data virtualization service will make to the existing processing: the time to formulate a query represents the time spent in defining the query; the average number of iterations required to get the query running and optimized; the existing expertise for different polyglot platforms; and the average processing freshness with respect to time lag between event and analysis. Also, understand if user-defined functions (UDFs) need to be supported as part of the query processing (they're typically not well supported by virtualization engines).

Need for application datastore isolation
> Data virtualization pushes the queries to the application data sources. The following are the key considerations: the current load on application stores and slowdown of the application queries; existing SLA violations in application performance due to datastore performance; and the rate of change in application data. For scenarios where the application datastores are saturated or with rapidly changing data, it may not be feasible to implement a data virtualization strategy.

Operational Requirements

Automation needs to take into account the current process and technology requirements. This will vary from deployment to deployment:

Interoperability with deployed technology
> The key considerations are the different data models and datastore technologies used to persist the data in the lake and applications. The supported query engines and programming languages correspond to the datastores.

Observability tools
> The data virtualization service needs to integrate with the existing monitoring, alerting, and debugging tools to ensure availability, correctness, and query SLAs.

Speeds and feeds
> In designing the data virtualization service, take into account the number of concurrent queries to be processed, the complexity of queries processed, and tolerable latencies for real-time analysis.

Functional Requirements

The key features of the data virtualization service are:

- Automated routing of queries to the right clusters without requiring any client-side changes. The routing is based on tracking the static configuration properties (such as number of cluster nodes and hardware configuration, namely CPU, disk, storage, and so on) as well as the dynamic load on the existing clusters (average wait time, distribution of query execution times, and so on).

- Simplifies formulating queries for structured, semi-structured, and unstructured data residing across polyglot datastores.

- Federated query support for joining data residing across different datastores in the lake as well as application microservices. Also, it has the ability to limit the number of queries pushed to the application datastores.

Nonfunctional Requirements

Similar to any software design, the following are some of the key NFRs that should be considered in the design of the data virtualization service:

Extensibility
> The service should be extensible for changing environments with the ability to be extensible in supporting new tools and frameworks.

Cost

Virtualization is computationally expensive, and it is critical to optimize the associated cost.

Debuggability

The queries developed on the virtualization service should be easy to monitor and debug for correctness and performance in production deployments running at scale.

Implementation Patterns

Corresponding to the existing task map, there are three levels of automation for the query virtualization service. Each level corresponds to automating a combination of tasks that are currently either manual or inefficient (as shown in Figure 10-1):

Automatic query routing pattern

Simplifies the tasks related to selecting the right tool for the job. This pattern hides the complexity of selecting the right processing environment for the query.

Single query language pattern

Simplifies the learning curve associated with writing queries on structured, semi-structured, and unstructured data.

Federated query pattern

Simplifies the tasks related to joining data across sources. The pattern provides a single query engine that can be accessed using a single query engine.

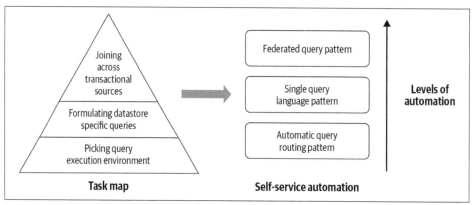

Figure 10-1. The different levels of automation for the data virtualization service.

Automatic Query Routing Pattern

The goal of this pattern is to automatically route the query to a processing cluster—the data users simply submit the job to the virtualization service. The routing pattern takes into account query and cluster properties as well as current cluster load. In other words, the pattern is a matchmaker between queries and available processing clusters.

Under the hood, the pattern broadly works as follows:

- A processing job is submitted to the jobs API. The properties of the job, such as job type (Hive, Presto, Spark), command-line arguments, and set of file dependencies, are specified.
- The data virtualization service generates a custom run script for each individual submitted job. The run scripts allow the jobs to be run on different processing clusters that are chosen at runtime.
- Based on current load and other properties, a cluster is selected for execution of the job. The request is submitted to the job orchestrator service for execution. The query routing pattern does not get involved with cluster scaling or job scheduling. In other words, the pattern focuses on fulfilling the user's tasks by starting their jobs on a cluster that matches their job needs.

Netflix's Genie (*https://oreil.ly/LQkQM*) is an example of an open source implementation. Variants of the pattern have been implemented internally by Web 2.0 companies like Facebook, where a query is analyzed for the data cardinality and complexity. Short-running, interactive queries are routed to the Presto cluster while long-running, resource-intensive queries are executed on the Hive cluster.

Genie was a project started at Netflix to simplify the routing of queries. It allows data users as well as various systems (schedulers, microservices, Python libraries, and so on) to submit jobs without actually knowing anything about the clusters themselves. The unit of execution is a single Hadoop, Hive, or Pig job. Data users specify to Genie the kind of processing cluster to pick by providing either cluster name/ID or properties like prod versus testing (as shown in Figure 10-2). Genie nodes use the appropriate application libraries to create a new working directory for each job, stage all the dependencies (including Hadoop, Hive, and Pig configurations for the chosen cluster), then fork off a Hadoop client process from that working directory. Genie then returns a Genie job ID, which can be used by the clients to query for status and to get an output URI, which is browsable during and after job execution. Genie has a leader node that runs tasks for inventory cleanup, zombie job detection, disk cleanup, and job monitoring. Leadership election is supported via either Zookeeper or by setting a single node to be the leader statically via a property.

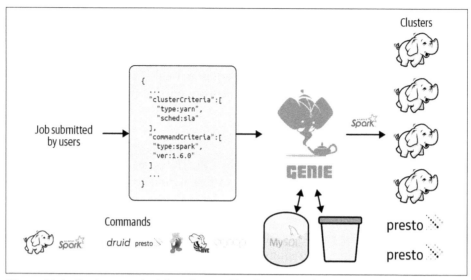

Figure 10-2. Genie maps the jobs submitted by the user to the appropriate processing cluster (from InfoQ (https://oreil.ly/TW2KO)).

With the growing complexity of query processing configurations, the query routing pattern is becoming increasingly important for hiding underlying complexities, especially at scale. The strength of the pattern is transparent routing based on the combination of static configuration and dynamic load properties. The weakness is that the routing service can become a bottleneck or single point of saturation.

Unified Query Pattern

This pattern focuses on unified query language and programming models. Data users can use the unified approach for structured, semi-structured, and unstructured data across different datastores. The pattern is illustrated by PartiQL (a unified SQL-like query language), Apache Drill (a programming model for semi-structured data), and Apache Beam (a unified programming model for streaming and batch processing).

PartiQL (*https://partiql.org/*) is a SQL-compatible query language that makes it easy to efficiently query data, regardless of where or in what format it is stored (as illustrated in Figure 10-3). PartiQL processes structured data from relational databases (both transactional and analytical), semi-structured and nested data in open data formats (such as an Amazon S3), and schema-less data in NoSQL or document databases that allow different attributes for different rows.

PartiQL has a minimum number of extensions over SQL, enabling intuitive filtering, joining, aggregation, and windowing on the combination of structured, semi-structured, and nested datasets. The PartiQL data model treats nested data as a fundamental part of the data abstraction, providing syntax and semantics that comprehensively and accurately access and query nested data while naturally composing with the standard features of SQL. PartiQL does not require a predefined schema over a dataset. PartiQL syntax and semantics are data format–independent— i.e., a query is written identically across underlying data in JSON, Parquet, ORC, CSV, or other formats. Queries operate on a comprehensive, logical type system that maps to diverse underlying formats. Also, PartiQL syntax and semantics are not tied to a particular underlying datastore.

In the past, languages addressed subsets of the requirements. For example, Postgres JSON is SQL-compatible but does not treat the JSON nested data as a first-class citizen. Semi-structured query languages treat nested data as first-class citizens but either allow occasional incompatibilities with SQL or do not even look like SQL. PartiQL is an example of a clean, well-founded query language that is very close to SQL and has the power needed to process nested and semi-structured data. PartiQL leverages work in the database research community, namely UCSD's SQL++ (*https:// oreil.ly/LMhdj*).

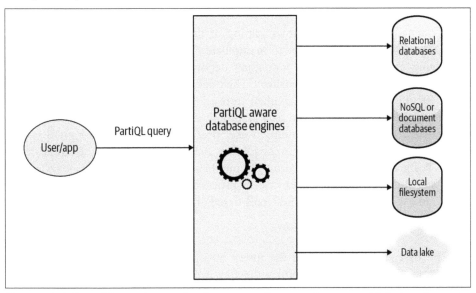

Figure 10-3. PartiQL queries are database-agnostic, operating on multiple data formats and models (from the AWS Open Source Blog (https://oreil.ly/qPexz)).

Apache Drill (*http://drill.apache.org*) is an example of an intuitive extension to SQL that easily queries complex data. Drill features a JSON data model that enables queries on nested data as well as rapidly evolving structures commonly seen in modern applications and non-relational datastores. Drill (inspired by Google Dremel) allows users to explore, visualize, and query different datasets without having to fix a schema using MapReduce routines or ETL. Using Drill, data can be queried just by mentioning the path in the SQL query to a NoSQL database, Amazon S3 bucket, or Hadoop directory. Drill defines the schema on the go so that users can directly query the data, unlike traditional SQL query engines. When using Drill, developers don't need to code and build applications like Hive to extract data; normal SQL queries will help the user get data from any data source and in any specific format. Drill uses a hierarchical columnar data model for treating data like a group of tables, irrespective of how the data is actually modeled.

Apache Beam (*https://beam.apache.org*) unifies batch and stream processing. It is an open source, unified model for defining both batch and streaming data-parallel processing pipelines. Data users build a program that defines the pipeline using one of the open source Beam SDKs. The pipeline is then executed by one of Beam's supported distributed processing backends, which include Apache Apex (*https://oreil.ly/lgOwh*), Apache Flink (*https://oreil.ly/veoIk*), Apache Spark (*https://oreil.ly/stk81*), and Google Cloud Dataflow (*https://oreil.ly/B9wAN*).

Federated Query Pattern

The federated query pattern allows joining of data residing across different datastores. Data users write the query to manipulate the data without getting exposed to underlying complexities of the individual datastores or having to first physically aggregate the data in a single repository. The query processing is federated under the hood, fetching data from the individual stores, joining the data, and generating the final result. Users operate on the data assuming it is available in a single, large data warehouse. Examples include joining a user profile collection in MongoDB with a directory of event logs in Hadoop, or joining a site's textual traffic log stored in S3 with a PostgreSQL database to count the number of times each user has visited the site. The pattern is implemented by query processing engines such as Apache Spark, Presto, and several commercial and cloud-based offerings.

Broadly, the pattern works as follows:

- The first step is converting the query into an execution plan. The optimizer (*https://oreil.ly/TpM0q*) compiles the physical plan for execution based on an understanding of the semantics of operations and structure of the data.

- As a part of the plan, it makes intelligent decisions to speed up computation, such as through predicate pushdown. Filter predicates are pushed down into the data source, enabling the physical execution to skip irrelevant data. In the case of Parquet files, entire blocks can be skipped and comparisons on strings can be turned into cheaper integer comparisons via dictionary encoding. In the case of relational databases, predicates are pushed down into the external databases to reduce the amount of data traffic. Ideally, most of the processing should happen close to where the data is stored, to leverage the capabilities of the participating stores to dynamically eliminate data that is not needed.

- The responses from the datastores are aggregated and transformed to generate the final query result that can be written back into a datastore. Appropriate failure retries are built to ensure data correctness.

An implementation of the pattern is the Spark query processing engine. Spark SQL queries can access multiple tables simultaneously in such a way that multiple rows of each table are processed at the same time. The tables can be located in the same or different databases. To support the datastores, Spark implements connectors to multiple datastores (*https://oreil.ly/sQksR*). The data across disparate sources can be joined using DataFrames abstraction. The optimizer compiles the operations that were used to build the DataFrame into a physical plan for execution. Before any computation on a DataFrame starts, a logical plan is created. Query pushdown leverages these performance efficiencies by enabling large and complex Spark logical plans (in their entirety or in parts) to be processed in datastores, thus using the datastores to do most of the actual work. Pushdown is not possible in all situations. For example, Spark UDFs cannot be pushed down to Snowflake.

Similarly, Presto supports federated queries. Presto is a distributed ANSI SQL engine for processing big data ad hoc queries. The engine is used to run fast, interactive analytics on federated data sources, such as SQL Server, Azure SQL Database, Azure SQL Data Warehouse, MySQL, Postgres, Cassandra, MongoDB, Kafka, Hive (HDFS, Cloud Object Stores), and so on. It accesses data from multiple systems within a single query. For example, it could join historic log data stored in S3 with real-time customer data stored in MySQL.

Summary

The concept of virtualization abstracts the underlying processing details and provides users with a single logical view of the system. It has been applied in other domains like server virtualization technologies where containers and virtual machines abstract the underlying details of physical hardware. Similarly, in the big data era where there are no silver bullets in datastore technologies and processing engines, data users should be agnostic in terms of how data is queried across sources. They should be able to access and query the data as a single logical namespace irrespective of the underlying data persistence models and query engines to process the query.

Data Transformation Service

So far, in the build phase, we have finalized the methodology to handle polyglot data models and the query processing required to implement the insight logic. In this chapter, we dig deeper into the implementation of business logic, which traditionally follows the Extract-Transform-Load (ETL) or Extract-Load-Transform (ELT) pattern.

There are a few key pain points associated with developing transformation logic. First, data users are experts in business logic but need engineering support to implement the logic at scale. That is, with the exponential growth in data, distributed programming models are required to implement the logic in a reliable and performant fashion. This often slows down the overall process since data users need to explain business logic and then user acceptance testing (UAT) to engineers. Second, there is an increasing need to build real-time business logic transformers. Traditionally, the transformation has been batch-oriented, involving reading from file, transforming the format, joining with different data sources, and so on. Data users are not experts in evolving programming models, especially for real-time insights. Third, running transformations in production requires continuous support to track availability, quality, change management of data sources, and processing logic. These pain points slow down the time to transform. Typically, transformation logic is not built from scratch but as a variant of the existing logic.

Ideally, a *data transformation service* allows users to specify the business logic without the actual details of the implementation. Under the hood, the service translates the logic into an implementation code that is performant and scalable. The service supports both batch and real-time processing. It implements monitoring of availability, quality, and change management. This reduces the *time to transform*, as data users can define and version-control their business logic without worrying about writing, optimizing, and debugging actual processing code. In addition to reducing the time required to build the transformation logic, the service reduces the time to execute in production in a performant fashion and operates in production at scale.

Journey Map

The transformation service helps data users with tasks related to data reporting, storytelling, model generation, and so on. In contrast to data wrangling, which implements dataset-specific functions (such as filling in missing values, outlier detection, and enriching), the transformation logic is written by data users in the context of solving a problem, and the logic typically evolves with business definitions.

Production Dashboard and ML Pipelines

Data analysts extract insights from data to produce business metrics for daily dashboards on marketing funnels, product feature usage, sign-ups and sign-ins, A/B testing, and so on. The business logic for the transformation is based on collaboration with stakeholders from finance, sales, marketing, and so on. Similarly, scientists develop ML models for data products and business processes. These pipelines are typically run on a scheduled basis with tight service level agreements (SLA). Today, business definitions are mixed with implementation code, making it difficult to manage and change the business logic.

Data-Driven Storytelling

Organizations are becoming increasingly data-driven. Data across multiple silos is combined and analyzed to make decisions. This data is stored in a wide variety of datastores, and in different formats. The data is structured, semi-structured, or unstructured. For instance, customer details may be in a flat file in one silo, in XML in another, and in a relational table in the other. Sometimes the data might be poorly designed, even if it is structured. Storytelling requires efficiently dealing with large amounts of data in different formats and datastores. As the amount of data increases, the processing can run for hours and days without distributed processing.

Minimizing Time to Transform

Time to transform includes the time to define, execute, and operate the business logic transformation. The time spent is divided into three buckets: transformation implementation, transformation execution, and transformation operations.

Transformation Implementation

The implementation of the transformation logic includes defining the business logic and coding for transformation logic code. This includes appropriate testing and verification, performance optimization, and other software engineering aspects.

There are two aspects that make this challenging and time-consuming. First, it is difficult to separate the correctness of the logic from the implementation issues—i.e., logic is mixed with implementation. When new team members join, they are unable to understand and extract the underlying logic (and the reasoning for those choices), making it difficult to manage. Second, data users are not engineers. There is a learning curve to efficiently implementing the primitives (aggregates, filters, groupby, etc.) in a scalable fashion across different systems. To increase productivity, there is a balance required between low-level and high-level business logic specifications. The low-level constructs are difficult to learn, while the high-level constructs need to be appropriately expressive.

Transformation Execution

Execution of the transformation includes a few tasks. The first is selecting the appropriate query processing engine. For example, a query can be executed in Spark, Hive, or Flink. Second, the transformation logic can be run either as batch or streaming, which require different implementations. Third, beyond the core transformation logic, the execution requires the data to be read, logic to be applied, and output to be written to a serving database. Data needs to be consumed as tables, files, objects, events, and other forms. The output may be written to different serving stores.

Several challenges make execution time-consuming. First, there is a plethora of processing technologies, and it is difficult for data users to pick the right query processing framework. Second, managing different versions of the transformation logic for batch as opposed to real-time processing is difficult to manage consistently. Third, whenever the logic changes, a data backfill is required for changes in logic. For data scale in petabytes, the logic needs to be efficient in incrementally processing updates and applied only on the new data.

Transformation Operations

Transformations are typically deployed in production with SLAs. Operating in production requires monitoring, alerting, and proactive anomaly detection for completion and data quality violations. Operating transformations in production is time-consuming; distinguishing between a hung and slow process is not easy and requires manual debugging and analysis. Logging across the system's metadata is critical for root-cause analysis and requires individual log parsers for different data systems.

Defining Requirements

The requirements for the transformation service vary based on the skills of the data users, the types of use cases, and the existing processes for building data pipelines. This section helps to understand the current state and the requirements for deployment of the service.

Current State Questionnaire

There are three categories of considerations related to the current state:

Current state for implementing transformation logic
> The key metrics to gather are time to modify the logic of existing transformations, time to verify the correctness of the implementation, and time to optimize a new transformation implementation. In addition to these stats, list the different data formats being used in the lake.

Current state for executing transformations
> The key aspects to consider are the number of use cases requiring real-time transformation (instead of traditional, batch-oriented transformation), the datastores to read and write, the existing processing engines, the existing programming models (such as Apache Beam), and the average number of concurrent requests.

Current state for operating transformations
> The key metrics to consider are time to detect, time to debug production issues, the number of SLA violation incidents, and issues related to transformation correctness.

Functional Requirements

The key features required in this service are:

Automated transformation code generation
> Data users specify the business logic for the transformation without worrying about the code details for the implementation.

Batch and stream execution
> Allows running the transformation logic as batch or streaming depending on the requirements of the use case. Execution runs at scale in a performant fashion.

Incremental processing
> Able to remember the data processed in the past invocation and applies the processing on the new incremental data.

Automated backfill processing
> Automatically recomputes the metric on changes in the logic.

Detecting availability and quality issues
> Monitors the availability, quality, and change management.

Nonfunctional Requirements

Following are some of the key NFRs that should be considered in the design of the data transformation service:

Data connectivity
    ETL tools should be able to communicate with any data sources.

Scalability
    Able to scale to the growing data volume and velocity.

Intuitive
    Given the broad spectrum of data users, the transformation service should be easy to use.

Implementation Patterns

Corresponding to the existing task map, there are three levels of automation for the transformation service (as shown in Figure 11-1). Each level corresponds to automating a combination of tasks that are currently either manual or inefficient:

Implementation pattern
    Simplifies specification and implementation of transformation logic and rapidly evolves based on the changing business requirements.

Execution pattern
    Unifies the execution of the transformation logic, allowing both batch and real-time processing based on the freshness requirements.

Operational pattern
    Tracks transformations in production seamlessly to meet SLAs. This pattern provides monitoring and alerting to ensure availability and quality of the transformation. We cover this pattern in Chapters 15 and 18 in the context of the query optimization service and the data quality service, respectively.

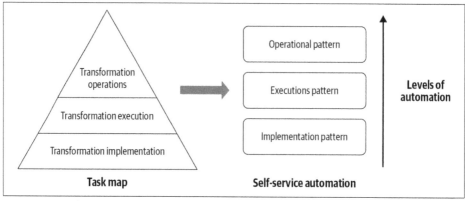

Figure 11-1. The different levels of automation for the data transformation service.

Implementation Pattern

This pattern focuses on simplifying the implementation of the business logic. The general approach is for data users to define the logic in terms of a high-level language of standard transformation functions (analogous to LEGO building blocks). By separating the logic specification from the actual code implementation, these specifications are easy to manage, modify, collaborate on, and understand. Given the spectrum of data users, this pattern improves the time to implement the transformation and ensures high quality. There are multiple commercial and open source solutions available, such as Informatica PowerCenter (*https://oreil.ly/nfVKS*), Microsoft SSIS (*https://oreil.ly/pNRI8*), Pentaho Kettle (*https://oreil.ly/i25Jr*), Talend (*https://oreil.ly/O27RK*), and so on.

At a high level, these solutions work as follows:

- Users specify the transformation logic using either a DSL language or a drag-and-drop UI. The transformation logic is defined in terms of standardized building blocks: namely extract, filter, aggregate, and so on. The specifications are version-controlled and managed separately from the code.

- The specifications are converted automatically into executable code. The code accounts for specific datastores, processing engines, data formats, and so on. The generated code can be in different programming languages or models.

To illustrate, we cover Apache NiFi and Looker's LookerML for GUI-based and DSL-based transformation, respectively. GUI-based tools are not a good replacement for a well-structured transformation code; they lack flexibility, and there are several scenarios where the limitations of the tools force users to adopt hacky ways to implement the logic.

Apache NiFi (*https://nifi.apache.org*) provides a rich, web-based GUI for designing, controlling, and monitoring data transformations (as shown in Figure 11-2). NiFi provides 250+ standardized functions out of the box, divided into three main types: *sources* (extract functions), *processors* (transform functions), and *sinks* (load functions). Examples of processor functions are enhance, verify, filter, join, split, or adjust data. Additional processors can be added in Python, shell, and Spark. Processors are implemented to be highly concurrent in their data processing, and they hide the inherent complexities of parallel programming from the users. Processors run simultaneously and span multiple threads to cope with the load. Once data is fetched from external sources, it is represented as a FlowFile inside NiFi dataflows. FlowFile is basically a pointer to the original data with associated meta-information. A processor has three outputs:

Failure
> If a FlowFile cannot be processed correctly, the original FlowFile will be routed to this output.

Original
> Once an incoming FlowFile has been processed, the original FlowFile is routed to this output.

Success
> FlowFiles that are successfully processed will be routed to this relationship.

Other GUI transformation modeling solutions similar to NiFi include StreamSets (*https://streamsets.com*) and Matillion ETL (*https://oreil.ly/nlzEu*).

An example of a DSL specification is Looker's LookML (*https://oreil.ly/SmJdc*), which is used to construct SQL queries. LookML is a language for describing dimensions, aggregates, calculations, and data relationships. A transformation project is a collection of model, view, and dashboard files that are version-controlled together via a Git repository. The model files contain information about which tables to use and how they should be joined together. The view files contain information about how to calculate information about each table (or across multiple tables if the joins permit them). LookML separates structure from content, so the query structure (how tables are joined) is independent of the query content (the columns to access, derived fields, aggregate functions to compute, and filtering expressions to apply). In contrast to UI drag-and-drop models, LookML provides an IDE with auto-completion, error highlighting, contextual help, and a validator that helps you fix errors. Also, LookML supports complex data handling for power users, with functions such as inequality joins, many-to-many data relationships, multilevel aggregation, and so on. Other examples of the DSL approach include Airbnb's metrics DSL (*https://oreil.ly/3pY-J*) and DBFunctor (*https://oreil.ly/ia-vZ*), which is a declarative library for ETL/ELT data processing that leverages functional programming and Haskell's strong type system.

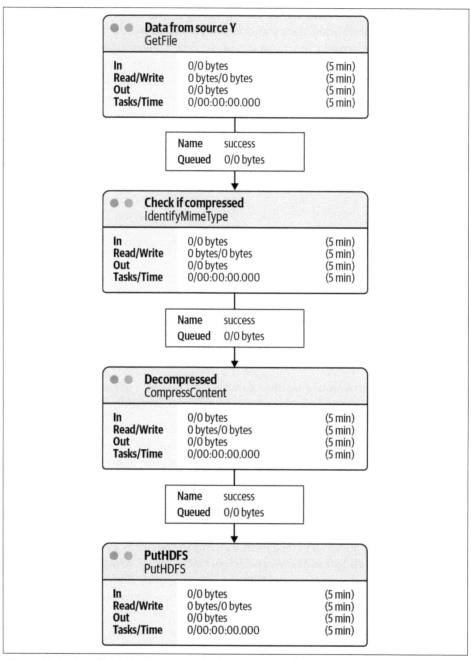

Figure 11-2. Apache NiFi schematic of a four-step transformation where data is read from source, checked for compression, decompressed, and finally copied into HDFS.

Execution Patterns

These patterns focus on making it self-service for data users to execute business transformation logic. Execution patterns differ in the time lag between event generation and the event processing time; the time lag ranges from daily or hourly batch processing to seconds or milliseconds lag using streaming patterns. In the early days, stream processing in Spark was implemented as microbatches, which evolved into per-event processing with Apache Flink. Further, in the early days of big data, the processing logic during streaming was lightweight counts and aggregates, while heavyweight analytical functions were executed in batch. Today, the distinctions between batch and streaming are blurred—data is treated as events, and the processing is a time-window function. Netflix's Keystone (*https://oreil.ly/cVf0M*) and Apache Storm (*https://storm.apache.org*) are examples of self-service streaming data patterns and treat batch processing as a subset of the stream processing.

The streaming data patterns work as follows: data is treated as events. The dataset is unbounded and operated using windowing functions. For batch processing, data (in tables) is replayed as events on a message bus for processing:

- Data is represented as events on a message bus. For instance, updates to tables can be represented as change data capture (CDC) events with the old and new values for the columns. Certain datasets like behavioral data can be naturally treated as events. Raw events are persisted in a store for replay.

- Transformation logic operates on the data events. The transformation can be stateless or stateful. An example of stateless processing is when each event is treated independently like when converting raw CDC events into business objects, such as customer creation, invoice created, and so on. Stateful processing operates across events, such as counts, aggregations, and so on.

- Similar to traditional ETL, the data user specifies the data source, transformation logic, and output where the data is to be written. The pattern automates execution, scaling, retries, backfilling, and other tasks related to executing the business logic transformation.

Netflix's Keystone platform (shown in Figure 11-3) simplifies reading events from the source, executing the processing job, and writing the data to a sink datastore. It also automates backfilling for processing logic changes, as well as running batch as a stream of events for processing. The data user focuses on the business logic and does not worry about data engineering aspects.

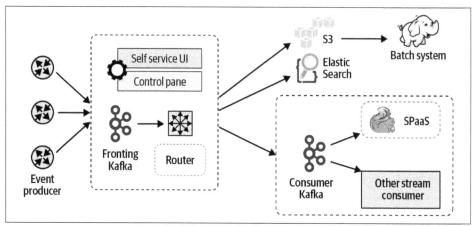

Figure 11-3. The Netflix Keystone service for self-service streaming data processing (from the Netflix Tech Blog (https://oreil.ly/HUr_a)).

Summary

In the journey of extracting insights from raw data, the data needs to be transformed based on business logic defined by data users with business domain expertise. These transformations are unique in the logic but are mostly composed of a common set of functions, such as aggregate, filter, join, split, and so on. The transformation service simplifies the complex task of building, executing, and operating these transformations in production.

CHAPTER 12

Model Training Service

So far, we have built the transformation pipeline for generating insights that can feed a business dashboard, or processed data for an application to share with end customers, and so on. If the insight is an ML model, model training is required; that will be covered in this chapter. A typical data scientist explores hundreds of model permutations during training to find the most accurate model. The exploration involves trying different permutations of ML algorithms, hyperparameter values, and data features. Today, the process of training ML models presents some challenges. First, with the growing dataset sizes and complicated deep learning models, training can take days and weeks. At the same time, it is nontrivial to manage training orchestration across a farm of servers consisting of a combination of CPUs and specialized hardware like GPUs. Second, iterative tuning of optimal values for model parameters and hyperparameter values relies on brute-force search. There is a need for automated model tuning, including tracking of all tuning iterations and their results. Third, for scenarios where the data is continuously changing (for instance, a product catalog, a social media feed, and so on), the model needs to be trained continuously. The ML pipelines for continuous training need to be managed in an automated fashion to continuously retrain, verify, and deploy the model without human intervention. These challenges slow down the time to train. Given that training is an iterative process, a slowdown in time to train has a multiplicative impact on the overall time to insight. Today, data engineering teams are building nonstandard training tools and frameworks that eventually become a technical debt.

Ideally, a *model training service* reduces the *time to train* by automating the training before deployment as well as continuous training post-deployment. For pre-deployment training, data users specify the data features, configuration, and model code, and the model training service leverages the feature store service and automatically orchestrates the overall workflow to train and tune the ML model. Given the growing amount of data, the service optimizes the training time by using distributed training as well as techniques like transfer learning. For continuous training, the service trains the model with new data, validates the accuracy compared to the current model, and triggers the deployment of the newly trained model accordingly. The service needs to support a wide range of ML libraries and tools, model types, and one-off and continuous training. Key examples of automated model training platforms include Google's TensorFlow Extended (TFX) (*https://oreil.ly/8ZKi5*), Airbnb's Bighead (*https://oreil.ly/uRB3e*), Uber's Michelangelo (*https://oreil.ly/n_7g-*), Amazon's SageMaker (*https://oreil.ly/kM5Dl*), Google Cloud's AutoML (*https://oreil.ly/3WIPK*), and so on.

Journey Map

Model training and validation is an iterative process that takes place before the model can be deployed in production (as shown in Figure 12-1). During the build phase, based on the results from the training, data users can go back to the data discovery and preparation phases to explore different combinations of features to develop a more accurate model. This section summarizes key scenarios in the journey map.

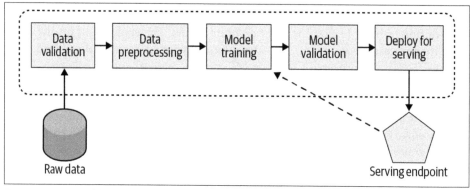

Figure 12-1. Model training and validation in the overall journey map of model deployment.

Model Prototyping

Data scientists explore different model permutations that involve feature combinations, model parameters, and hyperparameter values to find the best model for the business problem (as illustrated in Figure 12-2). For each permutation of values, a model is trained, validated, and compared for accuracy. Training involves a process of cross-validation, partitioning the dataset into two sets for training and testing (typically using a 70/30 split of the data for training and testing). The model is first trained using the data samples for training, then it is evaluated using the unseen samples in the testing dataset. It is computationally expensive and usually requires multiple passes over large datasets. Training models is iterative with diminishing returns. It generates a low-quality model at the beginning and improves the model's quality through a sequence of training iterations until it converges—it is an empirical process of trial and error that can take significant effort, both human and machine. Recording the permutations explored during prototyping is helpful for debugging and tuning at a later point.

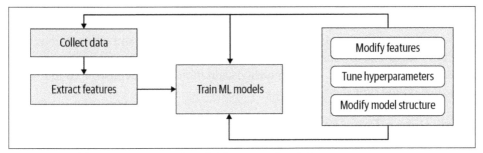

Figure 12-2. The iterive nature of model design and training.

With exponential growth of data volume and complexity of deep learning models, training models can take days and weeks. Given that training jobs are expensive, data users in experimental environments often prefer to work with more approximate models trained within a short period of time for preliminary validation and testing, rather than wait for a significant amount of time for a better-trained model with poorly tuned configurations.

Continuous Training

Data evolves continuously after the model is deployed in production. To account for these changes, data scientists either manually train on newer data and deploy the resulting model, or schedule training on new data to take place, say, once a week, and automatically deploy the resulting model. The goal is to ensure the highest accuracy with ongoing changes in data. An extreme example of refreshing models is online learning, which updates a model with every received request—i.e., the serving model is the training model. Online learning is applicable in environments where behaviors change quickly, such as product catalogs, video ranking, social feeds, and so on. During retraining, the new model quality needs to be verified and compared with the existing model in an automated fashion before being deployed in production.

In practice, it is more common to update a model in batches to ensure production safety by validating the data and models before they are updated. ML pipelines update models on an hourly or daily basis. The retraining can improve the accuracy for different segments of the data.

Model Debugging

Models may not perform well in production due to a wide variety of problems: data quality, incorrect feature pipelines, data distribution skew, model overfitting, and so on. Alternatively, a specific inference generated by the model needs to be audited for correctness.

In these scenarios, understanding and debugging models is increasingly important, especially for deep learning. Debugging model performance requires a model's lineage with respect to dependencies, how they were generated, and permutations that have been explored (considering the nontrivial amount of time it takes for exploring and training permutations). Using model visualization, data scientists need to understand, debug, and tune their models.

Minimizing Time to Train

Training today is time-consuming for two reasons:

- The inherent complexity due to growing dataset sizes and the complexity of deep learning models, which increases the time for each training iteration. Deciding on the right features to be used for the model (known as feature engineering), the values for model parameter values and hyperparameters is iterative, and requires data scientists to have the required expertise.

- Accidental complexity arising due to ad hoc scripts for training and tuning. These processes are nonstandard and vary for different combinations of ML libraries, tools, model types, and underlying hardware resources.

Reducing time to train is focused on eliminating accidental complexity through automation. Today, time in the training process is spent in training orchestration, tuning, and continuous training.

Training Orchestration

Training orchestration involves creating a training dataset for the model features, allocating compute resources across heterogenous hardware environments for training, and optimizing strategies for training. These tasks are time-consuming. Training used to be run by data scientists on their desktops. With growing dataset sizes, and considering that training can take days and weeks, there is a need to distribute training across a cluster of machines.

Creating training datasets requires creating the pipelines for getting training data that corresponds to each of the features in the model. As discussed previously, this can be automated using a feature store service (covered in Chapter 4). Resource allocation for training needs to leverage the underlying hardware combination of CPUs and

GPUs. There are different strategies to distribute the training tasks across the cores and aggregate the results (analogous to MapReduce approaches for data processing). Given the iterative nature of training, there is no need to start from scratch; optimization techniques like transfer learning can be automated to speed up the training process. Considering these tasks are manual and nonstandard, they are time-consuming as well as suboptimal.

Tuning

Model parameters and hyperparameter values are tuned to generate the most accurate and reliable model. Model parameters are learned attributes that define individual models derived directly from the training data (e.g., regression coefficients and decision tree split locations). Hyperparameters express higher-level structural settings for algorithms—for example, the strength of the penalty used in regularized regression, or the number of trees to include in a random forest. They are tuned to best fit the model because they can't be learned from the data.

Tuning values requires a trial-and-error approach of trying different value combinations. Different strategies are used to intelligently explore the search space of different combinations, and the time for tuning varies based on the techniques applied. At the end of each training iteration, the model is evaluated using a variety of metrics for measuring model accuracy.

Continuous Training

Models need to be updated continuously for changes in data. A key metric is model freshness, or how quickly new data is reflected by the model, which ensures high-quality inferences. There are two flavors of continuous training: updating the model on each new sample (known as online training) and periodically updating the model by creating a sliding window of the data, and retraining the model using windowing functions (analogous to streaming analytics). Retraining models involves tracking data changes and selective iteration for only the changes. This is in contrast to brute-force starting from scratch for each training iteration. Job orchestration frameworks today are not data-aware—i.e., they're not selective in rerunning only the pipelines that have new data.

In practice, it is more common to update a model in batches to ensure production safety by validating the data and models before they are updated. Continuous training is fairly complicated and error prone. Some of the common scenarios are:

- Feedback data points may belong predominantly in one category, leading to a model skew problem.
- The learning rate is too high, causing the model to forget everything that happened in the recent past (known as catastrophic interference).

- Model training results may overfit or underfit. Corner cases like distributed denial-of-service (DDoS) attacks may cause the models to go haywire. Similarly, regularization might be too low or too high.

Given that the arrival of new data is highly irregular, the pipeline architecture needs to be reactive and detect the presence of new inputs and trigger the generation of a new model accordingly. Continuous pipelines cannot be implemented effectively as the repeated execution of one-off pipelines at scheduled intervals—e.g., every six hours—if new data appears slightly after the scheduled execution of the pipeline; it can take more than one interval to produce a fresh model, which may be unacceptable in a production setting.

Defining Requirements

The model training service should be self-service. Data users specify the following specification details related to the training:

- Model type
- Model and hyperparameter values
- Data source reference
- Feature DSL expressions
- Schedule for continuous training (if applicable)

The service generates a trained model with details of the evaluation metrics and recommends the optimal values for model parameters and hyperparameters. Data users can specify the training details and review the results using a web UI, APIs, or notebooks. For advanced users, the service can optionally support options related to compute resource requirements, such as number of machines, how much memory, whether or not to use graphics processing units (GPUs), and so on.

Requirements for the model training service are divided into three categories: training orchestration, automated tuning, and continuous training.

Training Orchestration

There is no silver bullet for ML libraries and tools used by data users. There is a plethora of training environments and model types. Model training environments can be both in the cloud and in data scientists' local machines. The environments can be composed of traditional CPUs, GPUs, and deep learning–specific, custom-designed hardware like TPUs.

In addition to hardware, there is a wide variety of programming frameworks specialized for different programming languages and model types. For instance, TensorFlow is a popular deep learning framework used for solving a wide range of machine learning and deep learning problems, such as image classification and speech recognition. It operates at a large scale and in heterogeneous environments. Other examples of frameworks are PyTorch, Keras, MXNet, Caffe2, Spark MLlib, Theano, and so on. For non–deep learning, Spark MLlib and XGBoost are the popular choices; for deep learning, Caffe and TensorFlow are used most widely.

Similarly, there is a diverse set of ML algorithms that can be categorized into different taxonomies. In a task-based taxonomy, models are divided into:

- Predicting quantities using regression models
- Predicting categories using classification models
- Predicting outliers and fraudulent and novel values using anomaly detection models
- Exploring features and relationships using dimensionality reduction models
- Discovering structure of the data using clustering models

A popular alternative taxonomy is learning style–based taxonomy, which categorizes algorithms into supervised, unsupervised, and reinforcement learning. Deep learning is a variant of the supervised learning used for regression and classification. The popularity of deep learning is fueled by higher accuracy compared to most well-tuned and feature-engineered traditional ML techniques. It is important to realize that understandability of models is an important criteria for ML production deployments. As such, there is a trade-off of accuracy for manageability, understandability, and debuggability. Deep learning use cases typically handle a larger quantity of data, and different hardware requirements require distributed learning and a tighter integration with a flexible resource management stack. Distributed training scales to handle billions of samples.

The following are the considerations for training different model types:

- What amount of data will be used in training the model? Is the data going to be analyzed as sliding window batches or incrementally for new data points?
- What is the average number of features per model? Is there typically a skew in the training data samples distribution?
- What is the average number of parameters per model? More parameters means more tuning.
- Are the models single or partitioned? For partitioned models, one model per partition is trained, falling back to a parent model when needed—for example, training one model per city and falling back to a country-level model when an accurate city-level model cannot be achieved.

Tuning

Tuning is an iterative process. At the end of each iteration, the model is evaluated for accuracy. Informally, accuracy is the fraction of predictions the model got right and is measured using several metrics, namely area under the curve (AUC), precision, recall, F1, confusion matrix, and so on. Accuracy alone is not sufficient when working with a class-imbalanced dataset where there is a significant disparity between the number of positive and negative labels. Defining the evaluation metrics of a model is an important requirement for automation.

Another aspect of the tuning requirements is the cost and time available for tuning the model. Automated tuning explores multiple permutations in parallel for model parameters and hyperparameters. Given the abundance of compute resources available in the cloud, an increase in the number of permutations is easily possible.

Continuous Training

A key metric for continuous pipelines is model freshness. Depending on the use case, the need to update models can vary. For instance, personalizing the experience during a gaming session requires models to adapt to user behavior in near real time. On the other hand, personalizing a software product experience requires models to evolve in days or weeks depending on the agility of the product features. As the data distribution morphs due to changing customer behavior, the model needs to adapt on the fly to keep pace with trends in real time.

Online learning updates the model on every new sample and is applicable when data distribution is expected to morph over time or when data is a function of time (e.g., stock prices). Another scenario for using online learning is when data doesn't fit into memory and incremental new samples can be continuously used to fine-tune the model weights. Online learning is data efficient because once data has been consumed, it is no longer required (in contrast to the sliding windows required in schedule-based training). Also, online learning is adaptable because it makes no assumption about the distribution of data.

Nonfunctional Requirements

Similar to any software design, the following are some of the key NFRs that should be considered in the design of the model training service:

Scaling
   As enterprises grow, it is important that the training service scales to support larger datasets and an increased number of models.

Cost
Training is computationally expensive, and it is critical to optimize the associated cost.

Automated monitoring and alerting
Continuous training pipelines need to be monitored to detect production issues and generate automated alerts.

Implementation Patterns

Corresponding to the existing task map, there are three levels of automation for the model orchestration service, as shown in Figure 12-3. Each of the three patterns corresponds to automating a combination of tasks that are currently either manual or inefficient:

Distributed training orchestrator pattern
Automates resource orchestration, job scheduling, and optimizing the training workflows.

Automated tuning pattern
Automatically tunes the model parameters and hyperparameters. It tracks the results of training iterations and provides data users with a report of lineage iterations and their results.

Data-aware continuous training pattern
Automates the process of retraining the models by tracking the metadata associated with the ML pipeline components to intelligently retry. It also automates validation before pushing the model in production.

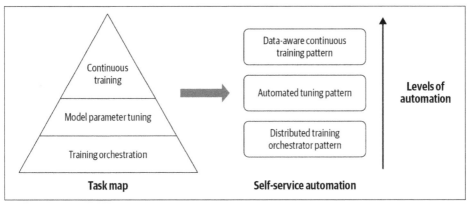

Figure 12-3. Levels of automation for the model training service.

Distributed Training Orchestrator Pattern

The distributed training orchestrator pattern automates the process of model training. The goal is to optimize the time and resources required across multiple other training jobs. Training is run on a cluster of machines optimized using techniques like transfer learning.

The pattern is composed of the following building blocks:

Resource orchestration
Distribution of training can be across compute cores (CPUs and GPUs) within the same machine or across machines. Different strategies are used to divide the training across the available hardware cores. There are two common approaches to distributing training with data parallelism: a) sync training with all workers training over different slices of input data in sync, and aggregate gradients at each step, and b) asynchronous training where all workers are independently training over the input data and updating variables asynchronously. The underlying sync training approach is the all-reduce pattern where the cores reduce model values and distribute results to all processes.

Job orchestration
For training, the feature datasets need to be either computed or fetched from the feature store. Often, it's a combination of computing the features as well as fetching from the store. Training is defined as a directed acyclic graph (DAG) of jobs. Standard schedulers like Apache Airflow are used under the hood.

Training optimization
Training typically runs through data samples within the training dataset. With each training sample, the model coefficients are refined via back propagation feedback. Optimizations are applied to speed up the training process. Sophisticated deep learning models have millions of parameters (weights), and training them from scratch often requires large amounts of data of computing resources. Transfer learning is a technique that shortcuts much of this by taking a piece of a model that has already been trained on a related task and reusing it in a new model.

An example of the distributed training orchestrator pattern is Google's TensorFlow Extended (TFX) (*https://oreil.ly/8ZKi5*). It implements multiple strategies to distribute the training tasks across CPUs and GPUs: MirroredStrategy, TPUStrategy, Multi-WorkerMirroredStrategy, CentralStorageStrategy, and OneServerStrategy. To handle processing of large amounts of data, distributed processing frameworks like Spark, Flink, or Google Cloud Dataflow are used. Most of the TFX components run on top of Apache Beam, which is a unified programming model that can run on several execution engines. TFX is extensible and supports Airflow and Kubeflow out of the box. It is also possible to add other workflow engines to TFX. If a new run of the pipeline only changes a subset of parameters, then the pipeline can reuse any data-preprocessing artifacts, such as vocabularies, and this can save a lot of time given that large data volumes make data preprocessing expensive. TFX optimizes training by pulling previous results of the pipeline components from cache.

The strengths of the distributed training orchestrator pattern are its ability to speed up training by distributing processing, as well as optimizing whenever possible. The weakness of the pattern is its integration with limited ML libraries, tools, and hardware. Overall, with growing dataset sizes, this pattern is critical to implement.

Automated Tuning Pattern

Automated tuning was originally defined in the context of tuning the model parameters and hyperparameters. Today, data scientists drive model tuning by analyzing the results of different combinations and systematically exploring the search space. Data scientists compare the results of multiple permutations and decide the best model values to use. The field of automated model tuning is exhaustive and beyond the scope of this book. It is built on neural architecture search, where evolutionary algorithms are used to design the new neural net architectures. This is useful because it allows for discovering architectures that are more complicated than humans, and optimized for particular goals. In their paper (*https://oreil.ly/xMT7W*), Google researchers Quoc Le and Barret Zoph used reinforcement learning to find new architectures for the computer vision problem Cifar10 and the natural language processing (NLP) problem Penn Tree Bank, and achieved similar results to existing architectures. There are several example libraries such as AutoGluon (*https://oreil.ly/LeA7B*), Auto-WEKA (*https://oreil.ly/AXw0O*), auto-sklearn (*https://oreil.ly/ZGQBq*), H2O AutoML (*https://oreil.ly/jwZOM*), TPOT (*https://oreil.ly/FTa5k*), AutoML (*https://www.automl.org*), and Hyperopt (*https://oreil.ly/1890p*). These libraries allow data scientists to specify the objective function and value bounds that can be applied to many types of ML algorithms, namely random forests, gradient-boosting machines, neural networks, and more.

Recently, the definition of automated tuning has become broader to include the entire life cycle, as shown in Figure 12-4. The pattern is known in the ML community as *AutoML*. An example of this pattern is Google's AutoML service, which automates the entire workflow of the model building, training, and deploy process (illustrated in Figure 12-5).

The strength of the automated tuning pattern is increased productivity for data scientists as the training service finds the optimal tuning values. The weakness of the pattern is the need for compute resources to explore brute-force permutations. Overall, with complex deep learning models, the pattern is important in finding the values.

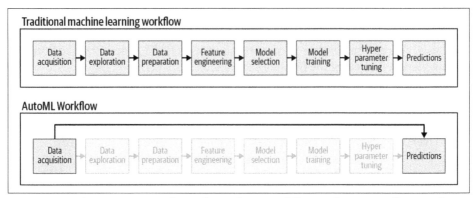

Figure 12-4. The comparison of a traditional ML workflow and AutoML (from Forbes (https://oreil.ly/3zG5Z)).

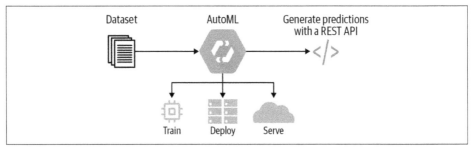

Figure 12-5. An example of the Google AutoML service (from Google Cloud (https://oreil.ly/tQ01a)).

Data-Aware Continuous Training

The data-aware continuous training pattern optimizes the training of deployed models to reflect changes in data. The retraining of models can be done either on a scheduled basis or in an online fashion, where each new data sample is used to retrain and create a new model. In contrast to patterns that invoke jobs on a fixed schedule, this pattern is data driven, allowing jobs to be triggered by the presence of a specific configuration of the pipeline components (such as the availability of new data or updated data vocabulary).

The pattern is composed of the following building blocks:

Metadata tracking

Metadata captures details associated with the current model, the execution stats of the pipeline components, and training dataset properties. Execution stats of pipeline components for each run are tracked to help debugging, reproducibility, and auditing. The training dataset can be configured either as a moving time window or the entire available data. The metadata helps the pipeline determine what results can be reused from previous runs. For instance, a pipeline that updates a deep learning model every hour needs to reinitialize the model's weights from a previous run to avoid having to retrain over all the data that has been accumulated up to that point.

Orchestration

The ML pipeline components are triggered asynchronously based on availability of data artifacts. As the ML components complete their processing, they record their state as a part of the metadata store. This serves as a communication channel between components and can react accordingly. This pub/sub functionality enables ML pipeline components to operate asynchronously at different iteration intervals, allowing fresh models to be produced as soon as possible. For instance, the trainer can generate a new model using the latest data and an old vocabulary without having to wait for an updated vocabulary.

Validation

Evaluates the models before pushing in production. Validation is implemented using different techniques based on the type of model. Validation involves model performance for individual data slices of the dataset. Besides checking the quality of the updated model to ensure high quality, validation needs to apply proactive safeguards on data quality and ensure that the model is compatible with the deployment environment.

Overall, data scientists can review how the data and results are changing over time as new data becomes available and the model is retrained. Comparison of model runs are required for long durations of time.

An example of the pattern is TFX. For metadata tracking, it implements ML-Metadata (MLMD), which is an open source library, to define, store, and query metadata for ML pipelines. MLMD stores the metadata in a relational backend and can be extended for any SQL-compatible database. TFX pipelines are created as DAGs. A TFX component has three main parts: a driver, an executor, and a publisher. The driver inspects the state of the world and decides what work needs to be done, coordinating job execution and feeding metadata to the executor. The publisher takes the results of the executor and updates the metadata store. The state published in the MLMD is used by other components of the pipeline, such as evaluation, training, and validation, to initiate their processing. The evaluator component takes the `EvalSavedModel` that the trainer created and the original input data and does deep analysis using Beam and the TensorFlow Model Analysis library. The component for validation in the TFX ModelValidator uses Beam to do that comparison, using criteria that you define, to decide whether or not to push the new model to production.

Overall, the need for the data-aware continuous training pattern depends on the rigor applied for model retraining. While the pattern can be applied to both online and offline models, it is most applicable for online models that need to be retrained either in an online fashion or on a scheduled basis.

Summary

Model training is inherently time-consuming and can slow down the overall time to insight. There is a trade-off between the time to train and quality of the trained model in terms of accuracy, robustness, performance, and bias. The model training service aims to eliminate the accidental complexity in managing training due to ad hoc approaches for distributed training, automated tuning, and continuous training. The service is indispensable for deployments with large amounts of data and using complex ML models.

CHAPTER 13

Continuous Integration Service

So far, we have covered building the transformation logic to implement the insight and training of ML models. Typically, ML model pipelines evolve continuously with source schema changes, feature logic, dependent datasets, data processing configurations, model algorithms, model features, and configuration. These changes are made by teams of data users to either implement new product capabilities or improve the accuracy of the models. In traditional software engineering, code is constantly updated with multiple changes made daily across teams. To get ready for deploying ML models in production, this chapter covers details of continuous integration of ML pipelines, similar to traditional software engineering.

There are multiple pain points associated with continuous integration of ML pipelines. The first is holistically tracking ML pipeline experiments involving data, code, and configuration. These experiments can be considered feature branches with the distinction that a vast majority of these branches will never be integrated with the trunk. These experiments need to be tracked to pick the optimal configuration as well as for future debugging. Existing code-versioning tools like GitHub only track code changes. There is neither a standard place to store the results of training experiments nor an easy way to compare one experiment to another. Second, to verify the changes, the ML pipeline needs to be packaged for deploying in a test environment. In contrast to traditional software running on one software stack, ML pipelines combine multiple libraries and tools. Reproducing the project configuration in a test environment is ad hoc and error prone. Third, running unit and integration tests in development or test environments does not provide realistic data similar to production. As such, issues leak into production, making it significantly more expensive to debug and fix compared to during code integration. These challenges slow down the time to integrate. Given the hundreds of changes to the ML pipeline made daily by members of the data team, the slowdown in time to integrate affects the overall time to insight.

Ideally, a *continuous integration service* automates the process of reliably integrating changes to ML pipelines. The service tracks the ML pipeline changes, creates a reproducible package for deploying in different test environments, and simplifies running of pipeline testing to detect issues. By automating these tasks, the service reduces the *time to integrate* and the number of issues that are leaked in production. The service allows for collaborative development among data users. As a part of testing the correctness of the pipeline changes, the ML model is trained and evaluated. We cover model training as a separate service in Chapter 12.

Journey Map

Figure 13-1 shows the traditional continuous integration pipeline for code. In a similar fashion, changes are made to ML models in the form of model code, configuration, and data features.

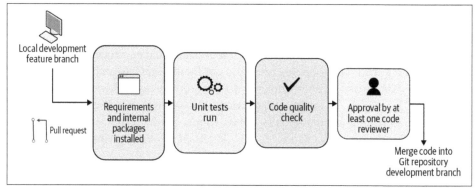

Figure 13-1. A traditional continuous integration pipeline for software.

Collaborating on an ML Pipeline

During the build phase, teams of data scientists and engineers work together to iterate and find the best model. Code for feature pipelines is developed in parallel with model algorithms, model parameters, and hyperparameters. Typically, the teams have tight deadlines to deliver ML pipelines and must experiment systematically with a large number of permutations before settling on the one to be integrated with the main trunk for deployment. Today, keeping track of experiments, building a deployable version, validating the pipelines, training the models, evaluating the model quality, and tracking the final results are accomplished in an ad hoc fashion.

Integrating ETL Changes

Feature pipelines are written as ETL code that reads data from different data sources and transforms them into features. ETL code evolves continuously. Some of the common scenarios are: moving to new versions of data processing frameworks like Spark, rewriting from Hive to Spark to improve performance, changes to the source schema, and so on.

The ETL changes need to be validated for correctness using a comprehensive suite of unit, functional, regression, and integration tests. These tests ensure the pipeline code is robust and operates correctly for corner cases. As a first step in the integration process, unit tests and a golden test suite of integration tests are run. These are also referred to as *smoke tests*, as they compare the results of sample input-output data. Ideally, integration tests should use actual production data to test both robustness and performance. Often, scaling issues or inefficient implementations are undetected in production. Today, tests can be written as a part of the code, or managed separately. Additionally, if the features are consumed for generating a business metrics dashboard, the data users need to verify the correctness of the results (this is known as user acceptance testing). The approach today is ad hoc, and the validation is typically done using small samples of data that aren't representative of production data.

Validating Schema Changes

Data source owners make changes to their source schema and typically do not coordinate with downstream ML pipeline users. These issues are typically detected in production and can have a significant impact. As a part of the change tracking, source schema changes need to be detected and trigger the continuous integration service to validate the effect of these changes proactively.

Minimizing Time to Integrate

Time to integrate is the time required to track, package, and validate an ML pipeline for correctness and production readiness. This also includes the time to train models (covered separately in Chapter 12). Today, time to integrate is spent on three processes that are either manual or ad hoc: experiment tracking, reproducible deployment, and testing validation.

Experiment Tracking

ML pipelines are a combination of datasets, code, and configuration. Tracking an experiment involves creating a single end-to-end view of the dataset versions, configuration of the model and pipeline, and code associated with feature pipelines and models. Traditionally, a continuous integration (CI) tool such as Jenkins listens for code commits in the code repository and triggers a validation process. Similarly, the experiments need to be tracked, and the corresponding results associated with the testing and model training need to be recorded back. Today, tracking experiments is time-consuming, making the final model selection process cumbersome given lack of consistent tracking of datasets, code, configuration, and corresponding results of the tests and model training.

Reproducible Deployment

Before changes can be integrated, they need to be validated for correctness. This requires the ML pipeline to be built and deployed in a test environment. Ensuring a reproducible environment is challenging. While code and configuration can be packaged using container technologies such as Docker, it is challenging to version the datasets, such that it is pointing to the right version of the dataset. A single reproducible packaging of the pipeline that can be deployed either locally or on a test cluster is ad hoc today, with manual scripts invoked in the orchestration.

Testing Validation

Testing involves running a battery of unit, functional, regression, and integration tests to uncover issues before the pipeline is deployed in production. There are three types of challenges:

Writing comprehensive tests to detect issues
Defining the right tests combines software engineering hygiene as well as team skills. Compared to traditional software, most organizations do not apply the same code coverage rigor to ML pipelines.

Using realistic production data
Most organizations have separate QA, E2E, and prod environments. The non-prod data typically contains samples of data and is not representative.

Running the tests takes a significant amount of time
Depending on the dataset size, tests may run for a significant amount of time since the resources allocated are typically limited.

Defining Requirements

There are three key modules required to build the continuous integration service:

Experiment tracking module
Tracks experiments as an E2E representation of the ML pipeline changes related to code, configuration, and datasets. The corresponding testing and model training results are also recorded.

Pipeline packaging module
Creates a reproducible package of the ML pipeline to be deployed either locally or in the cloud.

Testing automation module
Orchestrates optimal running of the tests using version production data.

This section covers the requirements for each module.

Experiment Tracking Module

The goal of this module is to holistically capture changes impacting the ML pipeline so that they can be integrated into the build-verify process. ML pipeline changes can be broadly divided into the following categories:

Config parameters
Any configurable parameter used within feature pipelines and ML models.

Code versions
Versions of libraries, programming languages, dependent code, and so on.

Datasets
Defines versions of data used as part of the ML pipeline. The versioning allows tracking the schema as well as data properties, such as distributions.

Additionally, experiment tracking records the attributes to analyze the results of the experiment. This includes user-defined metrics and record-specific details of the pipeline and model (e.g., code coverage metrics, model accuracy, and so on). Metrics are defined by users and consist of any measure useful for comparing experiments in order to pick the winning version.

Pipeline Packaging Module

The packaging of the ML pipeline needs to take into account the existing technologies used within the CI/CD stack. Key technology buckets include:

- Cloud providers like Azure, AWS, and so on
- Container orchestration frameworks like Docker, Kubernetes, and so on
- Artifact repos like Artifactory, Jenkins, S3, and so on
- CI frameworks like Jenkins, CircleCI, Travis, and so on
- Secrets management like AWS KMS, HashiCorp Vault, and so on

As a part of the packaging, it is important to clarify handling of the dataset versions. The input data to the pipeline is tracked as a read-only version of the production data. The output data generated by the experiment is managed in a separate namespace.

The pipeline can be packaged and deployed either locally or in the cloud. Typically, there are multiple environments, such as QA, dev, and E2E, where the pipeline is deployed for testing or training. Depending on the number of experiments that need to be run concurrently, the environments need to be appropriately sized.

Testing Automation Module

The size of the data used for testing should be large enough to be meaningful and small enough to speed up the testing. Typically, the issues encountered in production are added to the test suite patterns. For instance, if source data quality issues are rampant in production, the golden test suite needs to consist of quality integration tests that are run using actual production data.

The golden test suites are typically managed separately from the code. Requirements on code coverage and test pass criteria can be defined for these tests. Other considerations include the time to complete the test and the need to parallelize running of the tests.

Implementation Patterns

Corresponding to the existing task map, there are three levels of automation for the metadata catalog service (as shown in Figure 13-2). Each level corresponds to automating a combination of tasks that are currently either manual or inefficient:

Programmable tracking pattern
Allows user-defined metrics to be tracked for experiments for the ML models.

Reproducible project pattern
Packages the experiment for deployment in any environment to enable testing and model training.

Testing validation pattern
Tests in the form of unit, component, and integrated tests. This is similar to general software engineering practices and is outside the scope of this book.

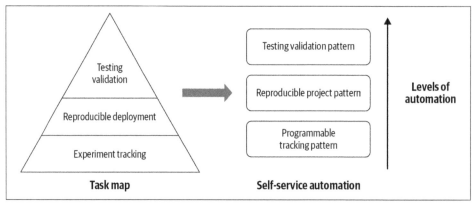

Figure 13-2. The different levels of automation for the continuous integration service.

Programmable Tracking Pattern

As a part of the ML pipeline experiments, the service tracks details about the code, configuration, and datasets. The programmable tracking pattern enables data scientists to add any metrics as part of the experiment tracking. The pattern to add metrics is consistent across any programming environment (for example, a standalone script or a notebook). Popular examples of the metrics tracked using this pattern are:

- Start and end time of the training job
- Who trained the model and details of the business context
- Distribution and relative importance of each feature
- Specific accuracy metrics for different model types (e.g., ROC curve, PR curve, and confusion matrix for a binary classifier)
- Summary of statistics for model visualization

The pattern is implemented by integrating tracking libraries for data processing and ML libraries such as Spark, Spark MLlib, Keras, and so on. An example of the pattern implementation is MLflow Tracking (*https://oreil.ly/QPDKd*) (as shown in Figure 13-3). It provides an API and UI for logging parameters, code versions, metrics, and output files. Data users can track parameters, metrics, and artifacts from within the ETL or model program. Results are logged to local files or a server. Using the web UI, data users can view and compare the output of multiple runs. Teams can also use the tools to compare results from different users.

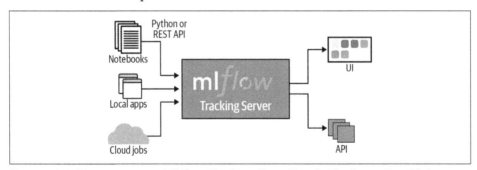

Figure 13-3. The open source MLflow Tracking (from Databricks (https://oreil.ly/12n_T)).

Without good experiment tracking, there have been real-world cases where models were built and deployed but were impossible to reproduce because the combination of data, code, and configuration details were not tracked systematically.

Reproducible Project Pattern

The goal of this pattern is to build a self-contained, reproducible package of the ML pipeline for deployment in a test or development environment; it's also appropriate for other use cases for reproducibility, extensibility, and experimentation. The pattern automates the creation of the environment for deployment with the right dependencies, and provides a standardized CLI or API to run the project.

To create a self-contained packaging of the ML pipeline, the pattern includes the following:

Invocation sequence of the pipeline components
> This is the order in which these components need to be invoked, typically represented as a DAG.

Version of the code
> This is essentially a feature branch in GitHub or another version-control repository. The code includes the pipeline components as well as the model algorithm. Typically, unit tests and golden test suite are also included in the same project packaging.

Execution environment for the components of the pipeline
> This includes the versions of the libraries and other dependencies. This is typically a Docker image.

Version of the data
> These are source datasets used with the pipeline.

An example of the pattern is MLflow Projects (*https://oreil.ly/FSfc1*), which provides a standard format for packaging reusable data science code. Each project is simply a directory with code or a Git repository, and uses a descriptor file to specify its dependencies and how to run the code (as shown in Figure 13-4). An MLflow Project is defined by a simple YAML file called *MLproject*. Projects can specify their dependencies through a Conda environment. A project may also have multiple entry points for invoking runs with named parameters. You can run projects using `mlflow run` in the command line. MLflow will automatically set up the right environment for the project and run it. In addition, if you use the MLflow Tracking API in a Project, MLflow will remember the project version executed (that is, the Git commit) and any parameters.

Overall, the strength of this pattern is its standardized approach to capturing all aspects of the ML pipeline, ensuring the results of the experiments are reproducible. The weakness is that the pattern does not take into account resource scaling requirements required for production deployments. Overall, the pattern is critical for automating packaging for ML pipelines and allows flexibility to reproduce in any environment.

Figure 13-4. The project structure defined by MLflow Project (from Databricks (https://oreil.ly/GeT3Z)).

Summary

Continuous integration is a software engineering practice that ensures changes to the code are continuously integrated and tested to uncover issues proactively. By applying the same principle to ML pipelines, the experiments can be treated as branches to the main code trunk. The goal of the continuous integration service is to track, build, and test the experiments with the goal of finding the most optimal ML pipeline. The process discards a majority of suboptimal experiments in the exploration process, but they are still valuable for debugging, and they help in designing future experiments.

CHAPTER 14

A/B Testing Service

Now we are ready to operationalize our data and ML pipelines to generate insights in production. There are multiple ways to generate the insight, and data users have to make a choice about which one to deploy in production. Consider the example of an ML model that forecasts home prices for end customers. Assume there are two equally accurate models developed for this insight—which one is better? This chapter focuses on an increasingly growing practice where multiple models are deployed and presented to different sets of customers. Based on behavioral data of customer usage, the goal is to select a better model. A/B testing (also known as bucket testing, split testing, or controlled experiment) is becoming a standard approach for evaluating user satisfaction from a product change, a new feature, or any hypothesis related to product growth. A/B testing is becoming a norm, and is widely used to make data-driven decisions. It is critical to integrate A/B testing as a part of the data platform to ensure consistent metrics definitions are applied across ML models, business reporting, and experimentation. While A/B testing could fill a complex, full-fledged book by itself, this chapter covers the core patterns in the context of the data platform as a starting point for data users.

Online controlled A/B testing is utilized at a wide range of companies to make data-driven decisions. As noted by Kohavi and Thomke (*https://oreil.ly/4jouE*), A/B testing is used for anything from frontend user interface changes to backend algorithms, from search engines (e.g., Google, Bing, Yahoo!), to retailers (e.g., Amazon, eBay, Etsy), to social networking services (e.g., Facebook, LinkedIn, Twitter), to travel services (e.g., Expedia, Airbnb, Booking.com). A/B testing is the practice of showing variants of the same web page to different segments of visitors at the same time and comparing which variant drives more conversions. Typically, the one that gives higher conversions is the winning variant. The metrics of success are unique to the experiment and specific hypothesis being tested.

As noted by Xu et al. (*https://oreil.ly/cVUEf*), running large-scale A/B tests is not just a matter of infrastructure and best practices, but it requires having a strong experimentation culture embedded as part of the decision-making process. Apart from building the basic functionalities any A/B testing platform requires, the experimentation culture requires comprehensive tracking of A/B testing experiments, simplifying multiple concurrent testing, and integration with business reporting. Producing trustworthy insights from A/B testing experiments requires a solid statistical foundation as well as seamless integration and monitoring and a variety of quality checks across all data pipelines.

The deployment of online controlled A/B experiments at scale requires supporting hundreds of concurrently running experiments across websites, mobile apps, and desktop applications, which is a nontrivial challenge. There are a few key pain points. First, configuring A/B testing experiments correctly is nontrivial, and you must ensure there is no imbalance that would result in a statistically significant difference in a metric of interest across the variant populations. Also, it's critical to ensure customers are not exposed to interactions between variants of different concurrently running experiments. Second, running A/B testing experiments at scale requires generating and delivering variant assignments in a performant and scalable fashion. For client-side experiments, the software is only updated periodically, requiring an online configuration to turn the features of the product on and off. Third, analyzing the A/B testing experiment results is based on metrics that need to be calculated. A significant amount of time is spent defining one-off metrics that are not consistent with respect to definitions, leading to nontrustworthy analysis. Ensuring the trustworthiness of the experiments, and automatically optimizing to ensure the customer experience is not being harmed, are difficult for a broad spectrum of data users. These pain points impact the *time to A/B test* in terms of correctly configuring the experiment, running at scale, and analyzing and optimizing the results. These aspects impact the overall time to insight.

Ideally, a *self-service A/B testing service* simplifies the process of designing A/B tests and hides the intricacies of statistical significance, imbalanced assignments, and experiment interactions. It automates scaling and performance-variant assignment. It provides a domain language for metrics definition, automating collection and wrangling to generate metrics. Finally, it automatically verifies experiment quality and optimizes allocation to the winning variant. Overall, the service enables data users to configure, start, monitor, and control the experiment throughout the life cycle of the service. It reduces the overall time to insight by informing experiment design, determining parameters of experiment execution, and helping experiment owners interpret the results. Many real-world companies use self-service experimentation platforms, namely Google (*https://oreil.ly/wSK9U*), Microsoft (*https://oreil.ly/LCwfy*), Netflix (*https://oreil.ly/IWBgc*), LinkedIn (*https://oreil.ly/JqAXV*), Uber (*https://eng.uber.com/xp*), and Airbnb (*https://oreil.ly/2RgVE*). A few open source examples are Cloudera's Gertrude (*https://oreil.ly/O2_0v*), Etsy's Feature Flagging (*https://oreil.ly/5K7rR*), and Facebook's PlanOut (*https://oreil.ly/sIXwy*). Figure 14-1 shows a screenshot of Intuit's open source experimentation platform, Wasabi.

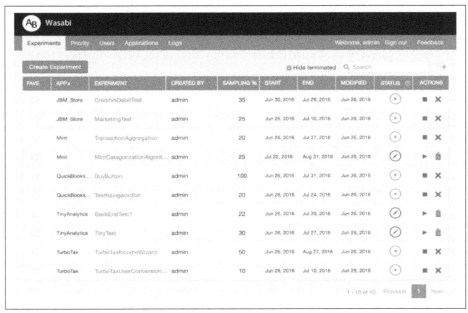

Figure 14-1. Screenshot of Intuit's open source experimentation platform, Wasabi (from GitHub (https://oreil.ly/u5jSl)).

Journey Map

We begin by covering the basic A/B testing concepts:

Factor (or variable)
> A variable that can change independently to create a dependent response. Factors generally have assigned values called levels. For example, changing the background color of a web page is a factor.

Treatment (or variant)
> The current system is considered the "champion," while the treatment is a modification that attempts to improve something and is known as the "challenger." A treatment is characterized by changing the level(s) in one or more factors.

Experimental unit
> The experimental unit is the physical entity that can be assigned, at random, to a treatment. It is an entity on which the experimentation or analysis is done (e.g., visitor, user, customer, etc.). As observed by Gupta et al. (*https://oreil.ly/Ov9OS*), if the experiment is designed and executed correctly, the only thing consistently

different between the two variants is the change in variable X. External factors are distributed evenly between control and treatment and therefore do not impact the results of the experiment. Hence, any difference in metrics between the two groups must be due to the change X (or a random chance that we rule out using statistical testing). This establishes a causal relationship between the change made to the product and changes in user behavior, which is the key reason for widespread use of controlled experiments for evaluating new features in software.

Sample
A group of users who are served the same treatment.

Overall Evaluation Criteria (OEC)
Refers to what measure, objective, or goal the experiment is aiming to achieve. It is a metric used to compare the response to different treatments. While the experiment is running, user interactions with the system are recorded, and metrics are computed.

Experimentation is an iterative cycle of design, execute, and analyze (as shown in Figure 14-2). Experiment analysis is conducted during the entire life cycle of an experiment, including during hypothesis generation, experiment design, experiment execution, and post-experiment during the decision-making process. The following are the specific phases of experimentation:

Generate hypothesis
Typically, the process starts off with collecting data to identify areas to improve, such as low conversion rates or high drop-off rates. With the goal identified, we generate A/B testing ideas and hypotheses about why the ideas are better than the current version. Results of historical experiments inform new hypotheses, help estimate how likely the new hypothesis is to impact the OEC, and help prioritize existing ideas. During this stage, the experiment owner examines other historical experiments, including those that improved the targeted metrics.

Design and implement features
The desired changes to an element on the website or mobile app experience are implemented and the changes are verified for correctness. The code that shows the elements needs to be deployed to the clients in such a way that it can be turned on and off via the experimentation system.

Experiment design
During experiment design, analysis is performed to answer the following key questions: What randomization scheme should be used for audience assignment? What's the duration of the experiment run? What's the percentage of allotted traffic? What randomization seed should be used to minimize the imbalance?

Execute experiment

The experiment is kicked off and users are assigned to the control or variant experience. Their interaction with each experience is measured, counted, and compared to determine how each performs. While the experiment is running, the analysis must answer two key questions: a) Is the experiment causing unacceptable harm to users? and b) Are there any data quality issues yielding untrustworthy experiment results?

Analyze results

The goal is to analyze the difference between the control and variants and determine whether there is a statistically significant difference. Such monitoring should continue throughout the experiment, checking for a variety of issues, including interactions with other concurrently running experiments. During the experiment, based on the analysis, actions can be suggested, such as stopping the experiment if harm is detected, looking at metric movements, or examining a specific user segment that behaves differently from others. Overall, the analysis needs to ascertain if the data from the experiment is trustworthy, and come to an understanding of why the treatment did better or worse than control. The next steps can be ship or no-ship recommendations or a new hypothesis to test.

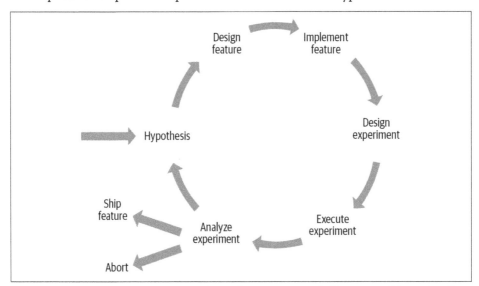

Figure 14-2. The iterative A/B testing loop (from Gupta et al. (https://oreil.ly/H6h7F)).

Minimizing Time to A/B Test

Time to A/B test includes designing the experiment, executing it at scale (including metrics analysis), and optimizing it. One success criterion is to prevent an incorrect experiment size from achieving statistical significance and wasting release cycle time.

Another criterion is to detect harm and alert the experiment owner about a bad user experience, which prevents lost revenue and user abandonment. The final criterion is to detect interactions with other experiments that may lead to wrong conclusions.

Experiment Design

This stage includes audience selection and depends on the design of the feature. This is accomplished using targeting or traffic filters, such as market segment, browser, operating system, version of the mobile/desktop app, or complex targeting of users who have logged into the product five times in the last month. The design needs to take into account single-factor versus multi-factor testing—i.e., testing in which treatments correspond to values of a single factor versus testing in which treatments corresponding to multiple values of multiple factors are compared. The experiment needs to ensure statistical significance of the sample size in the duration of the experiment. Typically, the duration of the experiment is extrapolated based on the historical traffic. To detect random imbalance, we start an experiment as an A/A (i.e., treatment and control are the same), run it for several days, and verify that no imbalance is detected. Typically, multiple experiments run concurrently, and the allocation is tracked to ensure the user is not allocated to multiple overlapping experiments.

Execution at Scale

This stage includes running the experiments at scale, either on the client side (e.g., a mobile app) or the server side (e.g., a website). For experimentation, the application requires a thin service client that calls the REST endpoint to determine the qualified experiments, treatments, and their factors. A simple experiment that does not involve segmentation can be executed locally, while other queries may need to query attributes for segmentation and typically require a remote call. The assignment rollouts are typically done gradually, starting with a canary rollout.

To scale experimentation, it is important to provide an easy way to define and validate new metrics that can be used by a broad range of data users. Generating the metrics to evaluate the experiment involves computing a large number of metrics efficiently at scale. There are several challenges. First, product users can browse when not logged in or signed up, making it difficult to correlate user actions. Product users also switch devices (between web and mobile), which further complicates correlation. It's important to ensure the metrics used for experimentation are consistent with the business dashboards. Second, thousands of reports are computed, processing terabytes of data, which is a significant challenge. Caching computations that are common across multiple experiments is helpful for reducing data size and performance.

Experiment Optimization

This stage includes monitoring the experiment and optimizing the allocations of the experiment. After the experiment is launched, the logs are analyzed continuously to ensure the experiment will reach statistical significance, that there are no negative impacts on customer experience, and that there is no cross-experiment interference. Another dimension of optimization is automatically increasing customer traffic to the variants that are doing well.

To track the experiment, rich instrumentation logs are used to produce self-service analytics and troubleshoot experiments. The logs contain information related to which qualified experiments, treatments, and pages were involved in the customer experience. The typical primary business OECs are acquisition (conversion of a prospect to a subscriber), engagement (how often the customer uses the product and how much time is spent on each visit), and retention (total number of subscribers and lifetime value of each customer).

These metrics take time to bake and reach a steady state. Secondary metrics (such as number of signups, logins, and so on) and operational metrics (such as availability, page performance, and so on) are tracked to confirm or deny that an experiment is trending well.

Implementation Patterns

Corresponding to the existing task map, there are three levels of automation for the experiment service (as shown in Figure 14-3). Each level corresponds to automating a combination of tasks that are currently either manual or inefficient:

Experiment specification pattern
Automates handling of randomization and experiment interactions related to experiment design.

Metrics definition pattern
Simplifies analysis of metrics to evaluate the experiment, reducing the time taken by experiment owners to extract insights related to the experiment.

Automated experiment optimization
Tracking the health of the experiment as well as automatically optimizing the allocation of the traffic among the variants.

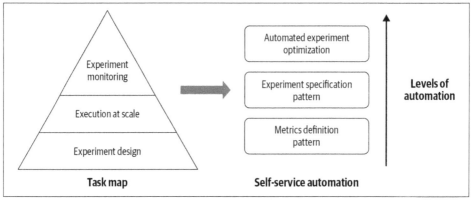

Figure 14-3. The different levels of automation for the A/B testing service.

Experiment Specification Pattern

This pattern focuses on making the experiment design turn-key, enabling experiment owners to configure, start, monitor, and control the experiment throughout its life cycle. For experimentation to scale, these tasks need to be simplified. The specification involves audience selection, experiment size and duration, interactions with other experiments, and randomization design. In this section, we cover popular approaches for randomization and experiment interactions.

When the users are randomized into variants, there is a probability of an imbalance that could result in a statistically significant difference between the variant populations. Disentangling the impact of such random imbalance from the impact of the treatment is nontrivial. One of the popular approaches to alleviating this problem is re-randomization (*https://oreil.ly/vOokI*)—i.e., if a random imbalance is detected, the experiment is restarted with re-randomization of the hash seed. There are a few different approaches to detecting random imbalance:

- Using an A/A experiment (i.e., treatment and control are the same) that is run initially for a few days as a sanity check before running the actual experiment.

- Using retrospective A/A analysis on the historical data, as described by Gupta et al (*https://oreil.ly/k8L2X*).

- Using the historical data, simulating the randomization on that data using the hash seed selected for the experiment. In the real world, many retrospective A/A analyses are conducted in parallel to generate the most balanced seed.

In the context of experiment interactions, there is a probability that users will be allocated to multiple experiments at the same time. This is problematic when interactions occur between variants of different experiments. A common example of experiment interaction is font color and background color both changing to the same value. To

---

execute multiple potentially interacting experiments concurrently, a common pattern is to create groups and assign variants of the experiment to one or more groups. The principle applied is that variants with no overlapping groups can be applied to concurrent experiments. Google's experimentation (*https://oreil.ly/FXofW*) refers to the groups as layers and domains; Microsoft's platform (*https://oreil.ly/OZ-0T*) refers to them as isolation groups.

Metrics Definition Pattern

This pattern simplifies defining the metrics required to analyze experiments. Instead of implementing one-off and inconsistent metrics, this pattern provides a DSL to define metrics and dimensions. Experiment owners use a vocabulary of business metrics (used for business dashboards and reports) to define dimensions for analyzing experiment results. The DSL gets translated into an internal representation, which can then be compiled into SQL and other big data programming languages. Having a language-independent DSL ensures interoperability across different backend data processing mechanisms. The goal of this pattern is to make the process of adding new metrics lightweight and self-service for a broad range of users. Examples of the DSL are Microsoft's experimentation (*https://oreil.ly/59XvI*) platform and Airbnb's metrics democratization (*https://oreil.ly/izJYp*).

The DSL is built-in on a catalog of metrics and attributes. They range from static attributes like user subscription status to dynamic attributes like a member's last login date. These attributes are either computed daily as batch or generated in real time. These metrics are certified for quality and correctness and managed consistently as part of the feature store covered in Chapter 3. A good example of the metrics platform is LinkedIn's Unified Metrics Platform (*https://oreil.ly/VTHNt*).

Automated Experiment Optimization

This pattern aims to automatically optimize the variant assignments across the users and ensures the experiment is trending correctly, both with respect to statistical significance as well as having no negative impact on customer experience. This pattern involves three building blocks: aggregation and analysis of user telemetry data, quality checks on the experiment metrics, and techniques for automated optimization. We cover details of each of these building blocks.

To track the health of the experiment, telemetry data in the form of qualified experiments, treatments, and pages the user is expected to experience are tracked. These are correlated with application logs on the experiments and treatments the users truly experienced. Telemetry data is usually collected from both the client and the server. There is a preference to collect from the server side, as it is easier to update, more complete, and comes with less delay.

As noted by Gupta et al. (*https://oreil.ly/Wy99H*), the most effective check for experiment metrics is the Sample Ratio Mismatch (SRM) test, which utilizes the Chi-Squared Test to compare the ratio of the observed user counts in the variants against the configured ratio. When an SRM is detected, the results are deemed invalid. Another verification mechanism is A/A experiments such that, given there are no treatment effects, the p-values are expected to be distributed uniformly. If p-values are not uniform, it indicates an issue. Other popular checks are T-test, negative binomial test, ranking test, and mix effect model.

There are many algorithms for automated optimization of variant assignment. The most popular approach is multi-armed bandits (*https://oreil.ly/Yr6pJ*). Each treatment (called an "arm") has a probability of success. The probability of success is unknown at the time of starting the experiment. As the experiment continues, each arm receives user traffic, and the Beta distribution is updated accordingly. The goal is to balance exploitation versus exploration by first exploring which experiment variants are performing well and then actively increasing the number of users being allocated to the winning variants. Multiple techniques are applied to accomplish this, such as a ε-greedy algorithm, Thompson sampling, Bayesian inference, and so on.

Summary

A/B tests help enterprises make better decisions and products. Democratizing the A/B testing platform is critical and allows a new team to easily onboard and start running experiments at low cost, with the goal that every single product feature or bug fix is evaluated via an experiment. A/B tests are increasingly evolving beyond answering *what* has been impacted to also answering *why* by utilizing the deep amount of information aggregated for each experiment, in terms of both the metrics and dimensions.

PART IV

Self-Service Operationalize

CHAPTER 15

Query Optimization Service

Now we are ready to operationalize the insights in production. The data users have written the business logic to generate insights in the form of dashboards, ML models, and so on. The data transformation logic is written either as SQL queries or big data programming models (such as Apache Spark, Beam, and so on) implemented in Python, Java, Scala, etc. This chapter focuses on the optimization of the queries and big data programs.

The difference between good and bad queries is quite significant. For instance, based on real-world experience, it is not unusual for a deployed production query to run for over 4 hours, when after optimization it could run in less than 10 minutes. Long-running queries that are run repeatedly are candidates for tuning.

Data users aren't engineers, which leads to several pain points for query tuning. First, query engines like Hadoop, Spark, and Presto have a plethora of knobs. Understanding which knobs to tune and their impact is nontrivial for most data users and requires a deep understanding of the inner workings of the query engines. There are no silver bullets—the optimal knob values for the query vary based on data models, query types, cluster sizes, concurrent query load, and so on. Given the scale of data, a brute-force approach to experimenting with different knob values is not feasible either.

Second, given the petabyte (PB) scale of data, writing queries optimized for distributed data processing best practices is difficult for most data users. Often, data engineering teams have to rewrite the queries to run efficiently in production. Most query engines and datastores have specialized query primitives that are specific to their implementation; leveraging these capabilities requires a learning curve with a growing number of technologies.

Third, query optimization is not a one-time activity but rather is ongoing based on the execution pattern. The query execution profile needs to be tuned based on the runtime properties in terms of partitioning, memory and CPU allocation, and so on. Query tuning is an iterative process with decreasing benefits after the initial few iterations targeting low-hanging optimizations.

Time to optimize represents the time spent by users in optimizing the query. It impacts the overall time to insight in two ways. First is the time spent by data users in tuning, and second is the time to complete the processing of the query. In production, a tuned query can run orders of magnitude faster, significantly improving the overall time to insight.

Ideally, the *query optimization service* should automatically optimize the queries without requiring the data users to have an understanding of the details. Under the hood, the service verifies if the query is written in an optimal fashion and determines optimal values for the configuration knobs. The knobs are related to the processing cluster and the query job, including continuous runtime profiling for data partitioning, processing skew among the distributed workers, and so on. In summary, query optimization is a balancing act between ensuring user productivity with respect to *time to optimize*, the time required to run the query, and the underlying resource allocation for processing in a multitenant environment.

Journey Map

The query optimization service plays a key role in the following tasks in the journey map.

Avoiding Cluster Clogs

Consider the scenario of a data user writing a complex query that joins tables with billions of rows on a nonindexed column value. While issuing the query, the data user may be unaware that this may take several hours or days to complete. Also, other SLA-sensitive query jobs can potentially be impacted. This scenario can occur during the exploration and production phases. Poorly written queries can clog the cluster and impact other production jobs. Today, such issues can be caught during the code review process, especially during the production phase. Code review is not foolproof and varies with the expertise of the team.

Resolving Runtime Query Issues

An existing query may stop working and fail with out of memory (OOM) issues. A number of scenarios can arise at runtime, such as failures, stuck or runaway queries, SLA violations, changed configuration or data properties, or a rogue query clogging the cluster. There can be a range of issues to debug, such as container sizes, configuration settings, network issues, machine degradation, bad joins, bugs in the query logic, unoptimized data layout or file formats, and scheduler settings. Today, debugging these issues is ad hoc. An optimization service that continuously profiles the query can help uncover the issues and potentially avoid them in production.

Speeding Up Applications

An increasing number of applications deployed in production rely on the performance of data queries. Optimizing these queries in production is critical for application performance and responsiveness for end users. Also, development of data products requires interactive ad hoc queries during model creation, which can benefit from faster query runs during exploration phases. Engineering teams currently follow the approach of reviewing the top 10 resource-consuming and long-running queries in production each week. They then target these queries for optimization, working with data users and potentially rewriting them if required.

Minimizing Time to Optimize

Time to optimize is a combination of the tasks involved to optimize the query, which in turn reduces the time required to run the query to generate results. The time is spent in three buckets:

- Aggregating monitoring statistics
- Analyzing the monitored data
- Invoking corrective actions as a result of the analysis

Aggregating Statistics

To holistically understand the performance of the query, statistics need to be collected across all layers of the software stack. They include statistics related to:

- Infrastructure-level (compute, storage, network, memory) performance
- Operating system health
- Container-level statistics from resource managers
- Query cluster resource allocation and utilization
- File access
- Pipeline and application performance

Monitoring details in the form of performance counters and logs are recorded and maintained for historic trend and anomaly analysis. Additionally, change management in configuration and data schema are recorded to help with debugging of issues.

Aggregating statistics is a heavy lift. It requires managing a variety of performance counters and log-message formats from different layers of the stack. The stats are collected using APIs that need to be interpreted and updated with software version upgrades.

Analyzing Statistics

The aggregated statistics need to be analyzed for prioritizing the knobs and optimizations that would be most effective for improving query performance. This differs across queries and requires analyzing the current state and correlating the statistics across different layers of the stack. For instance, Shi et al. (*https://oreil.ly/Raano*) compared the knob tuning in Hadoop for three different workloads: Terasort (sort a terabyte of data), N-gram (compute the inverted list of N-gram data), and PageRank (compute page rank of graphs). They discovered that for a Terasort job, a data compression knob was the most effective in improving performance. Similarly, for N-gram jobs, the configuration knobs related to Map Task count was critical, while the PageRank job was most impacted by the reduced task count.

The existing approaches for analysis are heuristic and time-consuming. They can be divided into three broad categories:

Query analysis
 Involves review of language constructs, cardinality checks of the tables involved, and appropriate use of indexes/partitions.

Job analysis
 Involves reviewing statistics related to data profiling, task parallelism, data compression, analysis of runtime execution stages, skew in data processing, efficiency of the map and reduce executors, and so on.

Cluster analysis
 Involves statistics related to job scheduling, sizing (hardware, bufferpool, and so on), container settings, number of execution cores, utilization, and so on.

The key challenge is the expertise required to correlate cluster, job, and query attributes to determine the prioritizing and ranking of the knobs that are critical for the given setup. The analysis also covers data schema design in terms of defining the right partitioning key to appropriately parallelize the processing.

Optimizing Jobs

Query optimization involves several factors, such as data layout, indexes and views, knob tuning, and query plan optimization. Lu et al. (*https://oreil.ly/ul3jm*) represent the factors as a Maslow's hierarchy based on their impact on query performance (as shown in Figure 15-1). The analysis step helps to shortlist and prioritize the knobs and query changes that can help optimize performance.

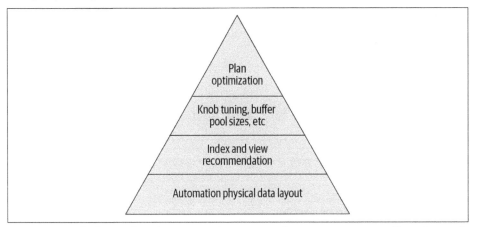

Figure 15-1. The hierarchy of aspects in the context of query optimization (from Lu et al. (https://oreil.ly/JuEnk)).

Optimization is an iterative process, and deciding on the new values across the jobs is challenging and time-consuming. Given the large number of knobs across the software stack, a high degree of correlation between the knob functionality needs to be taken into account (as shown in Figure 15-2). Knobs have a nonlinear effect on performance and require a certain level of expertise. Traditionally, query optimization has relied on data cardinality—in dealing with unstructured data with a lack of schema and statistics, estimating the impact is nontrivial. Finally, given the terabyte scale of data cycles, the iterative process requires time to evaluate the change.

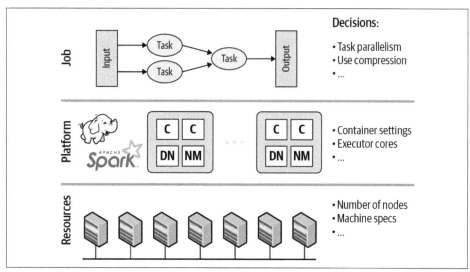

Figure 15-2. The knobs at different levels of the software stack (from Lu et al. (https://oreil.ly/aU5NL)).

Defining Requirements

The query optimization service has multiple levels of self-service automation. This section helps us to understand the current level of automation and the requirements for deployment of the service.

Current Pain Points Questionnaire

There are three categories of considerations to get a pulse of the current status:

Existing query workload
> The key aspects to consider are the percentage of ad hoc/scheduled/event-triggered queries running in production; and for scheduled and triggered queries, the typical frequency for these queries, which is an important indicator of the potential improvements. Also, understand the diversity of datastores and query engines involved in the query processing and the typical level of concurrency in the execution of the queries.

Impact of unoptimized queries
> The key indicators to evaluate are the number of missed SLAs, the level of utilization of the processing cluster, the number of failed queries, the wait time for the query to be scheduled on the cluster, and the variance in query completion times (i.e., the duration to complete a repeating query). These metrics are leading indicators of the potential improvements from implementing the query optimization service.

Existing tuning process
   Understand the existing processes followed for query optimization: a proactive
   versus reactive approach to tuning queries, code reviews, expertise with respect
   to understanding of underlying systems, and periodic review of resource-
   consuming queries.

Interop Requirements

Query optimization needs to interoperate with programming languages used for
writing queries (Python and Scala), backend datastores (Cassandra, Neo4j, Druid,
etc.), processing engines for streaming and batch (Spark, Flink, and Hive), and
deployment environments in the cloud and on-premise (EC2 and Docker).

Functionality Requirements

The optimization service needs to implement the following features:

Static query insights
   Recommendations for improving the query based on the right primitives, cardinalities of tables, and other heuristics. Ideally, poorly written queries that can
   impact processing on the cluster should not be allowed to run.

Dynamic query insights
   Based on runtime profiling, a single pane of glass of the entire stack, and recommendations on the knobs to tune. Job profiling is continuous and uses the statistics from every run of the query.

Automatically tune queries
   For common scenarios, the ability to have the queries automatically tuned
   instead of showing the recommendations.

Nonfunctional Requirements

Similar to any software design, the following are some of the key NFRs that should be
considered in the design of the query optimization service:

Explainability
   The service should be able to understand the reasoning of the recommendations
   generated by the optimization service.

Minimal disruption
   In using automatic tuning, the service should minimize the false positives and
   ensure there is no negative impact as a result of the tuning.

Cost optimization
> Given the high percentage of spend in query processing in the cloud, the optimization service should help reduce overall dollar costs.

Implementation Patterns

Corresponding to the existing task map, there are three levels of automation for the query optimization service (as shown in Figure 15-3). Each level corresponds to automating a combination of tasks that are currently either manual or inefficient:

Avoidance pattern
> Prevents bad queries from clogging the processing clusters and impacting other queries.

Operational insights pattern
> Provides insights based on analysis of runtime profiling statistics from the query runs. The operational insights can range from a single pane of glass for the monitoring of the entire stack, to recommendations on knobs.

Automated knob tuning pattern
> Takes actions to automatically tune job knob values.

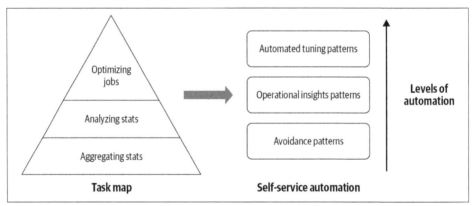

Figure 15-3. The different levels of automation for the query optimization service.

Avoidance Pattern

This pattern acts as a lint to prevent poorly written queries from clogging the processing cluster. It aims to prevent two types of errors. The first aim is to prevent accidental mistakes resulting from a lack of understanding of data models and cardinalities, such as complex joins on extremely large tables. The second aim is to prevent incorrect use of query constructs and best practices associated with different datastores. Given the spectrum of data users with varying expertise, this pattern plays a key role in providing self-service access while ensuring guardrails.

The avoidance pattern is applicable right at the time of writing the query, as well as during static analysis of queries before they are submitted for execution. Broadly, the pattern works as follows:

Aggregate metadata for the datasets
> The pattern leverages the metadata service to collect statistics (cardinality, data quality, and so on) and data types (refer back to Chapter 2).

Parse query
> It transforms the query from a raw string of characters into an abstract syntax tree (AST) representation.

Provide recommendations
> It applies rules on the query, including query primitives, best practices, physical data layout, and index and view recommendations.

To illustrate the pattern, Apache Calcite helps analyze queries before they are executed, while Hue provides an IDE to avoid creating poorly written queries.

Apache Calcite (*https://oreil.ly/H7AeG*) provides query processing, optimization, and query language support to many popular open source data processing systems, such as Apache Hive, Storm, Flink, Druid, and so on. Calcite's architecture consists of:

- A query processor capable of processing a variety of query languages. Calcite provides support for ANSI standard SQL as well as various SQL dialects and extensions (e.g., for expressing queries on streaming or nested data).

- An adapter architecture designed for extensibility and support for heterogeneous data models and stores, such as relational, semi-structured, streaming, and so on.

- A modular and extensible query optimizer with hundreds of built-in optimization rules, and a unifying framework for engineers to develop similar optimization logic and language support to avoid wasting engineering effort.

Hue (*https://gethue.com*) provides an example of avoiding bad queries within the IDE. There are similar capabilities in Netflix's Polynote (*https://oreil.ly/_B5I4*), Notebooks extensions, and so on. Hue implements two key patterns: a) Metadata browsing that lists and filters tables and columns automatically along with cardinality statistics, and b) Query editing with autocomplete for any SQL dialect, showing only valid syntax, and syntax highlighting of the keywords, plus visualization, query formatting, and parameterization.

The strengths of the pattern are that it saves significant debugging time in production and prevents surprises in production deployments. The weakness of the pattern is that it is difficult to enforce uniformly and typically varies with the team engineering culture.

Operational Insights Pattern

This pattern focuses on analyzing the metrics collected from multiple layers in the software stack and provides a rich set of actionable insights to data users. This is analogous to having an expert-in-a-box that correlates hundreds of metrics to deliver actionable insights. The pattern is a collection of correlation models on collected statistics to recommend tuning of knobs—for example, it correlates application performance to analyze application performance issues with code inefficiency, contention with cluster resources, or hardware failure or inefficiency (e.g., a slow node). Another example is correlating cluster utilization by analyzing cluster activity between two time periods, aggregated cluster workload, summary reports for cluster usage, chargeback reports, and so on.

Broadly, the pattern works (*https://oreil.ly/AhbDU*) as follows:

Collect stats
> It gets statistics and counters from all the layers of the big data stack. The statistics are correlated with a job history of recently succeeded and failed applications at regular intervals (job counters, configurations, and task data fetched from the job history server).

Correlate stats
> It correlates stats across the stack to create an E2E view for pipelines. The job orchestrator details can help stitch the view together.

Apply heuristics
> Once all the stats are aggregated, it runs a set of heuristics to generate a diagnostic report on how the individual heuristics and the job as a whole performed. These are then tagged with different severity levels to indicate potential performance problems.

To illustrate the pattern, Sparklens and Dr. Elephant are popular open source projects that provide operational insights.

Sparklens (*https://oreil.ly/5TLI4*) is a profiling tool for Spark applications that analyzes how efficiently the application is using the compute resources provided to it. It gathers all the metrics and runs analysis on them using a built-in Spark scheduler simulator. Sparklens analyzes application runs for bottlenecks, limiting scale-out by applying heuristic models for driver tasks, data skew, lack of worker tasks, and several other heuristics. Sparklens provides contextual information about what could be going wrong with the execution stages using a systematic method instead of learning by trial and error, saving both developer and compute time.

Dr. Elephant (*https://oreil.ly/_h8wW*) is a performance monitoring and tuning tool for Hadoop and Spark. It automatically gathers a job's metrics, analyzes them, and presents them in a simple way for easy consumption. Its goal is to improve developer productivity and increase cluster efficiency by making it easier to tune the jobs. It analyzes the Hadoop and Spark jobs using a set of pluggable, configurable, rule-based heuristics that provide insights on how a job performed, then uses the results to make suggestions about how to tune the job to make it perform more efficiently (as illustrated in Figure 15-4). It also computes a number of metrics for a job, which provides valuable information about the job performance on the cluster. Overall, the operational insights patterns avoid trial and error and provide recommendations based on analysis of the statistics.

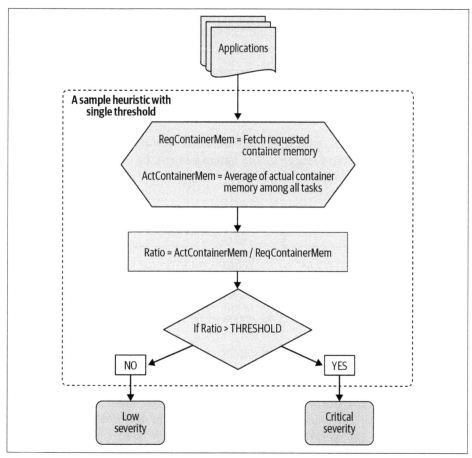

Figure 15-4. An example of rules used to make a recommendation in Dr. Elephant (from LinkedIn Engineering (https://oreil.ly/EglCm)).

Automated Tuning Pattern

The goal of this pattern is to develop an optimizer that invokes automatic tuning actions to improve the performance of the query. This is analogous to self-driving cars, where the actions require no intervention from the data users. The automated tuning takes into account configuration and statistics across the entire software stack. There are multiple different approaches for automated tuning of databases and big data systems. Broadly, as described by Lu et al. (*https://oreil.ly/nxr57*), the automated tuning optimizer works as follows:

- The optimizer takes as input the current knob values, current statistics, and performance goals, as shown in Figure 15-5.

- The optimizer models the expected performance outcome for different knob values to decide the optimal values. Essentially, the optimizer needs to predict the performance under hypothetical resource or knob changes for different types of workloads.

- New values are then applied or recommended. The tuning actions should be explainable to enable debugging. The optimizer typically implements a feedback loop to learn iteratively.

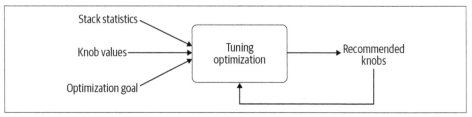

Figure 15-5. The input and output of the optimizer for the automated tuning pattern.

There are multiple approaches to building the automated tuning optimizer, as shown in Figure 15-6. In the 1960s, the techniques for automated database tuning were *rule-based*. This was based on the experience of human experts. In the 1970s, *cost-based* optimization emerged where statistical cost functions were used for tuning, which was formulated as constraint-based optimization. From the 1980s to the 2000s, *experiment-driven* and *simulation-driven* approaches were used where experiments with different parameter values were executed to learn the tuning behavior. In the last decade, *adaptive-tuning* approaches are employed to tune the values iteratively. The past several years have seen ML techniques based on reinforcement learning techniques employed.

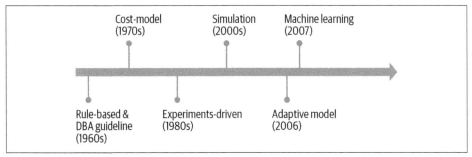

Figure 15-6. A timeline view of the approaches developed for the automated tuning optimizer (from Lu et al. (https://oreil.ly/9pHNt)).

The strength of the automated tuning pattern is improved productivity, as it enables data users who have little or no understanding of the system internals to improve query performance. The weakness is that an incorrect tuning has the potential to create negative impacts or cause disruption in production. Typically, deploying ML models requires significant training.

Summary

With hundreds of knobs in query engines and datastores, query tuning requires deep expertise in the underlying software and hardware stack. While it is a difficult problem, query tuning has become a must-have for the following needs of data teams:

Faster completion and strict SLAs
Given the growing volume of data, it is critical to tune the queries to complete in a timely fashion, especially if the queries need to complete within a strict time window for business reasons.

Better resource utilization
Being able to scale out the processing across distributed hardware resources is key. This also plays an important role in cost saving while running queries in the cloud, which can be quite expensive.

Performance isolation
Given multitenant deployments where processing clusters are shared by multiple teams, poorly written queries can bring down the system. It is critical to lint against bad queries impacting completion times in production.

CHAPTER 16

Pipeline Orchestration Service

So far, in the operationalize phase, we have optimized the individual queries and programs, and now it's time to schedule and run these in production. A runtime instance of a query or program is referred to as a job. Scheduling of jobs needs to take into account the right dependencies. For instance, if a job reads data from a specific table, it cannot be run until the previous job populating the table has been completed. To generalize, the pipeline of jobs needs to be orchestrated in a specific sequence, from ingestion to preparation to processing (as illustrated in Figure 16-1).

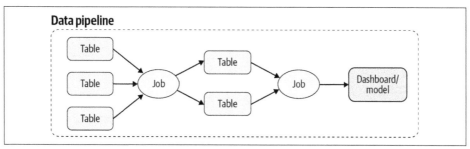

Figure 16-1. A logical representation of the pipeline as a sequence of dependent jobs executed to generate insights in the form of ML models or dashboards.

Orchestrating job pipelines for data processing and ML has several pain points. First, defining and managing dependencies between the jobs is ad hoc and error prone. Data users need to specify these dependencies and version-control them through the life cycle of the pipeline evolution. Second, pipelines invoke services across ingestion, preparation, transformation, training, and deployment. Monitoring and debugging pipelines for correctness, robustness, and timeliness across these services is complex. Third, orchestration of pipelines is multitenant, supporting multiple teams and business use cases. Orchestration is a balancing act in ensuring pipeline SLAs and efficient utilization of the underlying resources. As a result, there is a slowdown in time to orchestrate, which is a summation of the time to design job dependencies and the time to execute them efficiently in production. This in turn impacts the overall time to insight given that pipeline dependencies evolve iteratively and are executed repeatedly during their life cycles.

Ideally, an *orchestration service* should allow data users to define and version-control the job dependencies in a simplistic fashion. Under the hood, the service should automatically convert the dependencies into executable logic, manage the job execution by efficiently integrating with services, and retry for failures. The orchestration service ensures optimal resource utilization, pipeline SLAs, automated scaling, and isolation in a multitenant deployment. The service should be easy to manage with monitoring and debugging support at production scale. The service minimizes the *time to orchestrate*, helping reduce the overall time to insight.

Journey Map

Orchestrating pipelines is required during both the exploratory and production phases. The pipelines invoke a variety of jobs, such as data movement, wrangling, transformation, and model training (covered in earlier chapters). Pipelines can be invoked in a one-off fashion or scheduled or triggered based on events like new data becoming available, schema changes, and so on. The technologies involved in the E2E pipeline are raw datastores, data ingestion and collection tools, one or more datastores and analysis engines, serving datastores, and frameworks for data insights (as shown in Figure 16-2).

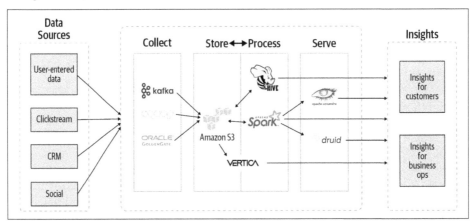

Figure 16-2. The anatomy of an E2E pipeline with example technologies.

Invoke Exploratory Pipelines

During the build process, pipelines are built to explore different combinations of datasets, features, model algorithms, and configuration. Users define the dependencies and manually trigger the pipeline. The goal of pipeline orchestration is to get quick responses and iterate on the pipelines. Exploratory pipelines should be run without affecting the production pipelines.

Run SLA-Bound Pipelines

In production, pipelines are typically scheduled on a regular basis with strict SLAs for completion. The orchestration needs to handle multiple corner cases, and build the appropriate retry logic and data quality checks between the execution steps. In case the pipeline does not complete, it needs to be debugged for issues like transformation logic bugs, OOM failures, improper change management, and so on. Data users rely on ad hoc tools for managing pipelines in production and collaborate with data engineering teams to debug issues that slow down the overall process.

Minimizing Time to Orchestrate

Time to orchestrate includes the time to design job dependencies, get them efficiently executed on available hardware resources, and monitor their quality and availability, especially for SLA-bound production pipelines. Time to orchestrate is spent in three different buckets: the design phase, the execution phase, and production debugging. The goal of the service is to minimize the time spent in each of these buckets.

Defining Job Dependencies

As a part of building the pipeline for transforming raw data into insights, data users need to specify the jobs involved in the pipeline, their dependencies, and the invocation rules. Jobs are invoked either ad hoc or scheduled or based on triggers. The job dependencies are represented as a DAG.

Ensuring correctness of dependencies at scale is nontrivial. Missing dependencies can lead to incorrect insights and is a significant challenge in production deployments. Tracking changes in dependencies with changes in code is difficult to version-control; while the dependent job may have completed, it may have failed to process the data correctly. In addition to knowing the dependent jobs, production deployments need ways to verify the correctness of the previous steps (i.e., they need circuit breakers based on data correctness).

The job dependencies are not constant but evolve during the pipeline life cycle. For instance, a change in the dashboard may create dependencies on a new table that is being populated by another job. The dependency needs to be updated appropriately to reflect the dependency on the new job.

Distributed Execution

Jobs are executed on a distributed cluster of machines allocated to the orchestrator. The pipeline DAGs are continuously evaluated. Applicable jobs across multiple tenants are then queued up for execution and scheduled in a timely fashion to ensure SLAs. The orchestrator scales the underlying resources to match the execution needs. The orchestrator does the balancing act of ensuring pipeline SLAs, optimal resource utilization, and fairness in resource allocation across tenants.

Distributed resource management is time-consuming thanks to a few challenges. First, ensuring isolation across multiple tenants such that a slowdown in one of the jobs doesn't block other unrelated jobs on the same cluster. Second, as the number of pipelines increases, a single scheduler becomes the bottleneck, causing long wait times for the jobs to be executed. Having an approach to partition the jobs across parallel schedulers allows scaling across the available resources. Third, given the heterogeneous nature of the jobs, there's a need to leverage a range of custom executors for data movement, schema services, processing, and ML tasks. In addition to resource management, job execution needs to handle appropriate retry for job execution errors, and jobs need to be recovered when failures occur at the crashed machines. Finally, the execution needs to fail over and continue execution with the appropriate leader election. Remembering the state of the pipeline for restart is critical.

Production Monitoring

Upon deployment of the pipeline in production, it needs to be monitored to ensure SLAs as well as to proactively alert on issues. In production, several issues can arise, from job errors to underlying hardware problems. Detecting these proactively is critical to meeting SLAs. Trend analysis is used to uncover anomalies proactively, and fine-grained monitoring combined with logging can help distinguish between a long-running job and a stalled job that's not making progress due to errors.

Monitoring the pipeline orchestration in production is complex. Fine-grained monitoring is needed to distinguish between a long-running job and a stalled job that is not making progress. Debugging for root-cause analysis requires understanding and correlating logs and metadata across multiple systems.

Defining Requirements

The orchestration service can have multiple levels of automation and self-service. This section covers the current level of automation and the requirements for initial deployment.

Current Pain Points Questionnaire

There are three categories of considerations to get a pulse of the current status:

How dependencies are defined
> Key considerations in this category are the time spent in getting a job ready for execution; how the dependencies are discovered and level of data user expertise required to define them; and how many orchestration issues have been encountered in production in terms of missing dependencies (i.e., are dependency errors a key issue related to correctness of insights in models and dashboards?).

How the pipelines are orchestrated
> Key considerations in this category are the time to get a job scheduled after being submitted (wait time); the variability in a job's completion time as a function of cluster load; the number of incidents related to missed SLAs; the number of issues with respect to cluster downtime; the average utilization of the underlying cluster resources; downtime associated with the orchestration cluster; and automatic retry after job errors.

How effectively the pipelines are monitored in production
> Key considerations in this category are whether data users can self-serve the monitoring and debugging and understand the current status of the jobs; whether notifications are available for failed jobs or missed SLAs; the number of false positives with anomaly-based proactive alerts; and the time to aggregate logs and understand the current job status.

Operational Requirements

Automation needs to take into account the processes that are currently deployed as well as technology tools and frameworks. These will vary from deployment to deployment. Operational requirements can be divided into three categories:

Types of pipeline dependencies
> Pipelines can be executed on schedule, ad hoc with user commands, or they can be triggered by data availability events. The service needs to provide support to the appropriate rules and triggers. Data users should also be able to specify priorities and SLAs of the pipelines.

Interoperability with deployed technology
> The starting point is understanding the different environments where pipelines are running: on-premise, in the cloud, or a hybrid of both. For each of these environments, list the technologies associated with executing the job, namely virtualization technologies (like Docker), job programming languages (like Python), frameworks for job dependency specifications, monitoring technologies, and serverless technologies for event-based execution.

Speeds and feeds
> This refers to the scale of job orchestration in terms of number of concurrent jobs to be supported (max and average), average length of jobs, number of tenant teams, typical number of server nodes, and uptime requirements.

Functional Requirements

Beyond the core functionality of simplifying job dependencies and providing reliable and optimal execution and automated monitoring, what follows is a checklist of additional features to consider as a part of the orchestration service:

Service-specific adapters
> Instead of generic shell command executors, the orchestrator can implement adapters to invoke specialized jobs, such as ingestion, real-time processing, ML constructs, and so on. A deep integration to service-specific APIs can improve job execution and monitoring compared to executing as a vanilla shell request.

Checkpointing of job execution
> For long-running jobs, checkpointing can help recover the jobs instead of restarting. Checkpointing can also help reuse previous results if the job is invoked without any change in data. Typically, if there are long-running jobs with strict SLAs, checkpointing becomes a key requirement.

Resource scaling
> The hardware resources allocated to the orchestrator should be able to auto-scale based on the queue depth of the outstanding requests. This is typically applicable in environments with varying numbers and types of pipelines such that static cluster sizing is either not performant or wasteful with respect to resource allocation.

Automatic audit and backfill
> Configuration changes associated with the pipeline orchestration, such as editing connections, editing variables, and toggling workflows, need to be saved to an audit store that can later be searched for debugging. For environments with evolving pipelines, a generic backfill feature will let data users create and easily manage backfills for any existing pipelines.

Nonfunctional Requirements

Similar to any software design, the following are some of the key NFRs that should be considered in the design of the orchestration service:

Cost
> Orchestration is computationally expensive, and it is critical to optimize the associated cost.

Intuitive design
> The service needs to be self-service and used by a wide range of users, namely data scientists, developers, machine learning experts, and operations employees.

Extensibility
> The service should be extensible for changing environments with the ability to be extensible in supporting new tools and frameworks.

Implementation Patterns

Corresponding to the existing task map, there are three levels of automation for the orchestration service, as shown in Figure 16-3. Each of the three levels correspond to automating a combination of tasks that are currently either manual or inefficient:

Dependency authoring patterns
> Simplify the specification of job dependencies, preventing dependency-related errors.

Distributed execution pattern
> Creates parallelism between the execution of SLA-bound pipelines from multiple tenant pipelines.

Pipeline observability patterns
> Make debugging and monitoring self-service for data users to proactively detect and avoid problems.

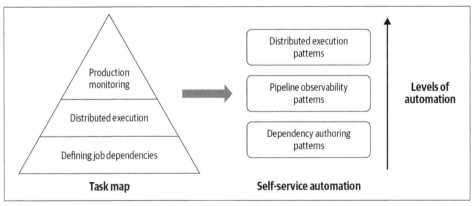

Figure 16-3. The levels of automation for the orchestration service.

Dependency Authoring Patterns

These patterns focus on simplifying authoring the job dependencies for data users. The goal is to provide the best trade-off between flexibility, expressiveness, and ease of use for a broad range of users to correctly define dependencies. In this category, a combination of patterns is implemented by open source pipeline orchestrators, namely Apache Airflow, Uber's Piper, Netflix's Meson, and Uber's Cadence (a generic orchestrator). The patterns for dependency authoring can be divided into three broad categories: domain-specific language (DSL), UI drag-and-drop, and procedural code.

At a high level, these patterns work as follows:

1. A user specifies dependencies using DSL, a UI, or code. The specification uses a collection of building blocks for defining dependency triggers and rules. The specifications are version-controlled.

2. The orchestrator interprets the specifications, which are represented internally as a DAG.

3. Dependencies are continuously evaluated during job execution. As the dependencies are satisfied, the jobs are scheduled for execution.

Apache Airflow (*https://oreil.ly/1PDuv*) implements a DSL-based definition of dependencies. For instance, there are three different ways to specify a dependency DAG Job A → Job B → Job C using Airflow's Python-based DSL:

- Using a downstream function: `a.set_downstream(b); b.set_downstream(c)`
- Using an upstream function: `c.set_upstream(b); b.set_upstream(a)`
- Using operators: `a >> b >> c` or `c << b << a`. Dependencies can also be lists or tuples: `a >> b >> (c, d)`

The dependencies are managed separately from the actual code and are represented internally as DAGs. In addition to dependencies, job trigger rules can be defined in Airflow using primitives like `all_success`, `all_failed`, `all_done`, `one_failed`, `one_success`, `none_failed`, `none_skipped`, and `dummy`. Another example of a DSL-based implementation is Netflix Meson, which uses a Scala-based DSL.

Uber's Piper orchestrator extends Airflow and implements visual drag-and-drop authoring for users not familiar with Python development. Domain-specific UIs help users create pipelines specific to verticals like machine learning, dashboarding, and ingestion. The visual specifications are converted and implemented as DAGs. On the other hand, Uber's Cadence orchestrator implements dependencies as part of the procedural code in Java, Python, and Go. It also allows pipeline definition using REST APIs.

Strengths of the DSL and UI authoring patterns compared to code are that they make authoring job dependencies accessible to a wide range of data users, avoid implementation errors, and separate tracking of the dependency logic from the implementation. The patterns make it easier to evolve and optimize the dependencies. The patterns' weakness is their limitations in specifying advanced dependencies.

Selecting the right authoring pattern is a balancing act between flexibility and ease of use for a range of data users within the organization. DSL authoring is a good middle ground between UI-based and code-based dependency authoring. Advanced data users prefer managing dependencies as code with version control and continuous integration.

Orchestration Observability Patterns

These patterns provide monitoring of the pipeline progress, alerts for SLA violations and errors, and assistance with pipeline-related debugging. Detecting issues proactively is critical for production data and ML pipelines. The goal is to make pipeline management self-service such that data users can visualize, manage, and debug both current and past runs of jobs and pipelines.

There is a collection of patterns used for pipeline observability. The general building blocks for these patterns are as follows:

Collect
Aggregates monitoring data from different services invoked by the pipeline jobs. Monitoring data is a collection of logs, statistics, job timings (time to complete, invocation schedule, and so on), data processed, and services-specific statistics like data ingestion, model training, and deployment.

Analyze
Correlates and analyzes details to understand the current status of the pipeline.

Alert
Compares current and historic values for anomaly alerting. Records feedback from the users to reduce the false positives over time.

Apache Airflow persists metadata associated with the pipelines in a database (typically MySQL or PostgreSQL). The metadata powers multiple visualizations to assist data users in managing and monitoring the pipelines. A few example visualizations are:

- A *DAG view* that lists DAGs in the environment, showing jobs succeeded, failed, or currently running
- A *graph view* to visualize the DAG's dependencies and their current status for a specific run
- A *Gantt chart view* showing job duration and overlap to identify bottlenecks and where the bulk of time is spent for specific DAG runs
- A *task duration view* that shows the duration of jobs over the past N runs and helps identify outliers

Another pattern is alerting on SLA misses. The time by which a job or DAG should have succeeded is set at the job level as a *timedelta*. If one or many instances have not succeeded by that time, an alert email is sent detailing the list of jobs that missed their SLA. The event is also recorded in the database and made available in the UI.

Netflix's Meson (*https://oreil.ly/TqLre*) orchestrator implements fine-grained progress tracking of pipeline jobs. When jobs are scheduled, a Meson job executor maintains a communication channel with the scheduler. The executor continuously sends heartbeats, percent complete, status messages, and so on. It also sends custom data that's richer than just exit codes or status messages on job completion. Another pattern is treating job outputs within the pipeline as first-class citizens and storing them as artifacts. Retries of a job can be skipped based on the presence or absence of an artifact ID.

Overall, the orchestration observability patterns are critical for self-service monitoring and alerting at production scale and meeting SLAs for critical pipelines.

Distributed Execution Pattern

This pattern focuses on distributing the pipeline jobs across available server resources. The pattern needs to balance utilization of heterogeneous hardware resources, parallelize pipeline execution to meet SLAs, and ensure fairness of resource allocation across multiple tenant jobs.

Essentially, the distributed execution pattern consists of two key building blocks:

Scheduler
Responsible for scheduling pipelines and jobs. The scheduler takes into account various factors, such as schedule interval, job dependencies, trigger rules, and retries, and uses this information to calculate the next set of jobs to run. Once resources are available, it queues the job for execution. Requests are queued and dispatched to execute on available resources.

Worker
Executes the jobs. Each worker pulls the next job for execution from the queue (stored in messaging frameworks or a datastore) and executes the task locally. The metadata database records the details of the executable job.

To illustrate, Airflow implements a singleton scheduler service that is multithreaded. Messages to invoke jobs are queued up in RabbitMQ (*https://www.rabbitmq.com*) or Redis (*https://oreil.ly/c-dhk*) databases. The jobs are distributed among multiple Celery (*https://oreil.ly/lk2CR*) workers. The Airflow scheduler monitors all tasks and all DAGs, and triggers the job instances whose dependencies have been met. Behind the scenes, it spins up a subprocess, which monitors and stays in sync with a folder for all DAG objects it may contain, and periodically (every minute or so) collects DAG-parsing results and inspects active jobs to see whether they can be triggered.

The Airflow scheduler is designed to run as a persistent service in an Airflow production environment.

Real-world deployments are prone to single points of failure and saturation. To improve availability, Uber's Piper (*https://oreil.ly/G5ZZU*) orchestrator implements the following patterns:

Leader election
> For any system components that are meant to run as a singleton, such as the executor, the leader election capability automatically elects the leader from available backup nodes. This eliminates single points of failure and also reduces any downtime during deployments, node restarts, or node relocations.

Work partitioning
> To manage an increasing number of pipelines, additional schedulers are assigned a portion of the pipelines automatically. As the new scheduler comes online, a set of pipelines is automatically assigned to it, and it can start scheduling them. As scheduler nodes come online or offline, the set of pipelines is automatically adjusted, enabling high availability and horizontal scalability.

High availability for hardware downtime
> Services must gracefully handle container crashes, restarts, and container relocations without any downtime. Piper uses Apache Mesos, which runs services within Docker containers and automatically monitors the health of the containers and spins up new instances on failures.

To efficiently execute jobs, Meson implements native integration with adapters of specific environments. Meson supports Spark Submit, allowing monitoring of the Spark job progress and the ability to retry failed Spark steps or kill Spark jobs that may have gone astray. Meson also supports the ability to target specific Spark versions, allowing users to leverage the latest version of Spark.

Given the growing amount of data and jobs, it is critical to have a highly scalable execution that scales automatically. Distributed execution patterns enable scaling based on available resources, balancing service time and wait time.

Summary

Orchestrating jobs is a balancing act between efficient resource utilization, performance SLAs of the jobs, and data dependencies between the jobs. In real-world deployments, it is critical to ensure a robust orchestration service that efficiently integrates with pipeline services and provides automated scaling and isolation in multitenant deployments.

CHAPTER 17

Model Deploy Service

In the journey of deploying insights in production, we have optimized the processing queries and orchestrated the job pipelines. Now we are ready to deploy ML models in production and periodically update them based on retraining.

Several pain points slow down time to deploy. The first is nonstandardized home-grown scripts for deploying models that need to support a range of ML model types, ML libraries and tools, model formats, and deployment endpoints (such as Internet of Things [IoT] devices, mobile, browser, and web API). The second pain point is that, once deployed, there are no standardized frameworks to monitor the performance of models. Given multitenant environments for model hosting, monitoring ensures automatic scaling of the models and performance isolation from other models. The third pain point is ensuring the prediction accuracy of the models with drifts in data distributions over time. *Time to deploy* impacts the overall time to insight during the initial model deployment and on an ongoing basis during monitoring and upgrading. Data users need to depend on data engineering to manage deployment, which slows down the overall time to insight even further.

Ideally, a self-service *model deploy service* should be available to deploy trained models from any ML library into any model format for deployment at any endpoint. Once deployed, the service automatically scales the model deployment. For upgrades to existing models, it supports canary deployments, A/B testing, and continuous deployments. The service automatically monitors the quality of the inference and alerts data users. Examples of self-service model deploy services include Facebook's FBLearner, Google's TensorFlow Extended (TFX), Airbnb's Bighead, Uber's Michelangelo, and Databricks' MLflow project.

Journey Map

Model deployment can be treated as a one-time or continuous process that occurs on a scheduled basis. A deployed model serves multiple clients and scales automatically to provide predictions in a timely fashion (as shown in Figure 17-1).

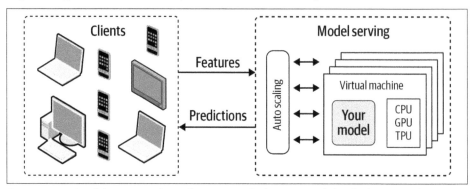

Figure 17-1. Model serving where clients provide features and the deployed model responds with the prediction.

Model Deployment in Production

Upon completion of training, the model is deployed in production. The goal is to ensure the model operates reliably in production, similarly to how it operated during training. During this phase of the journey map, the model is packaged and pushed out to an offline job for scheduled batch inference or to online endpoint containers for real-time request-response inference. An application invokes an online model via an API and responds back with the prediction, whereas an offline model is invoked on a schedule, then the inference is written back to the lake for downstream consumption by batch jobs, or accessed by users directly through query tools. Pipelines are set up to fetch features required for model inferencing. Data users need to have a ballpark estimate of the expected throughput (predictions per second) and response time latency. Monitoring is set up to track the accuracy of metrics and generate alerts based on thresholds. Today, given a lack of standardization, data users rely on engineering teams to manage this aspect of the journey map.

Model Maintenance and Upgrade

Models are retrained regularly to factor in new labeled data. For continuous online training, the model is updated on every new data record. During this phase of the journey map, the updated model needs to be deployed without impacting applications. Deployment needs to accommodate different scenarios, such as canary or A/B testing and partitioned models. These scenarios involve using different models to make predictions for different users and then analyzing the results. Canary testing allows you to validate a new release with minimal risk by deploying it first for a fraction of your users. The user split can be done based on policies and, once satisfied, the release can be rolled out gradually. A/B testing is about comparing the performance of different versions of the same feature while monitoring a high-level metric like click-through rate (CTR), conversion rate, and so on. Partitioned models are organized in a hierarchical fashion—for example, a ride-sharing service like Uber might have a single hierarchical model for all cities instead of separate models for each city. The processes of upgrading and A/B testing are nonstandard and managed differently by different teams.

Minimizing Time to Deploy

Time to deploy represents the time taken during deployment as well as post-deployment for scaling and drift monitoring in production. Time to deploy is spent in the following three categories: deployment orchestration, performance scaling, and drift monitoring.

Deployment Orchestration

Orchestration involves deployment of models on a production endpoint, such as a standalone web service, a model embedded within an application, a model on an IoT edge device, and so on. There is a plethora of combinations for ML libraries, tools, formats, model types, and endpoints; serializing the model seamlessly for deployment to a given endpoint is error prone and time-consuming. Managing multiple models for canary and A/B testing requires scripts to slice traffic among the models. Given that endpoints vary with respect to compute, memory, and networking resources, models need to be compressed and optimized specific to the endpoint. Upgrading models needs to be orchestrated in a nondisruptive way such that application requests are not impacted.

Teams today reinvent the wheel to apply the workflow to different permutations of deployment. It's not critical that one tool provides everything, but it is important to have an integrated set of tools that can tackle all steps of the workflow.

Performance Scaling

Performance scaling involves allocating the right amount of resources to adjust to the changing prediction load on the model. Detecting slowdown requires thresholds that take into account model type, input feature cardinality, online training data size, and several other factors. To handle the varying demands, models need to be scaled up and down. Given that models are stateless, additional instances can be spun up to manage increased load, allowing for horizontal scaling. For standalone service deployments, models are typically deployed on containers along with other models. Debugging the impact on performance from the interference of other models is difficult to manage. To take advantage of advanced hardware like GPUs, the requests sent to the models need to be batched for improving throughput while being within the latency bounds. Most of the tasks are handled in an ad hoc fashion, either manually or in a semi-automated way.

Drift Monitoring

Drift monitoring involves continuously verifying correctness of the inference that is impacted by shifts in feature distribution values, semantic labeling changes, distribution of data segments for inference, and so on. Measuring quality of inference is based on several metrics and varies based on the type of model. A challenge for data users is that complex engineering is required to join the actual results back with the predicted results. Tracking of feature value distributions and history of inputs for inference is ad hoc and often varies based on the engineering skills of the data users.

Defining Requirements

Given a trained model, the deploy service automates the endpoint deployment, scaling, and life cycle management of the deployed model. Data users should be able to self-serve without depending on engineering teams or ad hoc scripts with technical debt. Given the multitude of permutations, the requirements vary based on the specific needs and current state of the platform.

Orchestration

A model can essentially be treated as a combination of an algorithm and configuration details that can be used to make a new prediction based on a new set of input data. For instance, the algorithm can be a *random forest*, and the configuration details would be the coefficients calculated during model training. Once a model is trained based on the business needs, there are several requirements that need to be considered for deployment orchestration, namely endpoint configuration, model format, and production scenarios like upgrades.

Deployment endpoints

Model deployments in production are broadly divided into offline and online deployments. An offline deployment generates batch inference on a scheduled basis, whereas online deployment responds in near real time to application prediction requests (either sent individually or batched).

Deployment endpoints of the model can be packaged using one of the following patterns:

Embedded model

The model is built and packaged within the consuming application, and the model code is managed seamlessly as part of the application code. When building the application, the model is embedded inside the same Docker container such that the Docker image becomes a combination of application and model artifact that is then versioned and deployed to production. A variant of this pattern is library deployment, where the model is embedded as a library in application code.

Model deployed as a separate service

The model is wrapped in a service that can be deployed independently of the consuming applications. This allows updates to the model to be released independently.

Pub/sub model

The model is also treated and published independently, but the consuming application ingests the inference from a data stream instead of API calls. This is usually applicable in streaming scenarios where the application can subscribe to data streams that perform operations like pulling customer profile information.

Model formats

There are multiple different formats to serialize the model for interoperability. Model formats can be divided into language-agnostic and language-dependent exchange formats.

In the category of language-agnostic exchange formats, Predictive Model Markup Language (PMML) was originally considered a "de facto standard" and provided a way to share models like neural networks, SVM, Naive Bayes classifiers, and so on. PMML is XML-based and is not popular in the era of deep learning given that XML is no longer widely used. PMML's successor, Portable Format for Analytics (PFA), was developed by the same organization and is Avro-based. In the meantime, Facebook and Microsoft teamed up to create ONNX (Open Neural Network Exchange), which uses Google's Protocol Buffers as an interoperable format. ONNX focuses on the capabilities needed for inferencing and defines an extensible computation graph model as well as definitions of built-in operators and standard data types. ONNX is widely supported and can be found in many frameworks, tools, and hardware.

The following are popular formats in the category of language-dependent exchange formats:

- Spark MLWritable is the standard model storage format included with Spark. It is limited to use only within Spark.

- MLeap provides a common serialization format for exporting and importing Spark, scikit-learn, and TensorFlow models.

- Pickle is a standard Python serialization library used to save models from scikit-learn and other ML libraries to a file. The file can be loaded to deserialize the model and make new predictions.

Model deployment scenarios

Data users require multiple different deployment scenarios:

Nondisruptive upgrade
Updating the deployed model with a newer version should not impact the applications relying on the model. This is especially applicable for models packaged as standalone services.

Shadow mode deployment
This mode captures the inputs and inference of a new model in production without actually serving those inferences. The results can be analyzed with no significant consequences if a bug is detected.

Canary model deployment
As discussed previously, a canary release applies the new model to a small fraction of incoming requests. It requires mature deployment tooling, but it minimizes mistakes when they happen. The incoming requests can be split in many ways to determine whether they will be serviced by the old or new model: randomly, based on geolocation or specific user lists, and so on. There is a need for stickiness—i.e., for the duration of the test, designated users must be routed to servers running the new release. This can be achieved by setting a specific cookie for these users, allowing the web application to identify them and send their traffic to the proper servers. A typical approach is to use a switch web service and two single-model endpoints for canary testing.

A/B testing deployment
Using the A/B testing service (covered in Chapter 14), different models can be used for different user groups. Supporting A/B testing requires stickiness from the orchestration service—i.e., building user buckets, sticking them to different endpoints, and logging respective results. A key requirement is the ability to deploy multiple models to the same endpoint.

Model Scaling and Performance

It's important to answer the following questions related to scaling and performance:

- How many models are planned to be deployed? What percentage of these models is offline versus online?

- What is the maximum expected throughput in terms of predictions per second that models need to support?

- Are there online models that need to be served in real time? What is the ballpark for maximum tolerable response time latency? An order of milliseconds, or seconds?
- How fresh are the models with respect to reflecting new data samples? For online training of models, what is the ballpark data size that will be used? MB, GB, TB? How often is the model expected to be updated?
- If deployed in a regulated environment, what is the level of logging required for auditing the serving of requests?

Drift Verification

In general, there are two ways a model can decay: due to *data drift* or *concept drift*. With data drift, data evolves with time, potentially introducing previously unseen varieties and new categories of data, but there is no impact on previously labeled data. With concept drift, the interpretation of data changes with time even while the general distribution of the data does not. For example, what we agreed upon as belonging to class *A* in the past, we claim now that it should belong to class *B*, as our understanding of the properties of *A* and *B* have changed. Depending on the application, there might be a need to detect both data and concept drift.

Nonfunctional Requirements

Similar to any software design, the following are some of the key NFRs that should be considered in the design of a model deploy service:

Robustness
   The service needs to be able to recover from failures, and gracefully handle transient or permanent errors encountered during deployment.

Intuitive visualization
   The service should have a self-service UI serving a broad spectrum of data users with varying degrees of engineering expertise.

Verifiability
   It should be possible to test and verify the correctness of the deployment process.

Implementation Patterns

Corresponding to the existing task map, there are three levels of automation for the model deployment service (as shown in Figure 17-2). Each level corresponds to automating a combination of tasks that are currently either manual or inefficient:

Universal deployment pattern
> Deploys model types developed using different programming platforms and end-point types.

Autoscaling deployment pattern
> Scales the model deployment up and down to ensure performance SLAs.

Model drift tracking pattern
> Verifies accuracy of the model predictions to detect issues proactively before they impact application users.

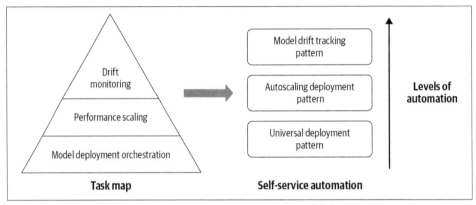

Figure 17-2. *The different levels of automation for the model deployment service.*

Universal Deployment Pattern

The universal deployment pattern standardizes the approach for data users to deploy models without being limited to specific programming tools or endpoints. Given the lack of a silver bullet with respect to model types, programming libraries and tools, and endpoint types, this pattern is becoming increasingly important.

The pattern is composed of three building blocks:

Model serialization
> Models are compiled into a single serialized format that is deployable at different endpoints. The serialized format is independent of the source code that created the model and contains all the required artifacts associated with the model, including model parameter weights, hyperparameter weights, metadata, and compiled DSL expressions of features. There are two approaches for model serialization: a) A single packaging standard across programming frameworks and deployment, and b) multiple formats of the model packaged together and applied to endpoints as applicable.

Model identification
> Multiple models can be deployed for canary and A/B testing scenarios. At the time of deployment, a model is identified by a universally unique identifier (UUID) and an optional tag. A tag can be associated with one or more models; the most recent model with the same tag is typically used. For online models, the model UUID is used to identify the model that will be used to service the prediction request. For offline models, all deployed models are used to score each batch dataset, and the prediction records contain the model UUID for result filtering.

Endpoint deployment
> A model can be deployed to different types of endpoints. A validation pre-step ensures the accuracy of the model being pushed to the endpoint. For standalone deployments, more than one model can be deployed at the same time to a given serving container, or the existing model can be replaced with the prediction containers, automatically loading the new models from disk and starting to handle prediction requests. For A/B testing of models, the experimentation framework uses model UUIDs or tags to automatically send portions of the traffic to each model and track performance metrics. This allows safe transitions from old models to new models and side-by-side A/B testing of models. To ship ML models and run inference tasks on mobile and IoT devices, large models need to be compressed to reduce energy consumption and accelerate computation. Compression usually prunes the unnecessary parameters of the model. This requires training the same job multiple times to get the best compression without compromising the quality of the model.

To illustrate the two approaches related to serialized model formats, we use the MLflow and TFX open source projects as examples:

Multiple flavors packaged together
> The MLflow Model (*https://oreil.ly/T9xdp*) defines a convention that lets us save a model in different "flavors" that can be understood by different downstream endpoints. Each MLflow Model is a directory containing arbitrary files and an *mlmodel* file in the root of the directory that can define multiple flavors the model can be viewed in. All of the flavors that a particular model supports are defined in its *mlmodel* file in YAML format. Flavors are the key concept that makes MLflow Models powerful: they are a convention that deployment tools can use to understand the model, which makes it possible to write tools that work with models from any ML library without having to integrate each tool with each library.

Single format with integration
> TensorFlow Extended (*https://oreil.ly/GJ3xZ*) integrates with programming environments to generate the model that can be deployed in multiple TFX endpoints. It generates two model formats: the SavedModel format includes a serialized description of the computation defined by the model in addition to the

parameter values. It contains a complete TensorFlow program, including weights and computation, and does not require the original model building code to run. The model's evaluation graph is exported to EvalSavedModel, which contains additional information related to computing the same evaluation metrics defined in the model over a large amount of data and user-defined slices. The SavedModel is deployed to the endpoint and EvalSavedModel is used for analyzing the performance of the model.

To illustrate how endpoint deployment works, we use Uber's Michelangelo. Models are deployed to a prediction service that receives the request (sent as Thrift requests via remote procedure call (RPC)), fetches the features from the feature store, performs feature transformation and selection, and invokes the model to make the actual prediction. In contrast, TFX embeds all the feature processing within the pipeline and represents it as a TensorFlow graph.

The universal deployment pattern's strength is its flexibility— i.e., you build once and deploy several times (similar to Java's value proposition of "write once, run anywhere"). The pattern's weakness is the cost to integrate with multiple programming libraries given there is no silver bullet. Overall, the pattern is a must-have for deployments where data users are dealing with heterogeneous models built using a variety of libraries and deployment on different endpoints.

Autoscaling Deployment Pattern

Upon deployment, ML models need to meet both the throughput SLA, measured in terms of number of predictions per second, as well as the latency SLA for the prediction, measured by TP95 response time. The SLA requirements are much more stringent for online models compared to offline models. The autoscaling deployment pattern ensures that model performance is automatically scaled up to keep with the changing invocation demands and scaled down to save cost.

The pattern has three building blocks:

Detecting slowdown
> It continuously measures model performance and detects slowdown based on defined thresholds. Thresholds vary based on the complexity of the model. For example, online serving latency depends on the type of model (deep learning versus regular models) and whether the model requires features from the feature store service. Typically, TP95 latency of online models is on the order of milliseconds and supports an order of a hundred thousand predictions per second.

Defining autoscaling policy
> The autoscaling policy adjusts the number of model serving instances up or down in response to throughput or when triggered by slowdown detection. The policy defines the target throughput per instance and provides upper and lower

bounds for the number of instances for each production variant. ML models are stateless and easy to scale out, both for online and offline models. For online models, they add more hosts to the prediction service cluster and let the load balancer spread the load. Offline inference with Spark involves adding more executors and letting Spark manage the parallelism.

Isolation and batching

Models are deployed in a multitenant environment. Enabling a single instance of the server to serve multiple ML models concurrently can lead to cross-modal interference and requires model isolation so that the performance characteristics of one model has minimal impact on other models. This is typically implemented by configuring separate dedicated thread pools for the models. Similarly, an important aspect of performance scaling is batching individual model inference requests together to unlock the high throughput of hardware accelerators like GPUs. The deployed endpoint implements a library for batching requests and scheduling the batches that process groups of small tasks.

Consider the example of the TFX Serving library. TFX automatically scales the model deployment. To reduce cross-modal interference, it allows any operation to be executed with a caller-specified thread pool. This ensures that threads performing request processing won't contend with long operations involved with loading a model from disk. The TensorFlow Session API offers many reasonable ways to perform batching of requests, since there is no single best approach for different requirements, such as online versus offline serving, interleaving requests to multiple models, CPU versus GPU compute, and synchronous versus asynchronous API invocation.

The strength of the autoscaling deployment pattern is that it provides the best combination of performance and cost. The weakness of the pattern is the time to spin up and scale out the model performance upon detection of saturation. For scenarios where the feature store is the scaling bottleneck, the pattern does not help. Overall, the pattern automates dealing with performance issues that would otherwise require a significant amount of data users' time monitoring and configuring in production.

Model Drift Tracking Pattern

The model drift monitoring pattern ensures that the deployed model is working correctly. There are three aspects of drift tracking. The first is the accuracy of the ML model for different ranges of feature values. For instance, the model will be inaccurate when predicting for outlier feature values instead of values it has seen in the past during training. The second aspect is tracking historical distribution of predicted values—i.e., detecting trends where the model predicts higher or lower values for similar values of input features. The third is that changes to model behavior can arise after retraining due to changes to training data distributions, data pipeline code and configuration, model algorithms, and model configuration parameters.

The pattern consists of the following building blocks:

Data distribution and result monitoring
> Monitors model features for distribution changes. The assumption is that model performance will change when the model is asked to make predictions on new data that was not part of the training set. Each inference is logged with a specific inference ID along with the input feature values. Also, a small percentage of the inferences are later joined with the observed outcomes or label values. The comparison of inferences against actuals helps compute precise accuracy metrics.

Model auditing
> Captures configuration and execution logs associated with each model inference. For instance, for decision tree models, the audit allows browsing through each of the individual trees to see their relative importance to the overall model, their split points, the importance of each feature to a particular tree, and the distribution of data at each split, among other variables. This helps in tracking why a model behaves as it does, as well as in debugging as necessary.

An example of the pattern is Uber's Michelangelo. The client sends Thrift requests via RPC to get the inference. Michelangelo fetches any missing features from the feature store, performs feature transformations as required, and invokes the actual model inference. It logs all the details as messages in Kafka for analysis and live monitoring. It tracks accuracy using different metrics for different model types. For instance, in the case of a regression model, it tracks R-squared/coefficient of determination (*https://oreil.ly/TLzuf*), root mean square error (*https://oreil.ly/NDcO_*) (RMSE), and mean absolute error (MAE) metrics (*https://oreil.ly/F1IUl*). The metrics used should be in the context of what matters for the problem, and it is critical to appropriately define the loss function as it becomes the basis of model optimization.

Summary

Writing a one-off script to deploy a model is not difficult. Managing those scripts for permutations of model training types (online versus offline), model inference types (online versus offline), model formats (PAML, PFA, ONNX, and so on), endpoint types (web service, IoT, embedded browser, and so on), and performance requirements (defined by predictions/second and latency) is difficult. Given a large number of permutations, one-off scripts used by individual teams soon become a technical debt and are nontrivial to manage. The higher the number of permutations, the greater the need to automate with a model deploy service.

CHAPTER 18

Quality Observability Service

So far, we have covered deployment of insights, and they're now ready to be used in production. Consider a real-world example of a business dashboard deployed in production that is showing a spike in one of the metrics (such as gross new subscribers). Data users need to ensure that the spike is actually reflecting reality and not the result of a data quality problem. Several things can go wrong and lead to quality issues: uncoordinated source schema changes, changes in data element properties, ingestion issues, source and target systems with out-of-sync data, processing failures, incorrect business definitions for generating metrics, and so on.

Tracking quality in production pipelines is complex. First, there is no E2E unified and standardized tracking of data quality across multiple sources in the data pipeline. This results in a long delay in identifying and fixing data quality issues. Also, there is currently no standardized platform that requires teams to apply and manage their own hardware and software infrastructure to address the problem. Second, defining the quality checks and running them at scale requires a significant engineering effort. For instance, a personalization platform requires data quality validation of millions of records each day. Currently, data users rely on one-off checks that are not scalable with large volumes of data flowing across multiple systems. Third, it's important not just to detect data quality issues, but also to avoid mixing low-quality data records with the rest of the dataset partitions. The quality checks should be able to run on incremental datasets instead of running on the entire petabyte dataset. *Time to insight quality* includes tasks to analyze data attributes for anomalies, debug the root cause of detected quality issues, and proactively prevent low-quality data from impacting the insights in dashboards and models. These tasks can slow down the overall time to insight associated with the pipelines.

Ideally, a self-service *quality observability service* should allow for registering data assets, defining quality models for the datasets, and monitoring and alerting when an issue or anomaly is detected. Anomalies in data characteristics are a potential signal of a quality issue. In scenarios where a quality issue is detected, the service gathers enough profiling details and configuration change tracking to help with the root-cause debugging. Finally, the service should be proactive in preventing quality issues by using schema enforcement and isolating low-quality data records before they are added to the dataset.

Journey Map

Monitoring the quality of insights is a continuous activity. The key contributor to the quality of insights is the quality of the underlying data, which is continuously evolving. Data of poor quality can lead to incorrect business insights, inferior customer experience when using ML model predictions, and so on. Quality observability is a must-have service, especially when using ML algorithms that are sensitive to data noise.

Daily Data Quality Monitoring Reports

Data users need to ensure that the generated insights are valid for consumption. Typically, the process involves verifying data correctness from origin to consumption. A dataset deployed in production is continuously tracked for daily ingestion quality. Several types of data quality issues, namely incomplete data, ambiguous data interpretation, duplicated data, and an outdated metadata catalog, can impact the quality of the resulting ML models, dashboards, and other generated insights.

The goal of the daily data quality report is to prevent low-quality data from impacting generated insights. A variety of techniques are used to verify data quality—for example, verifying data type matching, source-target cardinality, and value distributions, as well as profiling the statistics against historic trends to detect anomalies and potential quality issues. It is difficult and costly to validate data quality with large volumes of data flowing across multiple platforms. Today, the checks are ad hoc, non-comprehensive checks implemented in SQL. Data users typically reinvent the wheel to implement quality checks for different datasets.

Debugging Quality Issues

In the context of explaining insights (for example, an expected spike in traffic), the data user spends a significant amount of time determining whether it's indicative of a data problem or actually reflecting reality. Making this determination requires deep analysis of pipeline lineage and of monitoring statistics and event logs associated with different systems in the pipeline. It requires a significant amount of time spent detecting and analyzing every change. A variety of root-cause issues can affect the pipeline, such as empty partitions, unexpected nulls, and malformed JSON. Figure 18-1 illustrates the key issues we encountered in production. Given the variety of issues, there is no silver bullet for debugging.

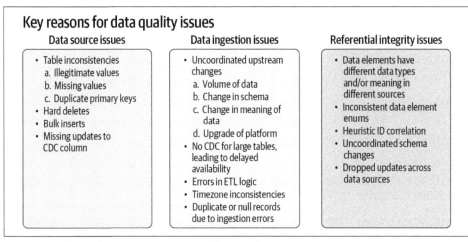

Key reasons for data quality issues

Data source issues	Data ingestion issues	Referential integrity issues

• Table inconsistencies
  a. Illegitimate values
  b. Missing values
  c. Duplicate primary keys
• Hard deletes
• Bulk inserts
• Missing updates to CDC column
	• Uncoordinated upstream changes
	  a. Volume of data
	  b. Change in schema
	  c. Change in meaning of data
	  d. Upgrade of platform
	• No CDC for large tables, leading to delayed availability
	• Errors in ETL logic
	• Timezone inconsistencies
	• Duplicate or null records due to ingestion errors
		• Data elements have different data types and/or meaning in different sources
		• Inconsistent data element enums
		• Heuristic ID correlation
		• Uncoordinated schema changes
		• Dropped updates across data sources

Figure 18-1. Key data issues encountered in production.

Handling Low-Quality Data Records

Beyond detecting quality issues, how do we ensure that low-quality data is proactively discarded or cleansed at the time of ingestion, before it pollutes the dataset in the data lake? Today, the process is ad hoc and involves back-and-forth between data engineering and data users. There are no clear strategies to isolate, clean, and backfill the partitions that have low-quality records. The definition of quality can be extended to other properties, namely detecting bias in the data. Bias is a growing concern for ML models where the dataset does not represent the normal distribution.

Minimizing Time to Insight Quality

Time to insight quality includes the time to verify accuracy of data, the profile data properties for anomalies, and proactively preventing low-quality data records from polluting the data lake.

Verify the Accuracy of the Data

The process of verification involves creating data quality models to analyze the individual samples of data in the E2E pipeline. The model defines quality rules for data, metadata, monitoring statistics, log messages, and so on. Models cover different data quality dimensions, such as accuracy, data profiling, anomaly detection, validity, and timeliness.

These quality checks can be applied at different data life cycle stages, which allows us to detect issues early:

Source stage
Data creation within the application tier (transactional databases, clickstream, logs, IoT sensors, etc.).

Ingestion stage
Data collected from the sources in batch or real time and stored in the lake.

Prep stage
Data available in the catalog documenting the attributes of the data as well as metadata properties like value distributions, enums, etc.

Metrics logic stage
Transformation of the data into derived attributes/aggregates made available as metrics/features.

Creating data quality models today is ad hoc and cannot be generalized across different datasets. Checks are implemented using SQL joins as well as one-off scripts for analysis of monitoring statistics and logs. A generic comparing algorithm is required to relieve data users of the burden of coding while being flexible enough to cover most accuracy requirements. The checks can be a combination of generic data properties as well as business-specific logic.

Detect Quality Anomalies

Anomaly detection involves profiling the data properties and comparing them with historic trends to define expected ranges. Anomalies are indications that something is changing, and can help uncover data quality issues. Not all anomalies are related to data quality problems and may simply be a result of changes in configuration or schema that can cause the metric to shift away from the previous pattern. Telling the difference between true data quality problems and simple anomalies is challenging. There is no single algorithm that works best for all scenarios. Anomaly training is a big problem. Defining normal regions is very difficult, as the boundaries between anomalies and normal data are not precise. The definition of normal keeps evolving —what is considered normal today may be not normal in the future. Each false positive leads to an increase in the amount of time spent debugging and explaining the reason for the change.

Prevent Data Quality Issues

While the previous tasks were related to detecting data quality issues, this task is about preventing low-quality data records from being used in generating insights. For instance, consider a scenario where the business reporting dashboard shows a dip in metrics due to missing data records, or an ML model with online training exhibits prediction errors due to corrupted records used in training. At the time of ingestion, records with data quality issues are flagged based on accuracy rules and anomaly tracking. These records or partitions are not visible as a part of the dataset, which prevents data users from using the data. With human intervention, the data needs to be either cleaned of inconsistencies or discarded. There is a trade-off between data quality and availability. An aggressive approach to detecting and preventing low-quality data can lead to data availability issues (as illustrated in Figure 18-2). Conversely, higher data availability can come at the expense of data quality. The correct balance depends on the use case. For datasets that feed several downstream pipelines, ensuring high quality is more critical. Once the issue is resolved, backfilling of the ETLs is required to address data availability.

Figure 18-2. Avoiding low-quality data can lead to data availability issues; leaving quality unchecked ensures high availability but requires post-processing to ensure consistent data quality.

Defining Requirements

The effectiveness of the data quality service depends on the domain and type of insights being generated. For insights that are sensitive to high data precision, quality observability is a must-have. Every enterprise has to decide what level of each criteria they need (on the whole and for particular tasks). Implementing quality checks can become an exercise in boiling the ocean. It is important to prioritize and phase the key quality requirements by implementing quality models incrementally.

Detection and Handling Data Quality Issues

There are multiple different quality checks (*https://oreil.ly/rBWNU*), such as null value check, specific value check, schema validation check, column value duplicates, and uniqueness check. Further, there are several different dimensions of data quality checks. Apache Griffin (*https://oreil.ly/FxJTq*) defines the following dimensions of data quality: consistency, accuracy, completeness, auditability, orderliness, uniqueness, and timeliness. An alternate taxonomy (as shown in Figure 18-3) of data quality checks is based on first verifying the consistency of a single column within the table, multiple columns, and cross-database dependencies.

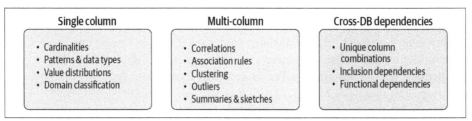

Figure 18-3. Taxonomy of data quality checks as defined by Abedjan et al. (https:// oreil.ly/mD7mz)

Data quality needs to support both batch and streaming data sources. The user can register the dataset to be used for a data quality check. The dataset can be batch data in an RDBMS or a Hadoop system or near real-time streaming data from Kafka, Storm, and other real-time data platforms. As a part of the requirements, an inventory of all the datastores needs to be created and prioritized for interoperability.

Another aspect of the requirements is defining the process of handling low-quality data once it is detected during the daily ingestion process. Handling of such records depends on how the datasets are structured. Append-only tables are easier to handle compared to in-place updates where older partitions can be modified. The process for handling low-quality data needs to define who is alerted, the response time SLA to resolve the issue, how to backfill the processing, and criteria for discarding the data.

Functional Requirements

The quality observability service needs to implement the following features:

Accuracy measurement
 Assessment of a dataset's accuracy made using absolute rules based on the data schema properties, value distributions, or business-specific logic.

Data profiling and anomaly detection
Statistical analysis and assessment of data values within the dataset and pre-built algorithmic functions to identify events that do not conform to an expected pattern in a dataset (indicating a data quality problem).

Proactive avoidance
Measures to prevent low-quality data records from mixing with the rest of the dataset.

Nonfunctional Requirements

Similar to any software design, the following are some of the key NFRs that should be considered in the design of the quality observability service:

Timeliness
The data quality checks can be executed in a timely fashion to detect issues faster.

Extensibility
The solution can work with multiple data systems.

Scalability
The solution needs to be designed to work on large volumes of data (on the order of PBs).

Intuitiveness
The solution should allow users to visualize the data quality dashboards and personalize their view of the dashboards.

Implementation Patterns

Corresponding to the existing task map, there are three levels of automation for the quality observability service (as shown in Figure 18-4). Each level corresponds to automating a combination of tasks that are currently either manual or inefficient:

Accuracy models pattern
Automates creation of models to verify accuracy of data at scale.

Profiling-based anomaly detection pattern
Automates detection of quality anomalies while reducing false positives.

Avoidance pattern
Proactively prevents low-quality records from polluting the dataset.

Data quality frameworks have been an active part of research. IEEE has a comprehensive survey (*https://oreil.ly/Gn_QT*) of data quality frameworks.

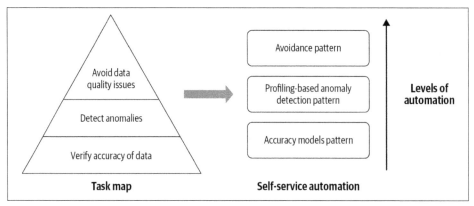

Figure 18-4. The different levels of automation for the query optimization service.

Accuracy Models Pattern

The accuracy models pattern calculates the accuracy of the dataset. The basic approach is to calculate the discrepancy between the incremental data records and the existing source dataset by matching their contents and examining their properties and relationships.

The pattern works as follows:

- The user defines the golden dataset as the source of truth. This is the ideal property associated with the dataset in terms of attribute data types, value ranges, and so on. The user defines mapping rules specifying the matching of the column values between the data records and the golden dataset. Data users or business small and medium-sized enterprises (SMEs) define the rules. For instance, a rule could specify that the phone number column cannot be null. Users also define their own specific functions.

- The mappings rules are run as quality jobs that are run continuously to calculate the data quality metrics. Metrics can be defined for different columns of data, such as rowcount, compressedBytes, nullCount, NumFiles, and Bytes. After retrieving the data, the model engine computes data quality metrics.

Popular open source implementations of the pattern are Amazon Deequ, Apache Griffin, and Netflix's Metacat.

Deequ (*https://oreil.ly/gYNoH*) is built on top of Apache Spark and is scalable for huge amounts of data. It provides constraint verification, allowing users to define test cases for quality reporting. Deequ provides built-in functionality for identifying constraints to be tested and computes metrics based on the tests. A common scenario in real-world deployments is growing datasets over time by appending new rows. Deequ supports stateful metrics (*https://oreil.ly/oV1ZS*) computations, providing a way to validate incremental data loads. Internally, Deequ computes states on data partitions, which can be aggregated and used to form the input to its metrics computations. These states can be used to update metrics for growing datasets cheaply.

Profiling-Based Anomaly Detection Pattern

This pattern focuses on detecting data quality issues based on automated analysis of historic data profiling. There are two parts to the pattern: a) Data profiling that aggregates historic characteristics of the dataset, and b) anomaly detection that provides the ability to predict data issues by applying mathematical algorithms. Overall, the goal of the pattern is to identify unusual data properties that are indicative of a quality issue.

The pattern works as follows:

- Data is profiled with different types of statistics:
  - Simple statistics that track for nulls, duplicate values, etc.
  - Summary statistics that track max, min, mean, deviation, etc.
  - Advanced statistics such as frequency distribution, correlated stats, etc.

  A history of these statistics is persisted along with other relevant events like configuration changes in systems and workloads.
- The historical trends are fed to mathematical and ML algorithms. The statistics are analyzed for the expected range of values. For instance, mean absolute deviation (MAD) calculates the average distance between each data record and the mean. The mean (average) of these differences is calculated based on the absolute value of each difference. Data records that fall outside the threshold are marked as an anomaly, indicating a quality issue. Similarly, ML algorithms like clustering techniques with Euclidean distances are also used. In reality, a diverse ensemble of algorithms is optimized for detecting diverse classes of anomalies and are capable of incorporating short- and long-term trends and seasonality.

There are multiple implementations of this pattern, namely Apache Griffin (*https:// oreil.ly/hCaAa*), LinkedIn's ThirdEye (*https://oreil.ly/isGfa*), and Amazon Deequ (*https://oreil.ly/GhP-d*).

To illustrate the pattern, we cover Apache Griffin. Data profiling is based on the column summary statistics calculated using Spark MLlib. The profiling jobs in Spark are automatically scheduled. The calculations are performed only once for all data type columns and persisted as metrics (as shown in Figure 18-5). For anomaly analysis, Griffin uses Bollinger Band and MAD algorithms.

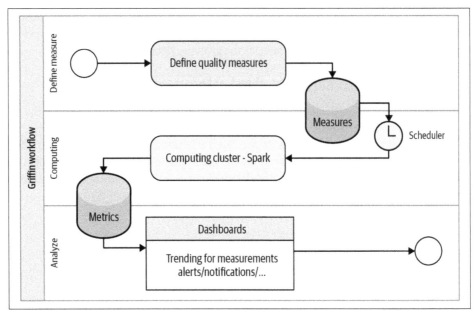

Figure 18-5. The internal workflow of Apache Griffin (from apache.org (https://oreil.ly/UMih1)).

Avoidance Pattern

This pattern prevents low-quality records from being merged with the rest of the dataset. It is a proactive approach to manage data quality in order to reduce the need for post-processing data wrangling. In the absence of this pattern, data with quality issues gets consumed by ML models and dashboards, leading to incorrect insights. Debugging insights for correctness is a nightmare that requires unsustainable fire-fighting on a case-by-case basis.

The following are popular approaches to implementing this pattern. Typically, both of these approaches are used together:

Schema enforcement
> In this approach, the schema is specified during data lake ingestion. The schema is verified and enforced at the time of ingestion to prevent data corruption before the data is ingested into the data lake. Databricks' Delta Lake implements this pattern.

Circuit breakers
> Analogous to the Circuit Breaker pattern in a microservices (*https://oreil.ly/GpPvt*) architecture, circuit breakers for data pipelines prevent low-quality data from propagating to downstream processes (as shown in Figure 18-6). The result is that data will be missing in the reports for time periods of low quality, but if

present, it is guaranteed to be correct. This proactive approach makes data availability directly proportional to data quality. Intuit's SuperGlue (*https://oreil.ly/-cYde*) and Netflix's WAP (*https://oreil.ly/3Rm9Z*) (Write Audit Push) implement this pattern.

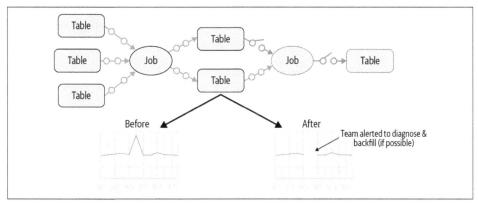

Figure 18-6. The data pipeline circuit breaker (from the O'Reilly Strata Conference, NY, 2018 (https://oreil.ly/HBPn4)).

To illustrate the circuit breaker approach, we first cover Netflix's WAP pattern. New data records are written in a separate partition. The partition is not added to the catalog and is not visible to applications. The partition is audited for quality. If the tests are passed, the partition details are pushed to the Hive catalog, making the records discoverable. A related pattern is Intuit's SuperGlue, which discovers pipeline lineage, analyzes data for accuracy and anomalies at each stage of the pipeline, and uses circuit breakers to prevent downstream processing. As shown in Figure 18-7, when quality issues are detected, the circuit moves from closed to open.

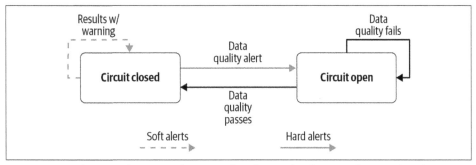

Figure 18-7. The state diagram of a circuit breaker in the data pipeline. A closed circuit lets the data continue flowing through the pipeline; an open circuit stops the downstream processing. (From the O'Reilly Strata Conference, NY, 2018 (https://oreil.ly/HBPn4)).

Depending on the confidence level, the circuit breaker pattern either generates an alert or completely stops the downstream processing. Figure 18-8 illustrates this with examples.

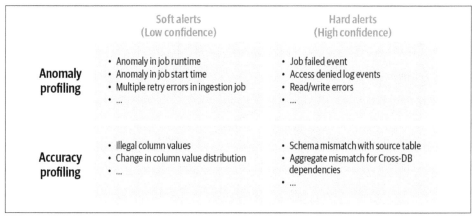

Figure 18-8. Examples corresponding to soft and hard alerts in the circuit breaker pattern (from the O'Reilly Strata Conference, NY, 2018 (https://oreil.ly/HBPn4)).

Summary

Ensuring the quality of the insights is one of the most challenging and critical aspects of the operationalize phase. Oftentimes, the issues are detected by end users who are using the dashboard or ML for decision making. The key success criteria of the quality observability service is to analyze the plethora of available signals for proactively detecting quality issues without inundating data users with false-positive alerts.

CHAPTER 19

Cost Management Service

We now have insights deployed in production with continuous monitoring for ensuring quality. The last piece of the operationalize phase is cost management. Cost management is especially critical in the cloud because the pay-as-you-go model increases linearly with usage (in contrast to a traditional buy-upfront, fixed-cost model). With data democratization, where data users can self-serve the journey to extract insights, there is a risk of wasted resources and unbounded costs; data users often spin up resources, and without actively leveraging them, which leads to low utilization. A single bad query running on high-end GPUs can accumulate thousands of dollars in a matter of hours, typically to the surprise of the data users. Cost management provides the visibility and controls needed to manage and optimize costs. It focuses on answering questions like:

- What are the dollars spent per application?
- Which teams are projected to spend more than their allocated budgets?
- Are there opportunities to reduce spend without impacting performance and availability?
- Are the allocated resources utilized appropriately?

Today, cost management presents a few pain points. First, there are many strategies for cost saving based on the specifics of the scenario. Data users are not experts in ever-evolving cloud offerings and aren't able to come up with strategies to save costs based on workload characteristics and performance SLAs. Second, data users struggle with efficiently scaling processing and taking advantage of the elasticity of the cloud. For instance, to process a backlog of queries, spinning 10 compute instances for an hour is equivalent in cost to one instance running for 10 hours. Third, cost allocation and chargeback to different teams with different budget allocations is difficult to track given that resources are not typically tagged, and discounts from cloud providers make true cost calculation difficult. Overall, cost management has no simple heuristic or approach, and is a balancing act of performance, spend, and utilization. *Time to optimize cost* slows down the overall time to insight given the time required for offline cost optimization of heavy production queries, continuous monitoring overhead (to avoid queries with significant cost), and periodically revisiting services used in the cloud to improve costs.

Ideally, the *cost management service* should be able to automatically manage resource supply and demand by scaling allocated resources in response to bursts in data processing workloads. It should automatically analyze and recommend cost-saving strategies by analyzing the running workloads, allocated resource properties, budgets, performance, and availability SLAs. It should provide cost observability in the form of fine-grained alerting and monitoring of budget usage across data pipelines, applications, and teams. By simplifying cost management for data users, the service improves the overall time to insight.

Journey Map

A large portion of today's massive amounts of data is being stored and processed in the cloud because of its many advantages, which author Abdul Quamar (*https://oreil.ly/wOKvX*) lists as scalability, elasticity, availability, low cost of ownership, and the overall economies of scale.

As enterprises move to the cloud, data users are expected to be aware of costs and actively optimize spend in all phases of the insight extraction journey. There are multiple choices in the pay-as-you-go model, especially with serverless processing, where cost is based on the amount of data scanned by the query. Data processing costs can be quite significant if not carefully governed.

Monitoring Cost Usage

Cloud processing accounts are usually set up by data engineering and IT teams. A single processing account supports multiple different teams of data scientists, analysts, and users. The account hosts either shared services used by multiple teams (interleaving of requests) or dedicated services provisioned for apps with strict performance SLAs. Budgets are allocated to each team based on business needs. Data users within these teams are expected to be within their monthly budget and ensure the queries are delivering the appropriate cost benefit.

This presents multiple challenges. In a democratized platform, it is important for users to be also responsible for their allocated budgets and be able to make trade-off decisions between budget, business needs, and processing cost. Providing cost visibility to data users is not easy for shared services. Ideally, the user should be able to get the predicted cost of the processing or training at the time they issue their request.

Resources spun up by teams are often not tagged, making accountability difficult. A lack of knowledge of the appropriate instance types, such as reserved versus on-demand versus spot-compute instances, can lead to significant money wasted.

Continuous Cost Optimization

There are several big data services in the cloud that have different cost models. Data users perform two phases of cost optimizations. The first phase takes place at the time of designing the pipeline. Here, options are evaluated for available pay-as-you-go models that best match the workload and SLA requirements. The second phase happens on an ongoing basis, analyzing the utilization and continuously optimizing the configuration. Cost optimization is a continual process of refinement and improvement. The goal is to build and operate a cost-aware system that achieves business outcomes while minimizing costs. In other words, a cost-optimized system will fully utilize all resources, achieve an outcome at the lowest possible price point, and meet functional requirements.

Considering the growing number of permutations associated with cloud offerings, it is nontrivial to pick the right design and configuration for the deployment. For example, for data processing, it is possible to pay for autoscaling compute instances or leverage the serverless model and pay based on the amount of data scanned by the query. The right option depends on workload patterns, data footprint, team expertise, business agility needs, and the predictability of SLAs.

Minimizing Time to Optimize Cost

Time to optimize cost involves selecting cost-effective services, configuring and operating the services, and applying cost optimization based on workload on an ongoing basis. The time spent is divided into three buckets: expenditure observability, matching supply and demand, and continuous cost optimization.

Expenditure Observability

This includes alerting, budgeting, monitoring, forecasting, reporting, and fine-grained attribution of costs. The goal is to provide visibility and governance to business and technical stakeholders. The capability of attributing resource costs to projects and teams drives efficient usage behavior and helps reduce waste. Observability allows for more informed decisions about where to allocate resources within the business.

Observability is built on aggregating and analyzing multiple different types of data, namely inventory of resources, dollar costs and associated discounts, resource tags, mapping of users to teams/projects, usage, and performance. Attribution of costs is a challenge that is currently accomplished using account structuring and tagging.

Accounts are structured as either one-parent-to-many-children or a single account for all of the processing. Tagging allows overlapping business and organizational information onto billing and usage data. For a shared managed service, attributing costs to projects is tricky to infer accurately. Another aspect of cost observability is alerting on configuration changes where resources are no longer being used or where orphaned projects no longer have an owner. A detailed inventory of resources and configuration needs to be tracked continuously.

Matching Supply and Demand

This includes automatically scaling up and down the allocated resources. There are three steps. First, the service automatically adds and removes server nodes to the processing cluster based on policies. Alternatively, the processing clusters can be considered as ephemeral and spun up to process a job. Second, as part of scaling, the service leverages different supply options like mixing CPU instance types, namely spot, reserved, and on-demand instances. Third, the service appropriately maps the workload characteristics to the available managed services. For a service processing a high load of queries, paying per query might be quite expensive compared to paying for allocated cluster resources.

The key challenge is achieving balance between the economic benefits of just-in-time supply needs and the need to provision for resource failures, high availability, and provision time. Spinning up on demand has an impact on performance.

Continuous Cost Optimization

These tasks aim to optimize spend and close the gap between resource allocations across projects and the corresponding business needs. Optimization is ongoing, and enterprises track (*https://oreil.ly/SC6aY*) various metrics:

- Reducing the cost per transaction or output of a system by x% every 6 or 12 months
- Increasing the percentage of on-demand compute instances that are turned on and off every day to 80–100%
- Keeping the number of "always on" instances running as reserved instances close to 100%

The key challenge today with cost optimization is the plethora of options available in the cloud; understanding the value of these strategies and their impacts is nontrivial. It requires both the expertise and understanding of a wide range of factors, namely storage tiering, compute instance types, flavors of managed services (serverless data versus traditional), and geographic distribution. Similarly, there is a growing range of compute options that require an understanding of hardware components related to compute, memory, and networking. The approaches for optimization differ based on workload types, such as transactional databases, analytical query processing, graph processing, and so on.

Defining Requirements

There are no silver bullet heuristics for cost optimization. The importance of the cost management service depends on the scale of cloud usage. For enterprises operating many of their data platforms in the cloud, a cost management service is a must-have. Each data team having siloed accounts simplifies expenditure observability, but it becomes a management nightmare, with continuous cost optimization across hundreds of accounts.

Pain Points Questionnaire

Depending on the specifics of the deployment, there are different cost management pain points that need to be prioritized. The following questions can help uncover the existing pain points:

- Is the budget out of control, with no clear path to reduce spend without impacting business needs?
- Is there an alignment gap between the cloud spend and business prioritization?
- Is there a low overall utilization of the allocated cloud resources?
- Is there a clear backlog of opportunities to lower cost by making configuration changes to the deployed pipelines?
- Is a significant percentage of resources untagged?
- Is a significant percentage of managed services being used?
- Are the cloud budget allocations for different projects based on forecasts?
- Is there proactive alerting to avoid costly processing that data users may not be aware of?
- Is the workload running on the cloud predictable instead of ad hoc?

Functional Requirements

The cost management service needs to support following core functionality:

Expenditure observability
    Providing alerting and monitoring on budget allocation, cost and usage reporting (CUR), resources used by different projects, forecast reports, and resource tag support.

Automated scaling

Policies to automatically scale resources up and down, as well as spin up processing clusters on demand.

Optimization advisor

Recommendation to improve costs through shutting down unused resources, changing configuration and policies, changing resource types, using different services for the workload type, recommendations on compute types, reservations, and managed services to better match the workload characteristics.

Interoperability

Interoperability with the inventory of existing services deployed in the cloud: databases, storage, serving datastores, compute instances, and managed services. Supporting different pay-as-you-go cost models.

Nonfunctional Requirements

Similar to any software design, the following are some of the key NFRs that should be considered in the design of the cost management service:

Intuitive dashboards

The goal is to create a culture of cost awareness and optimization among a spectrum of users. The dashboards and reports need to be intuitive.

Extensible support

The service should be easily extendable for a growing number of systems and services. Data users, finance, executives, and auditors should be able to customize the dashboards to extract actionable insights.

Implementation Patterns

Corresponding to the existing task map, there are three levels of automation for the cost management service (as shown in Figure 19-1). Each level corresponds to automating a combination of tasks that are currently either manual or inefficient:

Continuous cost monitoring pattern

Correlates actual cost, per-project usage, and data-user activity to create an actionable monitoring dashboard for forecasting and budget alerts.

Automated scaling pattern

Scales the resource allocation up and down, based on actual demand, to save costs.

Cost advisor pattern

Analyzes current usage for applicability of well-known heuristics and practices to recommend cost optimization strategies.

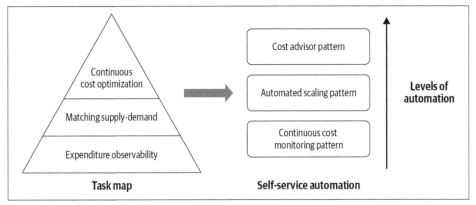

Figure 19-1. The different levels of automation for the cost management service

Continuous Cost Monitoring Pattern

The goal of this pattern is to aggregate the different aspects associated with cost tracking, and provide a correlated and actionable view to data users, finance, and executives. Today, users struggle between different views—for example, billing invoice, billing usage console, budgeting tools, cost forecast, and DIY dashboards.

At a high level, the pattern works as follows:

Defining budgets
Budgets are defined for different projects and their corresponding teams. These budgets include both the exploratory cost as well as running their insights in production.

Resource tagging
A tag is a simple label consisting of a user-defined key and an optional value that is used to make it easier to manage, search, and filter resources. Tags provide a more granular view of the resource consumption pattern and typically specify team, project, environment (dev, staging, prod), and application names associated with the resources. There are reactive and proactive approaches for tag governance. Reactive governance identifies improper tags, manually or using scripts. Proactive governance ensures standardized tags are applied consistently at resource creation. An example of proactive tags is a *createdBy* tag, which is available from some cloud providers (*https://oreil.ly/oh14t*) and applied automatically for cost allocation purposes and resources that might otherwise be uncategorized.

Aggregation of information
Cost monitoring requires an aggregation of multiple sources: a) Inventory of resources and corresponding tags, b) resource usage, c) billing rates and any discounted costs associated with the resources, and d) data users and their associated teams and projects (used for attribution of costs incurred in exploration or

sandbox environments). The information is aggregated and correlated into a single pane of glass.

Defining alerts
Alerts are set when costs or usage exceed (or are forecasted to exceed) the budgeted amount. Alerts are also defined on utilization drops below a defined threshold.

Forecasting costs
Based on usage trends, the future costs are forecasted for data users. Usage forecasting uses ML that learns usage trends and uses that information to provide a forecast of the future user needs.

An open source example of the continuous cost monitoring pattern is Intuit's Cost-Buddy (*https://oreil.ly/ar6KG*). It combines usage, pricing, resource tags, and team hierarchies to provide monitoring and forecasting for teams. It was built especially for shared data platforms where multiple teams are using the same data processing account. It calculates key cost-based KPIs, namely reserved instances coverage and utilization, daily run rate, underutilized resources, percentage of untagged resources, and percentage variance (budget to actual). Another example of the pattern is Lyft's AWS cost management (*https://oreil.ly/HyVvN*).

Automated Scaling Pattern

This pattern focuses on leveraging the elasticity of the cloud in response to increased workload requests. Traditionally, for on-premise deployments, given the lead time of weeks and months in adding resources, provisioning was planned with overallocation in mind. Given the elasticity of the cloud, the *just-in-case* provisioning has been replaced by *just-in-time* provisioning. This approach reduces idle resources and delivers consistent performance, even with surges in the number of requests. Automated scaling is a balancing act, with the goal of minimizing waste while at the same time taking into account boot-up times, availability, and performance SLAs.

At a high level, the pattern works as follows:

Scaling trigger
Monitoring solutions collect and track the number of outstanding requests, queue depth, utilization, service time latencies, and so on. Based on user-configured thresholds, a trigger is generated for scaling. The trigger can also be based on time.

Evaluating policies
Different types of policies can be used for scaling. Typically, a combination of demand-based scaling, time-based scaling, and buffering policies are used. The

most common policies are custom start and stop schedules of resources (e.g., turning off development resources over the weekend).

Mixing and matching resources

During scaling, a combination of resources can be used to best serve the requests at the cheapest cost. The scaling can mix spot-compute instances with reserved and on-demand instances.

Scaling needs to take into account the warm-up time of the newly provisioned resources and the transient impact on performance and availability SLAs. The speed of scaling can be reduced by using prebaked machine images that trade off configurability of these instances. Autoscaling is now a primitive capability for all cloud providers. Also, there are third-party solutions, such as GorillaStack, Skeddly, and ParkMyCloud.

There are different types of policies (*https://oreil.ly/7veSB*) for scaling matching supply with demand: demand-based, buffer-based, and time-based. Typically, deployments use a combination of these policy types:

Demand-based scaling

Automatically increase the number of resources during demand spikes to maintain performance and decrease capacity when demand subsides to reduce costs. The typical trigger metrics are CPU utilization, network throughput, latencies, and so on. Policies need to take into account how quickly new resources can be provisioned, and the size of the margin between supply and demand to cope with the rate of change in demand as well as resource failures.

Buffer-based scaling

A buffer is a mechanism for applications to communicate with processing platforms when they are running at different rates over time. The requests from the producers are posted in a queue, and decouple the throughput rate of producers from that of consumers. These policies are typically applied to background processing that generates significant load that doesn't need to be processed immediately. One of the prerequisites for this pattern is idempotence of the requests such that it allows a consumer to process a message multiple times, but when a message is subsequently processed, it has no effect on downstream systems or storage.

Time-based scaling

For predictable demand, a time-based approach is used. Systems can be scheduled to scale up or down at defined times. The scaling is not dependent on utilization levels of the resources. The advantage is resource availability without any delays due to startup procedures.

Cost Advisor Pattern

The cost advisor pattern analyzes the workloads and resource usage patterns to rec-ommend strategies for optimizing costs. Cost optimization is a continuous process, with recommendations evolving over time. Typically, the pattern is implemented as a collection of *if-then* rules that are periodically run within the cloud account. If the conditions in the rule match the deployment, then the recommendation is shown. Typically, the recommendations are applied based on the complexity of the change instead of the expected impact. There are multiple examples of this pattern, such as AWS Trusted Advisor and Azure Advisor. Cloud Custodian (*https://oreil.ly/MAvYr*) is an open source rule-based engine; Ice (*https://oreil.ly/tFPlX*) is an optimization tool originally developed by Netflix. There are third-party tools such as Stax, Cloudability, CloudHealth, and Datadog.

While a comprehensive list of cost optimization rules is beyond the scope of this book, there are certain principles that the rules implement, both generically as well as in the context of deployed managed services:

Eliminating idle resources
> This is low-hanging fruit where users often spin up resources and forget to shut them down.

Choosing the right compute instances
> The biggest percentage of cloud expenditure is related to compute costs. There are two aspects of picking the right instance types. The first is picking the instance with the right compute, network, and storage bandwidths based on the workload requirements. The second is picking the right purchasing options, namely on demand, spot, and reserved instances.

Tiering storage and optimizing data transfer costs
> Given the growing amount of data, ensure that data is archived to cheaper tiers, especially when it is not used frequently. Also, data transfer costs can accumulate significantly.

Leveraging workload predictability
> Separate workloads that are frequent and predictable (for instance, a 24/7 data-base workload) from infrequent, unpredictable workloads (for instance, interac-tive exploratory queries). Cost advisor rules apply different strategy recommendations to these workloads, such as using long-running processing clusters, versus per-job ephemeral clusters, versus serverless (such as pay-per-query) patterns.

Optimizing application design
> This includes more fundamental design choices, such as geographic location selection, use of managed services, and so on.

Summary

To harness the infinite resources available in the cloud, enterprises need infinite budgets! Cost management is critical to ensure that the finite budgets available for data platforms align effectively with business priorities. Given the multitude of choices, cost management is an expert-in-a-box for continuously improving costs for varying workload properties.

Index

A

A/B testing
  other terms for, 177
  uses of, 177
A/B testing deployment, 220
A/B testing service
  automated experiment optimization in, 185
  defined, 178
  experiment design in, 180, 182
  experiment execution in, 181
  experiment optimization in, 183
  experiment specification pattern in, 184
  experimental unit in, 179-180
  feature implementation and design in, 180
  implementation patterns in, 183-186
  iterative testing loop in, 181
  metrics definition pattern in, 185
  model deployment and, 217
  multi-armed bandits in, 186
  open source technology in, 178
  overall evaluation criteria in, 180
  re-randomization in, 184
  results analysis in, 181
  sample in, 180
  scaling in, 182
  time to A/B test metric in, 181-183
  treatment in, 179
access control
  attribute-based, 40, 47
  in data rights governance service, 121, 125-127
  in search service, 41
  out-of-bound, 125
  role-based, 40, 47

  in search service, 38, 40
  use-case dependent, 125-127
accuracy models pattern, 234
ACID
  data aggregation and, 6
  in data lake management service, 93, 94, 96, 102, 104
  in transactional pattern, 104
advanced data management pattern, 105-106
Amazon Macie, 123
Amundsen, 45
analytical transformation patterns, 113-114
Apache Airflow, 210, 211
Apache Atlas, 32, 126
Apache Beam, 140, 162
Apache Calcite, 127, 197
Apache Drill, 138-139
Apache Druid, 88
Apache Flume, 75-76
Apache Gobblin, 74, 125
Apache Griffin, 232, 235, 236
Apache Kafka, 73
  in quality observability service, 232
  metadata formats in, 25
  push-pull indexer pattern in, 43
  source-specific connectors pattern in, 30
Apache Nifi, 149, 150
Apache Pulsar, 87-88
Apache Ranger, 47, 126
Apache Sqoop, 71
artifacts
  in search service, 42
  indexing of, 37
  reusing for prototyping in search service, 36

Athena, 103
attributed-based access control (ABAC), 40, 47
automated experiment optimization, 185
automated tuning pattern
    in model training service, 161, 163
    in query optimization service, 200
automatic query routing pattern, 137-138
AutoML, 163, 164
avoidance pattern
    in quality observability service, 236-237
    in query optimization service, 196-197
Avro, 99
AWS Data Lake Formation, 126
Azkaban, 30

B
backfilling
    defined, 53
    in data transformation service, 145, 146, 151
    in feature store service, 53, 57
    in pipeline orchestration service, 208
    in quality observability service, 231
batch compute pipeline, 58
    weaknesses of, 72
batch ingestion pattern, 70-72
    map phase in, 71
    partition phase in, 71
    reduce phase in, 71
    strengths of, 72
big data, 2
    (see also data)
    immutability in, 96
    users vs. engineers in, 2
bot filtering, 81
    in clickstream tracking service, 83, 85-86
Brazilian General Data Protection Act, 115
bucket testing (see A/B testing)
build phase, in insight extraction, 7-8
business taxonomy, 33

C
California Consumer Privacy Act (CCPA), 65, 115
canary model deployment, 220
catalog access control pattern, 41, 46-49
    classification in, 47
    define phase in, 47
    enforcement phase in, 47
Celery, 212

change data capture (CDC) ingestion pattern
    in data movement service, 72-75
    generation of events in, 73
    merge of events in, 73
    onboarding in, 74
    open source technology in, 73
    phases of, 73
    published on event bus, 73
    strengths of, 74
    weaknesses of, 74
change management
    in data movement service, 65
change tracking
    in metadata catalog service, 25
classification
    in catalog access control pattern, 47
cleaning
    in insight extraction, 6
clickstream data
    defined, 77
    users of, 78, 79
clickstream events
    in insight extraction, 5
clickstream tracking service
    bot filtering in, 81, 83, 85-86
    building insights in, 82
    client-side events in, 82
    complex event processing in, 87
    consumption patterns in, 87-88
    defining requirements in, 82-84
    enrichment requirements checklist in, 83-84
    event attributes in, 82
    event collection in, 85
    event enrichment in, 81
    event proxy to targets in, 85
    event summarization in, 83
    event verification in, 85
    identity stitching in, 82
    implementation patterns in, 84-88
    instrumentation pattern in, 84-85
    instrumentation requirements in, 82-83
    managing instrumentation in, 80
    open source technology in, 85, 86
    privacy filtering in, 83
    rich context in, 81
    rule-based enrichment patterns in, 85
    server-side event collection in, 83
    sessionization in, 81, 83, 86
    third-party source collection in, 83

time to click metrics and, 79-82
user agent parsing in, 83
user context enrichment pattern in, 86
Cloudera, 99
cluster clogs, 190
complex event processing (CEP), 87
compliance, 6
(see also data rights)
data movement service and, 65, 66, 68
data rights, 6
compression
in data lake management service, 100
in data rights governance service, 123
in data transformation service, 150
in model deploy service, 223
in query optimization service, 192
concept drift, 221
connect phase, in push-pull indexer pattern, 42
consumption patterns, 87-88
continuous integration service
defined, 168
defining requirements in, 170-172
ETL change integration in, 168-169
experiment tracking in, 169
experiment tracking module in, 170, 171
implementation patterns in, 172-174
levels of automation in, 172
pipeline packaging module in, 171
programmable tracking pattern in, 172, 173
reproducible deployment in, 170
reproducible project pattern in, 172, 174
testing automation module in, 170, 172
testing validation in, 170
testing validation pattern in, 172
time to integrate metric in, 169-170
validation of schema changes in, 169
controlled experiment (see A/B testing)
cost
continuous monitoring of, 9
in data lake management service, 95
in data virtualization service, 136
in feature store service, 52, 53
in model training service, 160, 161
in pipeline orchestration service, 208
in query optimization service, 196
cost management service
automated scaling pattern in, 246-247
continuous cost monitoring pattern in,
245-246

cost advisor pattern in, 248
defined, 240
defining requirements in, 243-244
extensibility in, 244
implementation patterns in, 244
interoperability in, 244
levels of automation in, 245
nonfunctional requirements in, 244
pain point questionnaire for, 243
scaling in, 242, 244
time to optimize cost metric and, 241-243
cost optimization, continuous, 241, 242-243
cost usage monitoring, 240
Cost-Buddy (Intuit), 246
curation of data, 110
custom extractors, 30
customer data life cycle, 118

D
Dali, 126, 127
data, 1, 4
(see also big data)
(see also metadata)
clickstream, 77
in data warehousing era, 3
deficiencies in, 1
from raw, to insights, 3-4
self-service platform failures, 2-3
users vs. engineers, 2
data aggregation, in data movement service, 68
data cleaning
in clickstream tracking service, 84
in data wrangling service, 109
data documentation, 33
data drift, 221
data ingestion
data scale in, 67
refresh lag and, 67
source and target datastore technologies in,
66
data ingestion configuration, 65
data ingestion module, 66
data lake
data life cycle management and, 93
data movement service and, 64
kappa architecture with, 93-94
lambda architecture with, 93-94
data lake deletion pattern, 124-125
data lake management service

advanced data management pattern in, 105-106
Avro in, 99
batching and streaming data flows in, 96
CSV files in, 99
data access and usage tracking in, 95
data life cycle primitives pattern in, 102-104
data rollback in, 95
data updates in, 96
defined, 94
Delta lake transaction log in, 103, 104
document data model in, 101
file formats in, 98-100
graph data model in, 101
impact of, 134
incremental updates in, 104
JSON in, 99
key-value data model in, 101
namespace zones in, 97
ORCFile in, 99
primitive life cycle management with, 95-96
requirements in, 97-102
schema evolution in, 95, 103
SequenceFile in, 99
serving layers in, 100-102
text files in, 99
time to data lake management in, 97
transactional pattern in, 104
TSV files in, 99
versioning in, 95, 103
wide-column data model in, 101
data life cycle primitives pattern, 102-104
data movement service
  aggregation and, 63-64
  aggregation in, 68
  as pain point, 63
  batch ingestion pattern in, 70-72
  change data capture ingestion pattern in, 72
  change management in, 65
  compliance and, 65
  compliance module in, 66
  compliance requirements in, 68
  data ingestion configuration and, 65
  data lakes and, 64
  data quality verification and, 65-66
  data scale in, 67
  data store categories in, 66
  event aggregation pattern in, 75-76
  failure recovery in, 69

  filtering in, 68
  format transformation in, 68
  implementation patterns in, 70-76
  ingestion module in, 66
  ingestion requirements in, 66-67
  levels of automation in, 70
  microservices paradigm, 64
  monitoring in, 69
  need for, 63
  nonfunctional requirements in, 69
  onboarding in, 74
  open source technology in, 70, 73
  refresh lag and, 67
  requirements in, 66, 70
  source and target datastore technologies in, 66
  time to data availability, 64-66
  transformation module in, 66
  transformation requirements in, 68
  verification module in, 66
  verification requirements in, 69
  with exploratory analysis across sources, 64
  with processed data to serving stores, 64
  with raw data to specialized query engines, 64
data profiling stats, 25
data quality monitoring reports, 228
data quality verification, 65-66
data rights, 6
  (see also compliance)
  access to, 115
  collection of, 115
  compliance, 6
  data lakes and, 96
  deletion of, 115
  laws, 116
  use of, 115
data rights compliance, 6
  sensitive data discovery and classification pattern in, 123-124
data rights governance service
  access control in, 121
  customer data life cycle in, 118
  data formats in, 120
  data lake deletion pattern in, 124-125
  datasets in, 118
  defined, 117
  for execution of data rights requests, 117
  functional requirements in, 121

identification of customer data in, 120
implementation patterns in, 122-127
in-bound control in, 126
interoperability in, 120-121
levels of automation in, 122
limiting data access with, 119
lineage tracking in, 120
machine learning in, 123
metadata catalog in, 121
model retraining in, 118
nonfunctional requirements in, 122
out-of-bound control in, 125
pain point questionnaire for, 120
personally identifiable information in, 120,
    121, 123
processing engines in, 121
requirements in, 119-122
table management in, 120
time to compliance metric in, 118-119
use-case dependent access control in,
    125-127
data rollback, 95
data store categories, 66
data transformation module, 66
data transformation service
automated code generation in, 146
backfill processing in, 146
data-driven storytelling and, 144
defined, 143
defining requirements in, 145-147
execution patterns in, 151
functional requirements in, 146
implementation patterns in, 147-151
incremental processing in, 146
nonfunctional requirements in, 147
query processing in, 145
scalability in, 147
time to transform metric and, 144-145
transformation execution in, 145
transformation implementation in, 144-145
transformation operations in, 145
data updates
in data movement service, 67, 70, 72, 73
in clickstream tracking service, 87
in data lake management service, 96, 104
in search service, 42, 43
in metadata catalog service, 26
in search service, 39
data verification module, 66

data verification requirements, in data move-
    ment service, 69
data virtualization service
automatic query routing pattern in, 137-138
cost in, 136
data sources in, 132
debuggability in, 136
defined, 132
defining requirements in, 134-136
discovery phase in, 132
execution environment in, 133
extensibility in, 135
federated query pattern in, 140
functional requirements in, 135
interoperability in, 135
joining data across silos in, 134
levels of automation in, 136
need for, 134
observability in, 135
operational requirements in, 135
operationalization phase in, 132
pain point analysis in, 134
polyglot queries in, 133
processing cluster in, 132-133
unified query pattern in, 138-140
data wrangling
defined, 6
in feature computation, 56
pain points in, 107
requirements in, 110
time to wrangle metric and, 12
data wrangling service
analytical transformation patterns in,
    113-114
cleaning in, 109
data curation in, 110
defined, 108
discovery in, 108
enriching in, 109
exploratory data analysis patterns in,
    112-113
implementation patterns in, 111-114
levels of automation in, 112
machine learning in, 113
requirements in, 111
structuring in, 109
time to wrangle metric and, 109
validation in, 109
visualization in, 110

data-aware continuous training pattern, 161,
    164-166
Databricks Delta, 103
datasets
    analysis of, 23
    in data rights governance service, 118
    in experiment tracking module, 171
    in hybrid search ranking pattern, 45
    indexing of, 37
    in metadata catalog service, 23
    in search service, 36
    searching, in insight extraction, 4-5
    with owner-sourced description, 46
Debezium, 73
debuggability
    data lake management service and, 95
    data wrangling service and, 111
    in feature store service, 54
    in model training service, 156
    insight quality and, 9
    metadata catalog service and, 23, 27
    pipeline orchestration and, 9
    quality monitoring and, 228
Deequ (Amazon), 234
define phase, in catalog access control pattern,
    47
Delta Lake transaction log, 103, 104
dependency authoring patterns, 209-211
directed acyclic graph (DAG), 162, 165, 174,
    205, 210
discovery
    in data virtualization service, 132
    in data wrangling service, 108
    in insight extraction, 4-5
    of dataset metadata, 4
distributed training orchestrator pattern, 161,
    162-163
Divolte Collector, 86, 87
Docker, 170, 207, 219
document data model, 101
domain-specific language (DSL)
    in A/B testing service, 185
    in data transformation service, 148, 149
    in feature store service, 59
    in pipeline orchestration service, 210
Dr. Elephant, 198
drift monitoring, 218

E

ELT (Extract-Load-Transform)
    business logic and, 143
    in data transformation service, 149
enforcement phase, in catalog access control
    pattern, 47
enrichment, 6
    in data movement service, 68
    in clickstream tracking service, 77, 79, 81,
        84, 86
    in metadata catalog service, 22, 31, 32
ETL (Extract-Transform-Load)
    in data transformation service, 149
ETL (Extract-Transform-Load)
    business logic and, 143
    in continuous integration service, 168-169
    in data transformation service, 147
    in quality observability service, 231
    in query parsing, 31
event aggregation pattern
    in data movement service, 75-76
    event aggregation in, 75
    event forwarding in, 75
    strengths of, 76
    weaknesses of, 76
event enrichment, 81
event forwarding, 75
execution stats, 31
experiment specification pattern, 184-185
experiment tracking, 169
experiment tracking module, 170, 171
exploratory data analysis (EDA) patterns,
    112-113
extensibility
    in data movement service, 76
    in clickstream tracking service, 85
    in cost management service, 244
    in data rights governance service, 122
    in data virtualization service, 135
    in pipeline orchestration service, 209
    in quality observability service, 233
    in search service, 43
extract phase, in push-pull indexer pattern, 42
Extract-Load-Transform (ELT)
    in insight extraction, 7
Extract-Transform-Load (ETL)
    in insight extraction, 7

F

failure recovery, in data movement service, 69
FBLearner Flow, 2
feasibility analysis, for search service, 36
feature analysis, 57
feature groups, 56
feature registry pattern, 57
  feature registry store in, 61
  feature values store in, 60
  strengths of, 61
  weakness of, 62
feature serving
  feature groups in, 56
  in feature store service, 56-57
feature spec, 59
feature store service
  batch compute pipeline in, 58
  defined, 51-52
  defining requirements in, 55-57
  examples of, 58
  feature analysis in, 57
  feature computation in, 55
  feature pipeline and, 53
  feature registry pattern in, 57, 60-62
  feature serving and, 54
  feature serving in, 56-57
  feature spec in, 59
  feature values store in, 60
  finding available features for, 53
  hybrid feature computation pattern in, 57,
    58-60
  implementation patterns in, 57-62
  in model training service, 156
  intuitive interface in, 57
  minimization of time to featurize in, 53-55
  monitoring in, 57
  nonfunctional requirements in, 57
  open source technology in, 58
  scaling in, 56
  streaming compute pipeline in, 58
feature values store, 60
federated persistence, 30
federated query pattern, 140-141
feedback phase, in hybrid search ranking pattern, 45
file formats
  in data lake management service, 98-100
  in metadata catalog service, 25
filtering

bot, 81, 85-86
  in data movement service, 68
  privacy, 83
Fluent Bit, 76
Fluentd, 76
format transformation, 68

G

General Data Protection Regulation (GDPR),
  65, 115
graph data model, 101

H

Hadoop, 139
  (see also MapReduce)
  in data movement service, 66, 71
  in data lake management service, 104
  in quality observability service, 232
  in search service, 47
  metadata catalog service and, 30, 32
heuristics
  in query optimization service, 198
  in search service, 44, 45
Hopsworks feature store, 61
Hudi, 104
Hue, 197
hybrid feature computation pattern, 57
  batch compute pipeline in, 58
  feature spec in, 59
  streaming compute pipeline in, 58
  strengths of, 60
  weakness of, 60
hybrid search ranking pattern, 41, 44-46
  datasets in, 45
  feedback phase in, 45
  lineage fan-out in, 46
  ranking phase in, 44
  scoring in, 45

I

identity stitching, 82
implementation patterns
  in data movement service, 70-76
  in A/B testing service, 183-186
  in clickstream tracking service, 84-88
  in continuous integration service, 172-174
  in cost management service, 244-248
  in data rights governance service, 122-127

in data transformation service, 147-151
in data virtualization service, 136-141
in data wrangling service, 111-114
in feature store service, 57-62
in model deploy service, 221-226
in model training service, 161-166
in pipeline orchestration service, 209
in quality observability service, 233-237
in query optimization service, 196-201
in search service, 41-49
in metadata catalog service, 29-33
in-bound control, 126
indexer module, 38
indexing
    in search service, 39
indexing, in search service, 37
India Personal Data Protection Bill, 115
insight extraction
    cost monitoring in, 9
    discovery phase in, 4-5
    operationalization phase in, 8-10
    preparation phase in, 6
    quality monitoring in, 9
instrumentation pattern
    event collection in, 85
    event proxy to targets in, 85
    event verification in, 85
    in clickstream tracking service, 84-85
interoperability
    in data warehousing era, 3
    in cost management service, 244
    in data lake management service, 98, 99
    in data rights governance service, 120-121
    in data virtualization service, 135
    in pipeline orchestration service, 207
    in query optimization service, 195
IP2Geo, 81, 83, 86

J
JSON
    in clickstream tracking service, 80, 84, 88
    in data lake management service, 99
    in data quality monitoring, 229
    in data rights governance service, 125
    in data virtualization service, 133

K
kappa architecture, 93-94
key-value data model, 101

Keystone (Netflix), 151, 152
Knowledge Repo, 42
knowledge scaling, 24

L
label leakage, 54
lamda architecture, 93-94
lineage
    as metadata category, 40
    tracking in data rights governance, 120
lineage correlation pattern, 29, 31-32
lineage fan-out, 46
LookML, 149

M
machine learning, 153, 168
    (see also continuous integration service)
    (see also model training)
    data inefficiencies in, 1
    in data rights governance service, 123
    in data transformation service, 144
    in data wrangling service, 113
    feature store service and, 51-52
    in insight extraction, 7, 9
    insight platforms, 2
    model deployment, 9
    pipeline collaboration, 168
    taxonomies in, 159
    time to featurize metric and, 11
map phase, 71
MapReduce, 139
    (see also Hadoop)
    in data movement service, 71, 72, 74
    in data virtualization service, 139
    in model training service, 157
Marmaray, 74
Maslow's hierarchy of needs, 16
MaxMind, 81
Meson (Netflix), 212, 213
Metacat catalog, 30, 43
metadata
    as pain point, 21
    data quality and, 4
    in data rights governance service, 121
    discovery, in insight extraction, 4
    formats, 25
    in model training service, 164
    in query optimization service, 197
    lineage, 25

logical, 24
operational, 25
physical, 24
schema-on-read approach with, 21, 22
schema-on-write approach with, 21, 22
technical, 24
time to interpret metric with, 4
metadata catalog service
automation levels of, 29
change tracking in, 25
custom extractors in, 30
datasets in, 23
defined, 22
defining requirements in, 26-28
execution stats in, 31
federated persistence in, 30
implementation patterns in, 29-33
knowledge scaling with, 24
lineage correlation pattern in, 29, 31
open source technology in, 29
operational metadata extraction in, 25-26, 28
pipeline correlation in, 31
query parsing in, 31
schema inference and, 25
source-specific connectors pattern in, 29-30
team knowledge in, 26, 28
team knowledge pattern in, 32
technical metadata extraction in, 24-25, 27
time to interpret with, 24
Metadata extraction, from video
team knowledge pattern in, 29
metrics
time to A/B test, 13, 181-183
time to click, 12, 77, 79-82
time to click metrics, 5
time to compliance, 6, 10, 12, 118-119
time to data availability, 5, 12, 64-66
time to data lake management, 6, 12, 97-102
time to deploy, 9, 14, 217-218
time to featurize, 5, 11, 52, 53
time to find, 5, 10, 11, 37
time to insight, 10
time to insight quality, 9, 14, 229-231
time to integrate, 8, 13, 169-170
time to interpret, 4, 10, 11, 24
time to optimize, 8, 13, 191-193
time to optimize cost, 10, 14, 241-243
time to orchestrate, 9, 14, 205-206

time to train, 7, 13, 156-158
time to transform, 7, 13, 143, 144-145
time to virtualize, 7, 13
time to wrangle, 6, 12, 109
metrics definition pattern, 185
Michelangelo (Uber), 2, 59, 224, 226
microservices paradigm, 64
missing data aggregation, 5
MLeap, 219
MLflow Model, 223
MLflow Project, 174, 175
MLflow Tracking, 173
model debugging, 156
model deploy service
auditing in, 226
autoscaling deployment pattern in, 222-225
batching in, 225
data distribution in, 226
defined, 215
defining requirements in, 218-221
deployment endpoints and, 218-219
deployment orchestration in, 217
drift monitoring in, 218
drift verification in, 221
embedded model in, 219
endpoint deployment in, 223
implementation patterns in, 221-226
isolation in, 225
model drift tracking pattern in, 225-226
model formats in, 219-219
model identification in, 223
model serialization in, 222
nonfunctional requirements in, 221
performance scaling in, 217-218
pub/sub model in, 219
result monitoring in, 226
robustness in, 221
scaling in, 220-221
service level agreements and, 224
slowdown detection in, 224
time to deploy metric and, 217-218
universal deployment pattern in, 222
verifiability in, 221
visualization in, 221
model deployment, 154, 216
as separate service, 219
canary model, 220
non-disruptive upgrade scenario in, 220
scenarios, 220

shadow mode, 220
model freshness, 160
model maintenance and upgrade, 216, 217
model prototyping, 154-155
model training
    continuous, 157-158
    data life cycle management and, 95
    data rights governance service and, 118
    data versioning and, 103
    feature computation and, 54
    feature groups and, 56
    feature store service and, 51, 52, 53, 54, 57,
        60
    in data rights governance service, 118
    in insight extraction, 7
    nature of, 155
    time to featurize metric and, 11
model training service
    automated tuning pattern in, 161, 163
    continuous, 155
    continuous training in, 155, 157-158
    cost in, 161
    data-aware continuous training pattern in,
        161, 164
    defined, 153
    defining requirements in, 158-159
    distributed training orchestrator pattern in,
        161, 162-163
    feature store service and, 156
    implementation patterns in, 161-166
    job orchestration in, 162
    levels of automation in, 161
    metadata tracking in, 164
    monitoring in, 161
    nonfunctional requirements in, 160-161
    resource orchestration in, 162
    scaling in, 160
    TensorFlow Extended in, 162
    time to train metric and, 156-158
    training optimization in, 162
    tuning in, 157, 160, 163
    validation in, 165
monitoring
    cost usage, 240
    in data movement service, 69
    data quality, 228
    drift, 218
    in model deploy service, 226
    in model training service, 161

    in pipeline orchestration service, 206
    in search service, 41
    of insight quality, 9
multi-armed bandits, 186

N
namespace zones, 97
nonfunctional requirements (NFRs)
    in data movement service, 69-70
    in cost management service, 244
    in data rights governance service, 122
    in data transformation service, 147
    in feature store service, 57
    in model deploy service, 221
    in model training service, 160-161
    in pipeline orchestration service, 208
    in quality observability service, 233
    in query optimization service, 195-196
    in search service, 40

O
observability
    in data virtualization service, 135
onboarding
    in data movement service, 74
    in change data capture ingestion pattern, 74
    in search service, 41
ONNX (Open Neural Network Exchange), 219
open source
    A/B testing service, 178
    in change data capture ingestion pattern, 73
    in clickstream tracking service, 85, 86
    in data movement service, 70, 73
    in feature store service, 58
    in metadata catalog service, 29
    in search service, 42, 45, 47
OpenDSR, 125
operational insights pattern, 198-199
operationalization phase, in insight extraction,
    8-10
ORCFile, 99
out-of-bound control, 125

P
Parquet
    in data lake management service, 104
    in data virtualization service, 133, 139, 140
    in feature store service, 56

parsing phase, in hybrid search ranking pattern, 44
PartiQL, 138-139
partition phase, 71
personally identifiable information (PII)
    data movement service and, 65
    in data rights governance service, 120, 121, 123
    in team knowledge, 26
Pickle, 220
pipeline correlation, 31
pipeline jungles, 54
pipeline orchestration
    in insight extraction, 9
    pain points in, 203, 207
    pipeline anatomy in, 204
pipeline orchestration service
    audit in, 208
    backfill in, 208
    checkpointing of job execution in, 208
    cost in, 208
    defined, 204
    defining requirements in, 206-209
    dependency authoring patterns in, 209-211
    distributed execution in, 206
    distributed execution pattern in, 212-213
    exploratory pipelines in, 205
    extensibility in, 209
    implementation patterns in, 209
    interoperability in, 207
    job dependencies in, 205
    levels of automation in, 209
    nonfunctional requirements in, 208
    orchestration observability patterns in, 211-212
    pipeline dependencies in, 207
    production monitoring in, 206
    resource scaling in, 208
    service level agreements and, 205, 206
    service-specific adapters in, 208
    time to orchestrate metric and, 205-206
pipeline packaging module, 170, 171
Piper (Uber), 210, 213
pluggable validation, as team knowledge, 33
polyglot queries, 133
Portable Format for Analytics (PFA), 219
Predictive Model Markup Language (PMML), 219
preparation, in insight extraction, 6

privacy filtering, 83
profiling-based anomaly detection pattern, 235-236
programmable tracking pattern, 172, 173
pub/sub model, 219
push-pull indexer pattern, 41, 44
    connect phase in, 42
    extract phase in, 42
    update phase in, 42

Q
quality observability service
    accuracy measurement in, 232
    accuracy models pattern in, 234
    anomaly detection in, 233, 235-236
    avoidance pattern in, 236-237
    circuit breakers in, 236-237
    data accuracy verification in, 229-230
    data profiling in, 233
    data quality and, 232
    defined, 228
    defining requirements in, 231-233
    extensibility in, 233
    implementation patterns in, 233-237
    levels of automation in, 234
    low-quality records and, 229
    nonfunctional requirements in, 233
    prevention of data quality issues with, 231
    profiling-based anomaly detection pattern in, 235-236
    quality anomaly detection in, 230
    scaling in, 233
    schema enforcement in, 236
    time to insight quality metric and, 229-231
    timeliness in, 233
query optimization
    application speedup and, 191
    as ongoing, 190
    cluster clogs in, 190
    hierarchy of aspects in, 193
    importance of, 189
    in insight extraction, 8
    runtime query issues in, 190
query optimization service
    and impact of unoptimized queries, 194
    automated tuning pattern in, 200
    avoidance pattern in, 196-197
    cluster analysis in, 192
    cost optimization with, 196

defined, 190
defining requirements in, 194
explainability in, 195
functionality requirements in, 195
implementation patterns in, 196-201
interoperability in, 195
job analysis in, 192
job optimization in, 193
metadata aggregation in, 197
minimal disruption from, 195
nonfunctional requirements in, 195-196
operational insights pattern in, 198-199
pain points in, 194-195
parse query in, 197
query analysis in, 192
query workload and, 194
statistics in, 191-192, 198
time to optimize metric and, 191-193
tuning in, 195
query parsing, 31
query processing engines, 64

R

RabbitMQ, 212
ranking module, 38
ranking phase, in hybrid search ranking pattern, 44
ranking requirements, in search service, 40
RapidMiner, 112
re-randomization, 184
reduce phase, 71
refresh lag, 67
relevance
    in search service, 40
reproducible project pattern, 172, 174
requirements
    in data movement service, 66-70
    in clickstream tracking service, 82-84
    in continuous integration service, 170-172
    in cost management service, 243-244
    in data lake management service, 97-102
    in data rights governance service, 119-122
    in data transformation service, 145-147
    in data virtualization service, 134-136
    in data wrangling service, 110, 111
    in feature store service, 55-57
    in model deploy service, 218-221
    in model training service, 158-159
    in pipeline orchestration service, 206-209

in quality observability service, 231-233
in query optimization service, 194-196
in metadata catalog service, 26-28
in search service, 38-41
resource orchestration, 162
response times, in search service, 41
role-based access control (RBAC), 40, 47
rollback, data, 95
rule-based enrichment patterns, 85-87

S

Sample Ratio Mismatch (SRM) test, 186
scaling
    in A/B testing service, 182
    buffer-based, 247
    in cost management service, 242, 244
    in data transformation service, 147
    demand-based, 247
    in feature store service, 56-57
    feature store service and, 54
    in model deploy service, 217-218, 220-221
    in model training service, 160
    in pipeline orchestration service, 208
    in quality observability service, 233
    in search service, 41
    time-based, 247
schema evolution
    in data movement service, 68
    in data lake management service, 95, 103
schema inference, 25
schema-on-read, 21, 22
schema-on-write, 21, 22
scoring, in hybrid search ranking pattern, 45
search service
    access control in, 38, 40, 41
    access module in, 39
    artifacts in, 42
    automation levels of, 41
    catalog access control pattern in, 41, 46
    datasets in, 36
    defined, 35
    defining requirements in, 38-41
    existing artifacts for prototyping in, 36
    feasibility analysis for, 36
    hybrid search ranking pattern in, 41, 44-46
    implementation patterns in, 41-49
    indexer module in, 38
    indexing in, 37, 39
    monitoring in, 41

nonfunctional requirements in, 40
onboarding in, 41
open source technology in, 42, 45, 47
push-pull indexer pattern in, 41, 44
ranking module in, 38
ranking requirements in, 40
ranking results in, 37-38
relevance in, 40
response times in, 41
scaling in, 41
time to find metric in, 37-38
searching
in insight extraction, 5
Segment, 85
self-service data roadmap, 15-17
sensitive data recovery and classification pattern, 123-124
SequenceFile, 99
serialization
in data lake management service, 98
in model deploy service, 222
service level agreements
data rights governance service and, 119, 121
data transformation service and, 144, 145
data wrangling service and, 111
in model, 224
in pipeline orchestration service, 212
metadata catalog service and, 23, 28
pipeline orchestration and, 205, 206
query optimization service and, 194, 201
service level agreements (SLAs)
pipeline orchestration and, 9
sessionization
in clickstream tracking service, 81, 83
sessionization pattern, 86
source-specific connector pattern, 29-30
Sparklens, 198
split testing (see A/B testing)
statistics
aggregation of, 191-192
examples of, 191
in clickstream tracking service, 83
in query optimization service, 191-192, 198
storytelling, data-driven, 144
streaming compute pipeline, 58

T

team knowledge
business taxonomy as, 33

data documentation as, 33
in insight extraction, 4
in metadata catalog service, 26, 28
pluggable validation as, 33
time to interpret metric and, 11
team knowledge pattern, 29, 32
TensorFlow, 158
TensorFlow Extended (TFX), 2, 162, 165, 223, 225
testing automation module, 170, 172
testing validation pattern, 172
text files, in data lake management service, 99
time to A/B test, 8, 13, 181-183
time to click metrics, 5, 12, 77, 79-82
time to compliance metric, 6, 10, 12, 118-119
time to data availability metric, 5, 12, 64-66
time to data lake management, 6, 12, 97-102
time to deploy metric, 9, 14, 217-218
time to featurize metric, 5, 11-12, 52, 53-55
time to find metric, 5, 10, 11, 37-38
time to insight metric, 10
time to insight quality metric, 9, 14, 229-231
time to integrate metric, 8, 13, 169-170
time to interpret metric, 4, 10, 11, 24
time to optimize cost metric, 10, 14, 241-243
time to optimize metric, 8, 13, 191-193
time to orchestrate metric, 9, 14, 205-206
time to query, 133-134
time to train metric, 7, 13, 156-158
time to transform metric, 7, 13, 143, 144-145
time to virtualize metric, 7, 13
time to wrangle metric, 6, 12, 109
time-to-insight scorecard, 10-15
training (see model training)
transactional pattern, 104

U

unified query pattern, 138-140
update phase, in push-pull indexer pattern, 42
use case-dependent access control, 125-127
user agent parsing, 83
user context enrichment pattern, 86

V

validation
in continuous integration service, 169, 170
in data wrangling service, 109
in insight extraction, 6
in model training service, 165

of schema changes, 169
versioning
    in data lake management service, 95, 103
    in metadata catalog service, 27
visualization
    in data wrangling service, 110, 113
    in model deploy service, 221

W
WAP (Write Audit Push) (Netflix), 237

Wasabi, 179
wide-column data model, 101
Wrangler, 113

Y
YAML, 174, 223

About the Author

Dr. Sandeep Uttamchandani is the chief data officer and VP of Product Engineering at Unravel Data Systems. He brings nearly two decades of experience building enterprise data products and running petabyte-scale data platforms for business-critical analytics and machine learning applications. Most recently, he was at Intuit, where he ran the data platform team powering analytics and machine learning for Intuit's financial accounting, payroll, and payments products. Previously in his career, Sandeep was cofounder and CEO of a startup using machine learning for managing security vulnerabilities of open source products. He has held engineering leadership roles at VMware and IBM for more than 15 years.

Sandeep holds more than 40 issued patents, has more than 25 publications in key technical conferences, and has received several product innovation and management excellence awards. He is a regular speaker at data conferences and a guest lecturer at universities. He advises startups and has served as a program/steering committee member for several conferences, including serving as cochair of Gartner's SF CDO Executive Summit and Usenix Operational ML (OpML) conference. Sandeep holds a Ph.D. and a master's in computer science from the University of Illinois at Urbana-Champaign.

Colophon

The animal on the cover of *The Self-Service Data Roadmap* is a Townsend's big-eared bat (*Corynorhinus townsendii*). Native to western North America, these flying mammals have a large presence in the pine forests of the Rocky Mountain states like Utah and Colorado, but can be seen as far south as Mexico.

During the summer months they prefer open areas with low and steady temperatures such as caves, cliffs, and even abandoned mines. While males tend to roost alone, females will raise their pups in maternity colonies that can range from 12 to 200 members. With a large wing area to mass ratio, the Townsend's big-eared bat is capable of high maneuverability, low-speed flight, and the ability to hover while flying. Tests conducted on straight-line tracks have clocked their speeds ranging from between 6.4 to 12.3 mph.

The large ears of Townsend's big-eared bats are what enable them to navigate and hunt with accuracy. From their larynx they emit low-frequency pulses, which only last a few thousandths of a second, and bounce off objects and return back to their ears. With these quick signals, they can determine the shape, size, distance, and even texture of their main prey: moths. Moths make up about 80% of their diet. This bat is an effective pest-control that helps reduce the environmental and agricultural damage caused by insects.

O'REILLY®

There's much more
where this came from.

Experience books, videos, live online
training courses, and more from O'Reilly
and our 200+ partners—all in one place.

Learn more at oreilly.com/online-learning

Milton Keynes UK
Ingram Content Group UK Ltd.
UKHW030734130324
439333UK00001B/3